# MENUS FOR THE
# Microwave
# Hostess

## MARIE EMMERSON

OCTOPUS BOOKS

# RECIPE NOTES

The recipes in this book have been tested with microwave cookers operating on 650 and 700 watts. For microwave cookers with a lower wattage, extra cooking time may be necessary; check the food at the end of the cooking time given in the recipe and, if required, allow 20 seconds *more* per minute for a 500 watt model, and 15 seconds *more* per minute for a 600 watt model.

Like conventional cooking, certain factors can affect the cooking time. Food taken straight from the refrigerator will be colder than food at room temperature, so a longer cooking time will be needed. The size of egg used will give a different liquid ratio. The material, the shape and the size of the container may also affect timing (see page 119).

Here is a general guide to the capacities of the containers used throughout the book.

| | |
|---|---|
| Large or very large bowl | 2.75 1/4½-5 pints (6 pints) |
| Medium bowl | 2 l 3½ pints (4½ pints) |
| Small bowl | 1.2 l 2 pints (5 cups) |
| Large or very large jug | 1 l/1¾ pints (1 quart) |
| Jug or small jug | 600 ml/1 pint (2½ cups) |

Unless otherwise stated most quantities given are for 4 servings. The majority of recipes can be increased to serve 6 or 8, but if the capacity of the microwave cooker is small it may be preferable and quicker to use a conventional appliance when cooking for large numbers.

Standard spoon measurements are used in all recipes:
1 tablespoon = one 15 ml spoon
1 teaspoon = one 5 ml spoon
All spoon measurements are level

Where amounts of salt and pepper are unspecified in recipes the cook should use her discretion. Canned foods are used with their juices unless otherwise specified. Ovens and grills (broilers) should be preheated to the specified temperature or heat setting.

For all recipes, quantities are given in metric, imperial and American measures. Follow one set of measures only, because they are not interchangeable.

First published 1986 by Octopus Books Limited
59 Grosvenor Street, London W1

© 1986 Octopus Books Limited
ISBN 0 7064 2545 6

Produced by Mandarin Publishers Ltd
22a Westlands Road, Quarry Bay, Hong Kong
Printed in Hong Kong

# CONTENTS

Includes information on setting the scene, laying the table for the special occasions, cocktails to serve before the meal, the wines to choose and serve, advice on seating and serving – everything to ensure that the meal is a well ordered and unqualified success.

Menus that are effortless to put together, require no pre-planning or preparation, and that are suitable to serve at a host of informal occasions. Convenience foods are used to the full enabling you to create marvellous meals in minutes for family or friends.

Menus carefully designed for smarter evening affairs; the bulk of the food can be prepared in advance leaving the hostess free to enjoy her guests' company. The serving notes and table dressing hints lead to perfect presentation for more formal occasions.

Includes information on the microwave; how it works, the containers to use and golden rules on how to use your microwave.

A comprehensive guide to thawing and cooking all manner of foods – from apples through to zucchini.

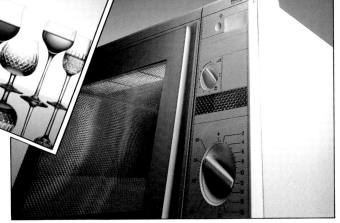

# Introduction

The microwave cooker is an exceptionally versatile piece of kitchen equipment with the advantages of speed and efficiency, as well as economy.
Its well known abilities to thaw and cook quickly are of great benefit and use in everyday cooking, but used alongside more conventional appliances they are a boon to the hostess who loves to entertain...

■ A multitude of food preparation methods can be carried out in the microwave which, under usual circumstances, would require one or more parts of a conventional cooker. Since it produces cooked food very quickly much more time can be spent on the garnishes and decorations which are particularly important when guests are expected. The microwave cooker does not brown or scorch food so there should be no last minute disasters. And finally, a wide variety of main dishes, side dishes, sauces and puddings can be prepared in advance and reheated in the microwave just before serving. This includes being able to reheat cooked vegetables without losing any of their quality.

■ Be selective about the food you cook in the microwave. There are many new users who feel that total loyalty must be given to the microwave at the expense of other kitchen appliances. In fact, there is still a use for small appliances like the electric toaster and kettle as indeed there is also a need for the conventional cooker. When cooking for large numbers the microwave may not be able to accommodate the quantity of food required, or indeed cook it as quickly as the conventional hob or oven. And in some instances, the results obtained from the microwave will be less acceptable – for example, most pastries, hot soufflés and many breads and cakes are better cooked conventionally.

■ When planning both impromptu and formal menus it is important to make your microwave work for you. With skill and experience it is possible to produce a meal of several courses using just the microwave cooker, but it is often more convenient to utilize the microwave in conjunction with other appliances. This practical approach to menu planning is highlighted throughout MENUS FOR THE MICROWAVE HOSTESS. If it is more practical to cook vegetables on the conventional hob while the main course is cooking in the microwave we tell you to do so. By following the carefully designed Action Plans situated alongside every menu in this book we promise you effortless entertaining…

# Hostess Notes

Table planning and setting are allimportant to successful entertaining. Allow yourself plenty of time to create the desired effect. There is nothing worse than a guest finding he or she has no knife, or if the hostess is continually bobbing up and down to get something that has been forgotten.

## SETTING THE SCENE

For formal occasions, if space permits, lay the table a day in advance and then cover the whole thing with a cloth. If this is not possible, then try to lay the table in the morning of the dinner party. Consider the colour of the linen, flowers, china and candles. Everything must please the eye and set the mood. Another mood setter is that of lighting. Soft lights around the room are always conducive to a welcoming atmosphere but if there is only a centre light then it is often more effective to turn it off and rely on candles.

Flowers enhance the look of a table but remember that they must not be too tall otherwise the guests will find themselves peering around the arrangement to hold a conversation with the person opposite them. See the box on page 76 for suggestions for different flower arrangements for your table.

A pretty table cloth or linen place mats can be used but for very formal occasions a white damask cloth is perhaps the classic choice. Napkins should match the table covering (and remember to protect a wood-finish table by positioning heavy baize or table mats beneath the cloth).

The china, glassware and cutlery should be spotlessly clean. When laying the table, set the end of the cutlery about 1 cm/½ inch from the edge of the table and arrange the cutlery in the order in which it is to be used, starting from the outside and working towards the plate. The dessert spoon and fork can be placed across the top of the plate with the bowl of the spoon to the left and the fork positioned underneath, the tines facing right.

Wine and water glasses are placed at the top right of the place setting, using the nearest to hand first.

*Glass adds sparkle to your table. A contemporary look can be achieved with modern table mats, or opt for something more classic by using lace and silver.*

*Paper comes into its own if you're catering for large numbers. There's a wide selection of paper cloths, napkins and plates available. For style use conventional napkin rings and cutlery.*

## SEATING PLAN

Decide the seating arrangements before the guests arrive. For formal occasions it is usual to have the host at the head of the table with the principal lady guest on his right. Whereas the the hostess sits at the foot of the table with the principal male guest on her right. Much depends upon the shape of the table but sometimes it is better to place partners next to each other, encouraging them to talk with the guest opposite rather than to each other. However, if the table is wide then separate them completely. Remember conversation is more likely to flow if the extroverts are situated with those who are quieter, and those guests who may clash on certain subjects are not seated near to each other.

## SERVING AND CLEARING

The main dish is usually placed on plates by the hostess and these are then handed to the lady guests first. Although everyone eats at a different rate, the host or hostess should ensure that they finish their course about the same time as the slowest guest, and the finished dishes must not be cleared until everyone has finished. Between each course, dishes, food and cutlery no longer required should be removed thus keeping the table clear and uncluttered.

## SELECTING AND SERVING WINE

Select the wines you intend to serve as soon as the menu has been decided upon.

Thankfully the snobbery that is often associated with wine is fast disappearing and it is now acceptable to serve the wine you like with what you like. However, it is still recommended that you serve a white wine with fish, and a red wine with meat. It is also recommended that you serve the driest wine at the beginning of the meal and finish with the sweetest. Likewise, you should serve the light bodied wines with the starter and move on to the fuller bodied wines as the meal progresses. The occasion has a certain bearing on the quality of wine you need to buy, but the flavour of fine ingredients, and dishes that have taken time to prepare, should be enhanced by the flavour of a good quality wine.

The temperature at which you serve your wines is important. White or rosé wines should be chilled for two to three hours before serving. Do not over chill them or you will loose the true flavour of the wine, and don't be tempted to 'fast chill' a wine by placing it in the freezer. If the wine freezes you will not only destroy its flavour but the bottle is likely to burst.

Red wines should be served at room temperature and need to be opened well in advance so that the wine is allowed to 'breathe' and develop in flavour. Do not be tempted to warm the wine in front of a radiator or hot oven and remember to uncork the wine at least an hour before you intend serving it.

Once the preparations are taken care of, sit back, relax and enjoy your guests, the occasion and the meal.

***Bon Appetit!***

# TIME FOR A TIPPLE

When entertaining family or friends, it is fun to get things off to a lively start by serving an exotic cocktail or fruity punch. It will prove to be an excellent aperitif and a wonderful conversation piece.

The word cocktail conjures up a world of sophistication and luxury but the making of cocktails is quite straightforward. It can simply be a pairing of two ingredients with the addition of ice and maybe a lemon slice or it can be a mixture of many ingredients served with an elaborate decoration.

Both types can be successfully made at home and they need not involve you spending a fortune. Start by serving the more simple cocktails that require the standard drinks found in any drinks cabinet – gin, vodka, vermouth, brandy. Add more exotic ingredients as your repertoire, and confidence in your cocktail making grows.

If you plan to indulge in cocktails on a regular basis it may be worth investing in a cocktail shaker. The standard cocktail measure is called a 'jigger' which is 45 ml/1½ fl oz (3 tablespoons). If you're planning on serving cocktails quite often you may find one of these useful. If not, you must ensure you use the same measure throughout, be it an egg cup or liqueur.

A punch is usually a more economical alternative to cocktails. It can be non-alcoholic or a concoction that is just as potent as the most powerful cocktail. Punches can be cool and refreshing for a summer's day, or hot and warming, perfect for a winter's evening.

## Blue Moon

| METRIC/IMPERIAL | AMERICAN |
|---|---|
| 1½ measures blue curaccao | 1½ measures blue curaccao |
| ½ measure brandy | ½ measure brandy |
| 2 measures whipping cream | 2 measures whipping cream |
| To decorate: | To decorate: |
| ½ egg white, lightly beaten | ½ egg white, lightly beaten |
| 1 tablespoon caster sugar | 1 tablespoon caster sugar |
| umbrella | umbrella |

Chill the curaccao, brandy and cream. Dip the rim of a cocktail or champagne glass (open type) into the egg white and then into the sugar to give a frosted rim. Mix together the chilled curaccao, brandy and cream. Pour into the glass and decorate with an umbrella. Serves 1.

## Summer Fruit Punch

| METRIC/IMPERIAL | AMERICAN |
|---|---|
| 50 g/2 oz caster sugar | ¼ cup sugar |
| 150 ml/¼ pint water | ⅔ cup water |
| 60 ml/2 fl oz orange juice | ¼ cup orange juice |
| 60 ml/2 fl oz lemon squash | ¼ cup lemon squash |
| 60 ml/2 fl oz pineapple juice | ¼ cup pineapple juice |
| 60 ml/2 fl oz grape juice | ¼ cup grape juice |
| 300 ml/½ pint cold tea | 1¼ cups cold tea |
| orange and apple slices | orange and apple slices |
| mint to decorate | mint to decorate |

Setting to use: HIGH

Place the sugar and water in a jug. Cook, covered, for 3 minutes. Stir well to dissolve the sugar. Set aside to cool. Mix together the orange juice, lemon squash, pineapple juice, grape juice, cold tea and cooled syrup. Place slices of fruit in a bowl. Add the punch and chill. Serve in tall glasses decorated with mint. Serves 4.

10

# Frosty Night Punch

| METRIC/IMPERIAL | AMERICAN |
|---|---|
| 250 ml/8 fl oz water | 1 cup water |
| 1 tea bag | 1 tea bag |
| 1 small orange, cut into pieces | 1 small orange, cut into pieces |
| 4 cloves | 4 cloves |
| 1/2 teaspoon lemon juice | 1/2 teaspoon lemon juice |
| 1/2 cinnamon stick | 1/2 cinnamon stick |
| 60 ml/2 fl oz whisky | 1/4 cup whisky |
| 60 ml/2 fl oz dry cider | 1/4 cup hard cider |
| 60 ml/2 fl oz orange juice | 1/4 cup orange juice |
| 25 g/1 oz brown sugar | 2 tablespoons brown sugar |
| 2 cinnamon sticks to decorate | 2 cinnamon sticks to decorate |

Setting to use: HIGH

Place the water in a large jug. Cook, uncovered, until boiling. Place the tea bag in a small bowl. Add the boiling water, orange, cloves, lemon juice and cinnamon. Stir, cover and stand for 3-4 minutes. Strain into a large jug. Stir in remaining ingredients. Cook, uncovered, for 3 minutes or until warm; do not boil. Pour into two heatproof tumblers. Add a cinnamon stick to each tumbler. Serves 2.

# Mitchell Magic

| METRIC/IMPERIAL | AMERICAN |
|---|---|
| 1/2 tumbler lightly crushed ice | 1/2 tumbler lightly crushed ice |
| 1 measure gin | 1 measure gin |
| 1/2 measure crème de menthe | 1/2 measure crème de menthe |
| 1/4 measure minted chocolate liqueur | 1/4 measure minted chocolate liqueur |
| 1/4 measure Maraschino syrup | 1/4 measure Maraschino syrup |
| orange juice | orange juice |
| Optional decoration: | Optional decoration: |
| slice orange | slice orange |
| a flower | a flower |
| an umbrella | an umbrella |

Place the ice in a tall glass. Pour over the gin, then the crème de menthe, followed by the chocolate liqueur and then the syrup.

Carefully top up with orange juice just before serving. Decorate with an orange slice, a flower or an umbrella. Serve with a straw. Serves 1.

NOTE: To give a layered effect, this cocktail must be made in the order given, and not stirred.

# Amethyst

| METRIC/IMPERIAL | AMERICAN |
|---|---|
| 1 measure Parfait Amour | 1 measure Parfait Amour |
| 1/2 measure vodka | 1/2 measure vodka |
| 1 measure dry vermouth | 1 measure dry vermouth |
| dash Angostura bitters | dash Angostura bitters |
| 2 ice cubes, crushed | 2 ice cubes, crushed |
| a purple umbrella to decorate | a purple umbrella to decorate |

Mix together the Parfait Amour, vodka, dry vermouth and bitters in a cocktail shaker. Shake to mix. Place the crushed ice in a chilled stemmed glass and pour over the cocktail. Decorate with an umbrella. Serves 1.

# Jenny Marie

| METRIC/IMPERIAL | AMERICAN |
|---|---|
| broken ice | broken ice |
| 3 drops Angostura bitters | 3 drops Angostura bitters |
| 1 measure Cointreau | 1 measure Cointreau |
| 1/2 measure apricot brandy | 1/2 measure apricot brandy |
| 1 measure Bianco vermouth | 1 measure Bianco vermouth |
| 1 teaspoon lemon juice | 1 teaspoon lemon juice |
| slice of lemon or strip of lemon peel to decorate | slice of lemon or strip of lemon peel |

Half fill a cocktail shaker with broken ice, then add the bitters and remaining ingredients.

Shake well and strain into a chilled cocktail glass. Decorate with the lemon slice or strip of lemon peel. Serves 1.

# Impromptu Entertaining

These impromptu menus enable you to entertain family or friends with barely any advance preparation. While your guests are enjoying a cocktail or a refreshing long drink you can be conjuring up a delicious meal to suit the occasion – knowing that the food can be prepared and cooked with the greatest of ease.

**WINE NOTE** The full flavours of a *Californian Chardonnay* echo the transatlantic inspiration behind the main course.

**ACTION PLAN**
1. Cook the chicken breasts and prepare the corn sauce. Set aside separately.
2. Cook the Brussels sprouts and potatoes on the conventional hob. When ready drain and keep warm, creaming the potatoes if necessary.
3. Meanwhile, prepare the fig pudding mixture and cook the eggs with tomatoes in the microwave.
4. Pour the corn sauce over the chicken and complete the cooking while eating the first course.
5. Cook the pudding while the main course is being served. You can heat 600 ml/1 pint (2¼ cup) canned or packaged custard in the microwave while you are turning out the pudding.

## ═══ Eggs with Tomatoes ═══

| METRIC/IMPERIAL | AMERICAN |
|---|---|
| 4 tomatoes, skinned and chopped | 4 tomatoes, skinned and chopped |
| 20 g/¾ oz butter | 4 teaspoons butter |
| ½ teaspoon chopped fresh tarragon | ½ teaspoon chopped fresh tarragon |
| salt | salt |
| freshly ground black pepper | freshly ground black pepper |
| 4 large eggs | 4 large eggs |
| tarragon sprigs to garnish | tarragon sprigs for garnish |

Setting to use: HIGH

Divide the tomatoes between four ramekin dishes. Dot with the butter and sprinkle with the tarragon, and salt and pepper to taste. Cook, covered, for 1½ minutes.

14

Break the eggs onto the tomatoes. Prick the yolks. Cover the dishes with plastic wrap and arrange in a circle in the microwave. Cook for 2¼ minutes. Rearrange the dishes halfway through cooking.

Let stand for 1 minute before serving, garnished with sprigs of tarragon.

## ═══ Chicken in Corn Sauce ═══

| METRIC/IMPERIAL | AMERICAN |
|---|---|
| 4 frozen chicken breasts on the bone, total weight about 1.2 kg/2½ lb | 4 frozen chicken breasts on the bone, total weight about 2½ lb |
| 1 × 300 g/10 oz can condensed cream of celery soup | 1 × 300 g/10 oz can condensed cream of celery soup |
| 2 tablespoons good quality mayonnaise | 2 tablespoons good quality mayonnaise |
| 50 g/2 oz button mushrooms, fresh or canned and drained | ½ cup fresh or canned and drained button mushrooms |

1 × 350 g/12 oz can sweetcorn
kernels, drained
salt
freshly ground black pepper

1 × 12 oz can whole kernel
corn, drained
salt
freshly ground black pepper

Setting to use: HIGH

Place the chicken breasts in a large bowl. Cook, covered, for 15 minutes. Rearrange after 5 and 10 minutes.

Remove the breasts and, using a knife and fork, remove the skin. Pour off the liquid from the bowl and reserve. Return the breasts to the bowl and cook, covered, for a further 4 minutes.

Meanwhile, mix together the reserved liquid, the soup (not diluted), mayonnaise, mushrooms, corn, and salt and pepper to taste. Pour over the chicken breasts. Cook, covered, for 6 minutes. Stir halfway through cooking.

Transfer to a warm serving dish. Serve any excess sauce separately.

▽ Weekend lunch: from right: eggs with tomatoes; Brussels sprouts; chicken in corn sauce; fig pudding

## Fig Pudding

| METRIC/IMPERIAL | AMERICAN |
| --- | --- |
| 125 g/4 oz butter | ½ cup butter |
| 125 g/4 oz caster sugar | ½ cup sugar |
| 2 large eggs | 2 large eggs |
| 175 g/6 oz self-raising flour | 1½ cups self-raising flour |
| 2 tablespoons milk | 2 tablespoons milk |
| 75 g/3 oz dried figs, chopped | ½ cups dried figs, chopped |
| caster sugar to dredge | sugar for dredging |

Setting to use: HIGH

Beat together the butter and sugar until light and fluffy. Beat in the eggs one at a time. Fold in the flour. Gently stir in the milk and figs.

Spoon into a greased 1.2 1/2 pint pudding basin (5 cup steaming mold). Cover and cook for 5 minutes. Turn around halfway through cooking, if necessary.

Remove the pudding and let stand, covered, for 2 minutes before turning out onto a warm serving dish.

Sprinkle with sugar and serve immediately.

NOTE: This pudding is best served immediately as it tends to toughen on cooling.

# Lunch with Friends

## scampi in white wine sauce
## crusty french bread
## ham steaks with almonds
## creamed potatoes
## peas
## fruit flan

### Serves 4

*A relatively smart menu that is suitable to serve family or friends. Instant potatoes can be used in place of creamed fresh potatoes, and fresh, canned or frozen corn kernels can be used.*

**WINE NOTE** A medium dry white wine is an exciting partner for ham garnished with almonds rather than fruit: look for the *Abboccato* version of *Orvieto*.

**ACTION PLAN**
1. Make the fruit flan and chill.
2. If using fresh potatoes, cook on the conventional hob. Drain and mash.
3. Meanwhile cook the ham dish in the microwave, transfer to a serving dish, spoon over the cooked onion mixture and set aside.
4. Make and serve the scampi in white wine sauce. Heat the bread before serving.
5. While eating the first course, cook the corn, (or heat canned or frozen vegetables in the microwave).
6. Pop the ham into the microwave to heat through before serving.

## Scampi in White Wine Sauce

| METRIC/IMPERIAL | AMERICAN |
|---|---|
| *1 medium onion, finely chopped* | *1 medium onion, finely chopped* |
| *25 g/1 oz butter* | *2 tablespoons butter* |
| *25 g/1 oz cornflour* | *1/4 cornstarch* |
| *150 ml/1/4 pint milk* | *2/3 cup milk* |
| *150 ml/1/4 pint dry or medium white wine* | *2/3 cup dry or medium white wine* |
| *500 g/1 lb peeled fresh or thawed scampi* | *1 lb shelled fresh or thawed jumbo shrimp* |
| *salt* | *salt* |
| *freshly ground black pepper* | *freshly ground black pepper* |
| *1 tablespoon double cream (optional)* | *1 tablespoon heavy cream (optional)* |
| *chopped spring onions or fresh parsley to garnish* | *chopped scallions or fresh parsley for garnish* |

Setting to use: HIGH

Place the onion and butter in a large bowl. Cook, covered, for 4 minutes. Stir in the cornflour (cornstarch). Gradually blend in the milk and wine. Cook uncovered, for 8½ minutes. Add the scampi (shrimp) halfway through cooking and stir well.

Season with the salt and pepper. Stir in the cream if using. Pile into warm serving dishes. Garnish with chopped spring onions (scallions) or parsley.

NOTE: If using frozen scampi (shrimp) increase the cooking time and use an extra teaspoon cornflour (cornstarch) to compensate for the extra liquid from the frozen shellfish.

## Ham Steaks with Almonds

| METRIC/IMPERIAL | AMERICAN |
|---|---|
| *4 gammon steaks, total weight 1 kg/2 lb, edges snipped* | *4 ham steaks, total weight 2 lb, edges snipped* |
| *3 spring onions, trimmed and chopped* | *3 scallions, trimmed and chopped* |
| *50 g/2 oz blanched almonds, split* | *1/2 cup sliced blanched almonds* |
| *50 g/2 oz raisins* | *1/3 cup raisins* |
| *25 g/1 oz butter* | *2 tablespoons butter* |

Setting to use: HIGH

Arrange the gammon (ham) steaks on the bottom of a large bowl. Cook, covered, for 10 minutes. Rearrange halfway through cooking. Set aside, covered.

Mix together the onions (scallions), almonds and raisins in a medium bowl. Add the butter. Cook, covered, for 4 minutes. Stir halfway through cooking.

Drain off the juice from the gammon (ham). Arrange the steaks on a warm serving dish. Spoon the almond mixture on top and serve.

## Fruit Flan

| METRIC/IMPERIAL | AMERICAN |
|---|---|
| *1 × 18 cm/7inch or 25 cm/ 10 inch frozen sponge flan case* | *1 × 7 or 10 inch frozen Mary Ann sponge cake* |
| *2 tablespoons sweet or medium sherry* | *2 tablespoons cream or medium sherry* |
| *1 × 400 g/14 oz can peaches, apricots or oranges, drained and syrup reserved* | *1 × 16 oz can peaches, apricots or oranges, drained and syrup reserved* |
| *1 teaspoon arrowroot (optional)* | *1 teaspoon arrowroot (optional)* |
| *whipped cream to decorate* | *whipped cream to decorate* |

Setting to use: HIGH/Conventional hob

Place the sponge case on a plate. Cook, uncovered, for 30 seconds.

Prick the cake with a fork and sprinkle over the sherry. Arrange the fruit in the sponge case. Set aside.

Measure 150 ml/1/4 pint (2/3 cup) of the syrup from the can

16

of fruit. Blend the arrowroot with some of the syrup, then add the remainder. Pour into saucepan and cook on the conventional hob, stirring all the time, until the syrup is thick and clear. Allow to stand for a few minutes to dispel bubbles.

Gently spoon the syrup over the fruit then decorate with a little whipped cream. Chill before serving.

△ *Lunch with friends from bottom: scampi in white wine sauce with crusty French bread; ham steaks with almonds; peas; fruit flan*

17

# Sunday Brunch

### pineapple with liqueur
### smoked salmon with scrambled eggs
### melba toast
### cold pork salad
### cucumber and tomato vinaigrette
### fresh orange juice

#### Serves 4

*This light summer menu can easily be converted into a lunch by serving the pineapple with liqueur at the end of the meal.*

**WINE NOTE**  Like poultry, pork goes well with either red or white wine. Try a light red *Anjou* or *Chinon* with the salad. Serve your guests fresh orange juice as they arrive.

**ACTION PLAN**
1. Cook the pork and set aside to cool.
2. Meanwhile, make the pineapple liqueur and chill.
3. Slice the tomato and cucumber, pour over a little vinaigrette dressing and chill.
4. Collect together the ingredients for the smoked salmon and scrambled eggs but only cook just before serving.
5. Complete the pork salad.

## Pineapple with Liqueur

| METRIC/IMPERIAL | AMERICAN |
|---|---|
| 1 × 425 g/15 oz can pineapple slices, drained; or 1 fresh pineapple, sliced | 1 × 16 oz can pineapple slices, drained; or 1 fresh pineapple, sliced |
| 4-6 tablespoons any liqueur or spirit such as kirsch, Benedictine or brandy | 4-6 tablespoons any liqueur or spirit such as kirsch, Benedictine or brandy |
| Optional decoration: | Optional decoration: |
| whipped cream | whipped cream |
| glacé or maraschino cherries | candied or maraschino cherries |

Arrange the pineapple in a shallow serving dish. Sprinkle over the liqueur. Chill if possible.

**NOTE:** If serving this dish as a dessert decorate with swirls of cream and cherries.

18

## Smoked Salmon with Scrambled Eggs

| METRIC/IMPERIAL | AMERICAN |
|---|---|
| 4 eggs | 4 eggs |
| 2 tablespoons double cream | 2 tablespoons heavy cream |
| salt | salt |
| freshly ground black pepper | freshly ground black pepper |
| 25 g/1 oz butter | 2 tablespoons butter |
| 4 large thin slices smoked salmon | 4 large thin slices smoked salmon |
| lime slices to garnish | lime slices for garnish |
| To serve: | For serving: |
| 150 ml/¼ pint soured cream | ⅔ cup sour cream |
| Melba toast | Melba toast |

Setting to use: HIGH

Place the eggs, cream, and salt and pepper to taste in a medium bowl. Whisk well and add the butter. Cook, uncovered, for 5 minutes or until the mixture is cooked. Using a fork, break up the mixture after 2, 3 and 4 minutes.

Spread out the salmon slices, cut each in half. Spread over the scrambled egg. Roll up each slice of salmon. Garnish with lime slices and serve immediately. Hand around sour cream and Melba toast separately.

# Cold Pork Salad

**METRIC/IMPERIAL**
625 g/1¼ lb pork fillet, diced
1 stick celery, chopped
2 spring onions, trimmed and chopped
2 cloves garlic, crushed
½ cucumber, peeled and finely diced
1 teaspoon dry mustard
150-300 ml/¼-½ pint mayonnaise
**To garnish:**
spring onions
thin lemon slices

**AMERICAN**
1¼ lb pork tenderloin, diced
1 stalk celery, chopped
2 scallions, trimmed and chopped
2 cloves garlic, minced
½ cucumber, peeled and finely diced
1 teaspoon dry mustard
⅔-1¼ cups mayonnaise
**For garnish:**
scallions
thin lemon slices

Setting to use: HIGH

Place the pork in a medium bowl. Cook, covered, for 6 minutes. Stir halfway through cooking. Drain the pork and set aside to get cold.

Mix together the celery, onions, garlic and cucumber. Stir in the cold pork. Stir the mustard into 150 ml/¼ pint [⅔ cup] mayonnaise, and mix with the pork then add more mayonnaise if desired to coat the vegetables and pork lightly. Garnish with spring onions (scallions) and lemon.

# Vinaigrette Dressing

**METRIC/IMPERIAL**
2 tablespoons wine vinegar or lemon juice
6 tablespoons oil (olive, sunflower, walnut or groundnut)
pinch of mustard powder
pinch of salt
freshly ground black pepper

**AMERICAN**
2 tablespoons wine vinegar or lemon juice
6 tablespoons oil (olive, sunflower, walnut or groundnut)
pinch of mustard powder
pinch of salt
freshly ground black pepper

Place all the ingredients in a screw-top jar and shake vigorously until well blended. Shake again just before using. Alternatively, whisk together well in a small bowl until well blended.

The dressing will keep for 1 week or longer in a screw-top jar in a cool place.

▽ Sunday brunch: clockwise from top: pineapple with liqueur; cold pork salad; smoked salmon with scrambled eggs served with melba toast; cucumber and tomato vinaigrette

**WINE NOTE** Any *Gewürztraminer* wine will lend an aromatic, slightly spicy note to this fine cold chicken dish.

**ACTION PLAN**
1. Prepare the grapefruit for cooking and leave to macerate.
2. Prepare the cake base for the trifle.
3. Cook the new potatoes in the microwave or on the conventional hob, toss in dressing and leave to cool.
4. Make the chicken dish and refrigerate.
5. Cook the grapefruit and serve.
6. Complete the trifle after serving the main course.

## Grapefruit with Ginger

| METRIC/IMPERIAL | AMERICAN |
|---|---|
| 2 large grapefruit, halved and segments loosened | 2 large grapefruit, halved and sections loosened |
| 3 tablespoons sherry | 3 tablespoons sherry |
| pinch grated nutmeg | pinch grated nutmeg |
| good pinch of ground ginger | 1/8 teaspoon ground ginger |
| 1 tablespoon preserved stem ginger, chopped | 1 tablespoon preserved stem ginger, chopped |
| 1 tablespoon caster sugar | 1 tablespoon sugar |
| 4 maraschino cherries | 4 maraschino cherries |

Setting to use: HIGH

Place the grapefruit halves in individual dishes.

Mix together the sherry, nutmeg, ground ginger and chopped ginger. Pour the mixture over the grapefruit. If possible, leave to macerate for 1 hour.

Sprinkle over the sugar. Cook, uncovered, for 3 minutes or until hot. Rearrange halfway through cooking.

Decorate with the maraschino cherries.

## Chicken with Tarragon Mayonnaise

| METRIC/IMPERIAL | AMERICAN |
|---|---|
| 1 × 1.5 kg/3 lb chicken, cooked | 1 × 3 lb chicken, cooked |
| salt | salt |
| freshly ground black pepper | freshly ground black pepper |
| 2 teaspoons chopped fresh tarragon | 2 teaspoons chopped fresh tarragon |
| 1 egg yolk | 1 egg yolk |
| 1/4 teaspoon dry mustard | 1/4 teaspoon dry mustard |
| 150-300 ml/1/4-1/2 pint olive oil | 2/3-1 1/4 cups olive oil |
| 4 teaspoons tarragon vinegar | 4 teaspoons tarragon vinegar |
| To garnish: | For garnish: |
| 50 g/2 oz white grapes, peeled, halved and pips removed | 1/2 cup green grapes, peeled, halved and seeded |
| 50 g/2 oz black grapes, peeled, halved and pips removed | 1/2 cup purple grapes, peeled, halved and seeded |
| tarragon sprigs | tarragon sprigs |

Setting to use: HIGH

Carve the chicken. Arrange the small pieces on a serving dish and the larger slices on top. Sprinkle salt, pepper and tarragon between the slices. Chill while making the mayonnaise.

Place the egg yolk in a small bowl and whisk in 1/4 teaspoon each salt and pepper and the mustard. Add the oil very slowly from the point of a teaspoon, beating throughout. Beat in the vinegar.

Spoon the tarragon mayonnaise over the chicken, and garnish with the grapes and tarragon sprigs.

NOTE: To save time, make the tarragon mayonnaise in a blender or food processor. Alternatively add 2 teaspoons chopped fresh tarragon to 300 ml/1/2 pint (1 1/4 cups) of a good quality commercial mayonnaise.

To cook the chicken, place it in a roasting bag and tie with a piece of string or an elastic band. Prick the bag and place it breast side down in a shallow dish. Cook on HIGH for 24 minutes. Turn over halfway through cooking. Remove from the bag, wrap in foil, and stand for 15 to 20 minutes. Remove the skin while the chicken is warm.

Chicken portions can be used in place of the whole chicken.

## New Potato Salad

To prepare this salad, simply scrub 500 g/1 lb baby new potatoes and cook in the microwave cooker or conventionally.

Drain and toss in a well seasoned Vinaigrette dressing (see page 19) and 1 tablespoon chopped fresh herbs. Leave to cool and serve at room temperature.

NOTE: For additional flavour add 1 tablespoon drained capers, 2 tablespoons grated blue cheese or 2 tablespoons crumbled crispy fried bacon.

20

△ *Smart summer lunch: clockwise from right: grapefruit with ginger; chicken with tarragon mayonnaise; new potato salad green salad; hot triffle*

# Hot Trifle

**METRIC/IMPERIAL**
*1 Swiss roll, sliced, or sponge cake*
*4 tablespoons sherry or fruit juice*
*1 × 400 g/14 oz can fruit cocktail, drained, or frozen fruit*
**Custard:**
*2 tablespoons custard powder*
*1-2 tablespoons caster sugar*
*600 ml/1 pint milk*
*1 egg, lightly beaten*
**To decorate:**
*Ratafias or macaroons*
*glacé cherries and candied angelica, or a can of fruit such as Mandarin oranges or peaches, drained*

**AMERICAN**
*1 jelly roll, sliced, or sponge cake*
*¼ cup sherry or fruit juice*
*1 × 16 oz can fruit cocktail, drained, or frozen fruit*
**Custard:**
*2 tablespoons English dessert powder*
*1-2 tablespoons sugar*
*2½ cups milk*
*1 egg, lightly beaten*
**To decorate:**
*Ratafias or macaroons*
*candied cherries and angelica, or a can of fruit such as Mandarin oranges or peaches, drained*

Setting to use: HIGH

Place the cake in the bottom of a 1 1/2 pint (1 quart) serving dish. Sprinkle over the sherry or fruit juice.

Place the canned or frozen fruit in a medium bowl. Cook covered, for 3 minutes. If frozen, allow 6-8 minutes. Let it stand while making the custard sauce.

Make the custard, place the custard powder in a large jug. Stir in the sugar and milk. Cook, uncovered, for 5 minutes. Stir frequently to avoid lumps. Whisk in the egg.

Spoon the fruit over the cake. Pour over the custard sauce. Decorate with ratafias or macaroons and fruit.

**NOTE:** You can use 600 ml/1 pint (2½ cups) canned or packaged custard instead of making your own.

21

# Supper with Friends

avocado with orange
cod with cheese sauce
broccoli
parsley potatoes
tomato and bean salad
chocolate mousse

Serves 4

*The tartness of the orange complements the
creaminess of the avocado, making this the
perfect spur-of-the moment starter.*

**WINE NOTE** A German *Kabinett* wine is a popular choice and it matches the light taste of the cod to perfection.

**ACTION PLAN**
1. Prepare the chocolate mousse and refrigerate.
2. If using fresh rather than canned potatoes, put them to cook on the conventional hob.
3. Cook the fish dish and set aside.
4. Prepare the avocado and orange while cooking the vegetables in the microwave.
5. Brown the fish dish under the grill (broiler) reheating it in the microwave if necessary.

## Avocado with Orange

| METRIC/IMPERIAL | AMERICAN |
|---|---|
| *2 large, or 3 small oranges* | *2 large, or 3 small oranges* |
| *2 large, or 3 small avocados* | *2 large, or 3 small avocados* |
| *vinaigrette dressing (see page 19)* | *vinaigrette dressing (see page 19)* |
| *chopped fresh parsley to garnish* | *chopped fresh parsley for garnish* |

Setting to use: HIGH

Using a sharp knife, peel the oranges making sure all the pith is removed. Cut into segments and arrange on 4 serving plates, retain any juice.

Halve the avocados and remove the stones (seeds). Peel and slice the flesh lengthwise and arrange with the orange segments.

Mix the reserved orange juice with a little of the dressing and pour over each plate. Sprinkle with parsley and serve.

22

## Cod with Cheese Sauce

| METRIC/IMPERIAL | AMERICAN |
|---|---|
| *4 × 150 g/5 oz frozen cod steaks* | *4 × 5oz frozen cod steaks* |
| *1 × 300 g/10 oz can condensed cream of mushroom soup* | *1 × 10 oz can condensed cream of mushroom soup* |
| *1 teaspoon dry mustard* | *1 teaspoon dry mustard* |
| *2 tablespoons mayonnaise* | *2 tablespoons mayonnaise* |
| *salt* | *salt* |
| *freshly ground black pepper* | *freshly ground black pepper* |
| *40 g/1½ oz Cheddar cheese, grated* | *⅓ cup grated Cheddar cheese* |

# ═ Tomato and Bean Salad ═

| METRIC/IMPERIAL | AMERICAN |
|---|---|
| 500 g/1 lb frozen French or runner beans | 1 lb frozen green beans |
| ½ cucumber, peeled and diced | ½ cucumber, peeled and diced |
| 250 g/8 oz tomatoes, cut into pieces | ½ lb tomatoes, cut into pieces |
| 50 g/2 oz black olives | ⅓ cup ripe olives |
| 4-6 tablespoons vinaigrette dressing, (see page 19) | 4-6 tablespoons vinaigrette dressing, (see page 19) |
| **To garnish:** | **For garnish:** |
| chopped fresh parsley anchovies | chopped fresh parsley anchovies |

Setting to use: **HIGH**

Place the beans in a medium bowl. Cook, covered, for 9 minutes. Stir halfway through cooking. Set aside until cold.

Drain the beans and lightly mix with the cucumber, tomatoes and olives. Toss in the dressing.

Pile into a serving bowl. Sprinkle with chopped parsley and arrange anchovy fillets in a lattic pattern over the tomato and bean salad.

NOTE: Canned beans or cold cooked beans can be used if more convenient.

# ═══ Chocolate Mousse ═══

| METRIC/IMPERIAL | AMERICAN |
|---|---|
| 250 g/8 oz plain chocolate, broken into pieces | 8 squares semi-sweet chocolate, broken into pieces |
| 25 g/1 oz butter | 2 tablespoons butter |
| 4 eggs, separated | 4 eggs, separated |
| **To decorate:** | **To decorate:** |
| 150 ml/¼ pint double cream, whipped | ⅔ cup heavy cream, whipped |
| chocolate curls | chocolate curls |
| sponge fingers or langue de chat (optional) | sponge fingers or langue de chat (optional) |

Setting to use: **HIGH**

Place the chocolate in a medium bowl. Cook, uncovered, for 2 minutes or until melted. Beat in the butter, rum and egg yolks.

Whisk the egg whites until stiff and fold gently into the chocolate mixture. Spoon into 4 glasses. Chill. Serve decorated with whipped cream, chocolate curls and sponge fingers, if using.

NOTE: For additional flavour, add 2 tablespoons of your favourite liqueur to the melted chocolate.

Setting to use: HIGH/Conventional Grill (Broiler)

Arrange the frozen fish in a shallow wide-based casserole. Cook, covered, for 10 minutes. Rearrange the fish halfway through cooking.

Meanwhile, mix together the soup (do not dilute), mustard powder, mayonnaise, and salt and pepper to taste.

Pour the liquid from the fish into the sauce and stir to mix. Pour the sauce over the fish.

Cook, uncovered, for 5 minutes. Gently stir the sauce halfway through cooking.

Sprinkle over the grated cheese and brown under a preheated conventional grill (broiler).

# Family Fare

## taramasalata with pitta bread
## liver in red wine
## creamed potatoes
## peas
## peach melba

### Serves 4

*If you are short of time use commercially prepared taramasalata which is readily available from supermarkets or delicatessen.*

taste and a drop or so of food colouring. If desired, a blender or food processor can be used.

If necessary add more cream to make a soft, peaky mixture.

Serve on four small plates garnished with parsley and gherkin.

## Liver in Red Wine

| METRIC/IMPERIAL | AMERICAN |
| --- | --- |
| 6 bacon rashers, rinds removed and chopped | 6 bacon slices, chopped |
| 25 g/1 oz butter | 2 tablespoons butter |
| 2 cloves garlic, crushed | 2 cloves garlic, minced |
| 1 medium onion, finely chopped | 1 medium onion, finely chopped |
| 25 g/1 oz cornflour | 1/4 cup cornstarch |
| 150 ml/1/4 pint red wine | 2/3 cup red wine |
| 150 ml/1/4 pint hot beef stock | 2/3 cup hot beef stock |
| 250 g/8 oz tomatoes, skinned and chopped | 1/2 lb tomatoes, skinned and chopped |
| 1 tablespoon tomato purée | 1 tablespoon tomato paste |
| 1/2 teaspoon chopped fresh parsley | 1/2 teaspoon chopped fresh parsley |
| 1/2 teaspoon chopped fresh basil | 1/2 teaspoon chopped fresh basil |
| | salt |

**WINE NOTE** Liver calls for a vigorous red wine: a *Beaujolais Nouveau* or *Villages* provides the perfect solution.

**ACTION PLAN**
1. Make the taramasalata, garnish and chill.
2. Prepare the Melba sauce. Drain or peel the peaches and refrigerate.
3. Cook the liver in red wine in the microwave, keep warm.
4. Cook the potatoes in the microwave, drain and cream. Meanwhile cook the peas in the microwave.
5. Warm the pitta bread for a few minutes in the microwave then serve with the taramasalata.
6. Assemble the peach Melba just before serving.

## Taramasalata

| METRIC/IMPERIAL | AMERICAN |
| --- | --- |
| 1 slice white bread, crusts removed and made into crumbs | 1 slice white bread, crusts removed and made into crumbs |
| 3 tablespoons olive oil | 3 tablespoons olive oil |
| 250 g/8 oz smoked cod's roe, skin removed | 1/2 lb smoked cod roe, skin removed |
| 1 clove garlic, crushed | 1 clove garlic, minced |
| 1 tablespoon lemon juice | 1 tablespoon lemon juice |
| 2-4 tablespoons double cream | 2-4 tablespoons heavy cream |
| salt | salt. |
| freshly ground black pepper | freshly ground black pepper |
| red food colouring | red food colouring |
| **To garnish:** | **For garnish:** |
| chopped gherkin | chopped gherkin |
| parsley | parsley |

Mix the breadcrumbs with the olive oil. Beat in the cod's roe, garlic, lemon juice, 2 tablespoons cream, salt and pepper to

24

salt
freshly ground black pepper
500 g/1 lb lamb's liver, thinly
    sliced
chopped fresh parsley to
    garnish (optional)

freshly ground black pepper
1 lb lamb's liver, thinly sliced
chopped fresh parsley for
    garnish (optional)

2 teaspoons cornflour
1 tablespoon white wine
1/2 teaspoon lemon juice
8 peeled fresh or canned
    peach halves
4 scoops vanilla ice cream

2 teaspoons cornstarch
1 tablespoon white wine
1/2 teaspoon lemon juice
8 peeled fresh or canned
    peach halves
4 scoops vanilla ice cream

Setting to use: HIGH

Place the bacon, butter, garlic and onion in a large bowl. Cook, covered, for 5 minutes.

Blend the cornflour (cornstarch) with the red wine to make a smooth paste. Stir this into the onion mixture with the hot stock, tomatoes, tomato purée (paste), parsley, basil, and salt and pepper to taste. Add the liver. Cook, covered, for 10 minutes, stirring halfway through cooking.

Let stand, covered, for 5 minutes before serving, sprinkled with chopped parsley if using.

Setting to use: HIGH

Place the frozen raspberries in a medium bowl. Cook, covered, for 5 minutes. If using canned raspberries, cook for 3 minutes. Stir in the sugar.

Blend in the cornflour (cornstarch) with the wine and lemon juice and stir into the raspberries. Cook, uncovered, for 4 minutes or until thickened. Stir every minute. Cool quickly by standing the bowl of raspberry sauce in another bowl of ice.

Place two peach halves in each of four glass dishes or wine glasses and top with scoops of ice cream. Pour over the sauce and serve with fan wafers.

# Peach Melba

METRIC/IMPERIAL
350 g/12 oz frozen raspberries,
    or 1 × 350 g/12 oz can
    raspberries, drained
3 tablespoons caster sugar

AMERICAN
3/4 lb frozen raspberries, or
    1 × 350 g/16 oz can
    raspberries, drained
3 tablespoons sugar

▽ Family fare: anticlockwise from centre: taramasalata with pitta bread; creamed potatoes; peas; liver in red wine; peach melba

25

# Italian Summer Gathering

## shrimps in garlic butter
### brown bread or toast

---

## spaghetti milanaise
## tomato salad

---

## selection of cheeses
## and fresh fruit

### Serves 2

*This is an intimate meal for two, but double up on the quantities and it would be the perfect casual supper to feed friends.*

---

**WINE NOTE** Look for *Lugana* or *Gavi* to match the first two courses of the light menu; they are among Italy's finest, most delicate white wines.

**ACTION PLAN**
1. Prepare the salad, set aside. Cook the spaghetti.
2. Cook the frozen shrimp if using and set aside.
3. Prepare the sauce for the spaghetti.
4. Cook and serve the first course.
5. Drain the spaghetti, toss with the sauce (warming it in the microwave again if necessary) and serve.
6. Toss the salad before serving.

## Shrimps in Garlic Butter

| METRIC/IMPERIAL | AMERICAN |
| --- | --- |
| 250 g/8 oz cooked peeled shrimps, fresh, frozen or canned | 1/2 lb cooked shelled shrimp, fresh, frozen or canned |
| 1 clove garlic, crushed | 1 clove garlic, minced |
| 125 g/4 oz butter | 1/2 cup butter |
| 1 tablespoon chopped fresh parsley | 1 tablespoon chopped fresh parsley |
| parsley sprigs to garnish | parsley sprigs for garnish |

Setting to use: HIGH

If using frozen shrimps, place in a medium bowl and cook, uncovered, for 3-4 minutes. After 2 minutes, gently separate the shrimps and stir with a fork. Spread out the shrimps on kitchen paper towels to drain.

Place the garlic and butter in a medium bowl. Cook, uncovered, for 2 minutes, until melted.

Stir in the shrimps and parsley. Cook, uncovered, for 4 minutes or until hot.

Pile the shrimps into two small serving dishes. Garnish each with a sprig of parsley. Serve with toast or brown bread.

## Spaghetti Milanaise

| METRIC/IMPERIAL | AMERICAN |
| --- | --- |
| 1 tablespoon oil | 1 tablespoon oil |
| salt | salt |
| 1.75 l/3 pints boiling water | 7 1/2 cups boiling water |
| 250 g/8 oz spaghetti | 1/2 lb spaghetti |
| 50 g/2 oz button mushrooms, sliced | 1/2 cup button mushrooms, sliced |
| 1 × 410 g/14 oz can chopped tomatoes | 1 × 16 oz can chopped tomatoes |
| 2 cloves garlic, crushed | 2 cloves garlic, minced |
| 50 g/2 oz cooked ham, cut into matchsticks | 1/4 cup cooked ham, cut into matchsticks |
| 50 g/2 oz cooked tongue, cut into matchsticks (optional) | 2 oz cooked tongue, cut into matchsticks (optional) |
| 25 g/1 oz butter, cut into pieces | 2 tablespoons butter, cut into pieces |
| freshly ground black pepper | freshly ground black pepper |
| 25 g/1 oz Parmesan cheese, grated | 1/4 cup Parmesan cheese, grated |

Setting to use: HIGH

Place the oil, a pinch of salt and the boiling water in a very large bowl. Put the spaghetti in the water. Cook, uncovered, for 1 minute, then gently push the spaghetti into the water until it is immersed. Cook covered, for 8 minutes. Check occasionally to ensure the spaghetti is totally covered with water during the cooking process. Let stand, covered, for 10 minutes.

Place the mushrooms in a medium bowl. Cook, covered, for 1 minute. Stir in the tomatoes, garlic, ham, tongue, butter, and salt and pepper to taste. Cook, covered; for 4 minutes. Stir halfway through cooking.

Drain the spaghetti. Toss together the spaghetti, tomato sauce and cheese. Pile into a warm serving bowl.

## Tomato Salad

| METRIC/IMPERIAL | AMERICAN |
| --- | --- |
| 4-5 large ripe tomatoes | 4-5 large ripe tomatoes |
| 5-6 large basil leaves | 5-6 large basil leaves |
| 1-2 tablespoons olive oil | 1-2 tablespoons olive oil |
| salt | salt |
| freshly ground pepper | freshly ground pepper |
| squeeze lemon juice | squeeze lemon juice |

Setting to use: HIGH

Finely slice the tomatoes. Shred the basil leaves, but do not chop as they tend to bruise. Arrange the tomatoes and basil in a bowl. Drizzle over a little oil, season with salt to taste, a fresh grinding of pepper and a squeeze of lemon juice. Toss lightly.

▷ *Italian summer gathering: from front: shrimps in garlic butter; tomato salad: spaghetti milanaise; selection of fresh fruit*

# Alfresco Lunch

## gazpacho
## french bread
## quick moussaka
## tossed green salad
## ice cream with apricot sauce

### Serves 4

*The moussaka is best served with tossed green salad although on cooler days you could serve a selection of vegetables. Select an ice cream of your choice, coffee and walnut, or hazelnut would make a change from vanilla.*

WINE NOTE  A dry rosé such as *Côtes de Provence* will make a pretty (and deceptively strong) background for this fresh menu.

ACTION PLAN
1. Make the gazpacho and chill.
2. Make the apricot sauce and set aside. (Chill if desired.)
3. Prepare the moussaka up to the point where you layer the ingredients in the casserole.
4. Prepare the green salad. Alternatively cook the vegetables conventionally on the hob while you are eating the first course.
5. Complete cooking the moussaka in the microwave then brown under the grill (broiler) before serving.

Place the bread in a bowl. Stir in the vinegar and as much oil as the bread will absorb.

Mix in the remaining ingredients. Purée in a blender or food processor with the ice cubes until smooth. Add more tomato juice or water to thin the soup. Chill in the refrigerator if possible; if not, pour the soup into a bowl and stand the bowl in a second bowl of ice cubes. Alternatively drop an ice cube or two into each bowl before serving.

## ═══ Gazpacho ═══

METRIC/IMPERIAL
*3 slices thick white bread, crusts removed and crumbled*
*1 tablespoon wine vinegar*
*oil*
*2 cloves garlic, crushed*
*150 ml/¼ pint tomato juice*
*1 large onion, grated*
*1 small cucumber, peeled and grated*
*salt*
*freshly ground black pepper*
*1 × 400 g/14 oz can tomatoes*
*1 small pepper, cored, seeded and chopped*
*2 tablespoons mayonnaise*
*2-4 ice cubes*

AMERICAN
*3 slices thick white bread, crusts removed and crumbled*
*1 tablespoon wine vinegar*
*oil*
*2 cloves garlic, minced*
*⅔ cup tomato juice*
*1 large onion, grated*
*1 small cucumber, peeled and grated*
*salt*
*freshly ground black pepper*
*1 × 400 g/16 oz can tomatoes*
*1 small sweet pepper, cored, seeded and chopped*
*2 tablespoons mayonnaise*
*2-4 ice cubes*

## ═══ Quick Moussaka ═══

METRIC/IMPERIAL
*350 g/12 oz frozen minced beef*
*1 tablespoon tomato purée or tomato sauce*
*1½ teaspoons mixed dried herbs*
*1 beef stock cube, crumbled*
*1 × 250 g/8 oz can tomatoes, chopped*
*salt*
*freshly ground black pepper*
*350 g/12 oz potatoes, peeled and sliced (not too thinly)*
*3 tablespoons water*

AMERICAN
*¾ lb frozen ground beef*
*1 tablespoon tomato paste or tomato sauce*
*1½ teaspoons mixed dried herbs*
*1 beef bouillon cube, crumbled*
*1 × 8 oz can tomatoes, chopped*
*salt*
*freshly ground black pepper*
*¾ lb potatoes, peeled and sliced (not too thinly)*
*3 tablespoons water*

△ Alfresco lunch : clockwise from front: gazpacho; tossed green salad; quick moussaka; ice cream with apricot sauce

15-25 g/¹/₂-1 oz Cheddar
  cheese, grated
Sauce:
25 g/1 oz butter
25 g/1 oz plain flour
300 ml/¹/₂ pint milk
1 egg, lightly beaten
40 g/1¹/₂ Cheddar cheese,
  grated

2-4 tablespoons grated
  Cheddar cheese
Sauce:
2 tablespoons butter
¹/₄ cup all-purpose flour
1¹/₄ cups milk
1 egg, lightly beaten
¹/₃ cup grated Cheddar cheese

Setting to use: HIGH

Place the frozen beef in a medium bowl. Cover and cook for 6 minutes. Break up with a fork, then stir in the tomato purée (paste) or sauce, herbs, stock (bouillon) cube, tomatoes, and salt and pepper to taste. Cook for 8 minutes. Stir halfway through cooking.

Meanwhile, place the butter in a saucepan and heat on a conventional hob until melted. Stir in the flour and cook for 1 minute. Gradually add the milk and cook, stirring all the time, until thick. Remove from the heat. Beat in the egg and cheese and stir until melted. Keep warm.

Place the potatoes and water in a medium bowl. Cook, covered, for 5 minutes.

Layer the meat, potatoes and sauce in a 1.2 l/2 pint (5 cup) casserole. Finish with the sauce. Cook, uncovered, for 4 minutes. Sprinkle with the cheese. Brown under a preheated conventional grill (broiler).

# Apricot Sauce

METRIC/IMPERIAL
4 tablespoons apricot jam,
  made up to 300 ml/¹/₂ pint
  with water
2 teaspoons arrowroot
drop of red food colouring

AMERICAN
4 tablespoons apricot jam,
  made up to 1¹/₄ cups with
  water
2 teaspoons arrowroot
drop of red food coloring

Setting to use: HIGH

Stir together the jam and water in a jug, reserving 2 tablespoons of the water to mix with the arrowroot. Cook, uncovered, for 3 minutes.

Mix together the arrowroot and reserved water to make a paste. Gradually add the apricot mixture, stirring all the time. Cook, uncovered, for 1 minute until clear. Stir after 30 seconds.

Add the food colouring. Pass through a strainer if liked.

NOTE: Any flavoured jam can be used, try strawberry, plum or black cherry.

# Designed to Impress

## consommé with sherry
## sautéed steak with herb butter
## stuffed potatoes
## tossed green salad
## zabaglione

### Serves 4

*This splendid dinner is for special occasions. Although the consommé is canned the addition of sherry turns the soup into something special.*

**WINE NOTE** The best meat deserves the best wine: look for a *Bordeaux Cru Classé* (classed growth claret) to accompany this steak.

**ACTION PLAN**
1. Prepare a green salad and vinaigrette dressing but do not toss.
2. Heat the consommé on the conventional hob while baking the potatoes in the microwave.
3. Let the potatoes stand then complete them and return to the microwave to reheat.
4. Brown the steaks and continue cooking in the microwave while you are eating the first course.
5. Make the zabaglione just before serving.

## Consommé with Sherry

| METRIC/IMPERIAL | AMERICAN |
|---|---|
| 2 × 42.5 g/15 oz cans consommé | 2 × 16 oz cans consommé |
| 4 tablespoons dry sherry | 1/4 cup dry sherry |
| finely grated carrot or chopped fresh parsley to garnish | finely grated carrot or chopped fresh parsley for garnish |

Heat the soup on the conventional hob according to the can instructions.

Stir in the sherry and allow to warm through. Pour into warmed serving bowls. Garnish with finely grated carrot or chopped parsley and serve.

▷ *Designed to impress: from front: consommé with sherry; stuffed potatoes; sautéed steak with herb butter; tossed green salad; zabaglione*

30

## Sautéed Steak

| METRIC/IMPERIAL | AMERICAN |
|---|---|
| 4 fillet steaks cut 2.5 cm/1 inch thick, total weight about 500 g/1 lb | 4 boneless sirloin steaks or filet mignon, cut 1 inch thick, total weight about 1 lb |
| butter for frying | butter for frying |
| **To garnish:** | **For garnish:** |
| herb butter (see opposite) | herb butter (see opposite) |
| watercress or sprigs of fresh parsley | watercress or sprigs of fresh parsley |

Setting to use: **HIGH**

# Herb Butter

Cream 125 g/4 oz (½ cup) butter until soft then add freshly ground black pepper to taste and three tablespoons chopped fresh herbs. (If using a food processor you can add whole herbs, these will be chopped as the butter is softened.)

Roll the butter into a sausage shape between sheets of greaseproof (wax) paper and refrigerate. When firm, cut into slices and serve on top of the hot steaks. Herb butter can also be served on top of grilled fish, baked potatoes and corn-on-the-cob (see page 46).

*Garlic Butter* Peel and crush 2 cloves garlic and add to the creamed butter with freshly ground black pepper to taste.

# Stuffed Potatoes

| METRIC/IMPERIAL | AMERICAN |
| --- | --- |
| *4 medium potatoes, scrubbed, dried and pricked* | *4 medium potatoes, scrubbed, dried and pricked* |
| *2 tablespoons tomato purée or tomato sauce* | *2 tablespoons tomato paste or tomato sauce* |
| *15-25 g/½-1 oz butter* | *1-2 tablespoons butter* |
| *salt* | *salt* |
| *freshly ground black pepper* | *freshly ground black pepper* |
| *chopped fresh parsley to garnish (optional)* | *chopped fresh parsley for garnish (optional)* |

Setting to use: HIGH

Place the potatoes in a circle on a piece of kitchen paper towel on the floor of the microwave.

Cook, uncovered, for 13 minutes. Turn over and rearrange halfway through cooking.

Remove the potatoes and wrap each one tightly in foil. Let them stand for 5 minutes.

Cut the tops off the potatoes. Scoop out the potato flesh and mash with the tomato purée (paste) or sauce, butter, and salt and pepper to taste.

Place one-third of the potato in a forcing (pastry) bag fitted with a large star nozzle. Pile the remaining potato into the potato skins. Pipe the potato in the bag over each.

If necessary, reheat for 3 minutes. Serve garnished with chopped parsley if using.

# Zabaglione

| METRIC/IMPERIAL | AMERICAN |
| --- | --- |
| *6 large egg yolks* | *6 large egg yolks* |
| *75 g/3 oz caster sugar* | *6 tablespoons sugar* |
| *4 tablespoons marsala wine* | *¼ cup marsala wine* |
| *boudoir biscuits to serve (optional)* | *ladyfingers to serve (optional)* |

Setting to use: HIGH

Using an electric whisk beat together the egg yolks and sugar in a medium bowl.

Cook, uncovered, for 15 seconds. Beat for a further minute. Continue alternately cooking for 15 seconds and beating until the dessert is pale and thick. Take care not to overcook.

Gradually beat in the wine. Pour into four wine glasses and serve at once, with boudoir biscuits (ladyfingers).

Lightly beat the steaks to make them thinner. Melt a little butter in the microwave and use it to brush the steaks on both sides.

Heat a very heavy frying pan and quickly fry each side of the steaks to sear and brown the surface.

Place the steaks in a casserole dish. Cook uncovered, for 3-5 minutes, depending on how well cooked you want the steaks to be.

Place a pat of herb butter on each steak and serve immediately with watercress or parsley to garnish.

NOTE: If preferred, steaks may be completely fried or grilled (broiled) conventionally.

# Economical Family Lunch

## egg mayonnaise
## spiced-up beef
## brown rice
## strawberry creams

### Serves 4

*This is the perfect menu to serve when the family are feeling hungry but you are not in the mood to cook.*

**WINE NOTE** This rather humble menu is best served without wine but if you want to splash out try serving an *Australian Shiraz*. This wine has the body and power needed to match the spicy flavour of the beef.

**ACTION PLAN**
1. Hard-boil the eggs on the conventional hob, drain and hold under cold running water for a few minutes then cool.
2. Cook the rice on the conventional hob according to packet directions.
3. Meanwhile, cook the beef in the microwave. While the beef is cooking make the egg mayonnaise.
4. Thaw the strawberries and set aside.
5. Make up the strawberry creams after serving the main course.

## Egg Mayonnaise

| METRIC/IMPERIAL | AMERICAN |
| --- | --- |
| 4 eggs | 4 eggs |
| 4 lettuce leaves, torn into pieces | 4 lettuce leaves, torn into pieces |
| 4-6 tablespoons well seasoned mayonnaise | 4-6 tablespoons well seasoned mayonnaise |
| To garnish: | For garnish: |
| paprika or cayenne pepper | paprika or cayenne pepper |
| lemon slices | lemon slices |

Hard boil the eggs on the conventional hob. Plunge in cold water to cool, then drain and remove the shells. Cut each egg in half lengthways.

Arrange the lettuce on four small plates or one larger serving dish.

Place the egg halves, yolks downwards, on the dish or dishes. Spoon over the mayonnaise and garnish with paprika or cayenne and lemon slices.

32

## Spiced-up Beef

| METRIC/IMPERIAL | AMERICAN |
| --- | --- |
| 1 stick celery (optional) | 1 stalk celery (optional) |
| 1 medium onion, chopped | 1 medium onion, chopped |
| 1 clove garlic, crushed | 1 clove garlic, minced |
| 1 tablespoon mild curry paste | 1 tablespoon mild curry paste |
| 1½ tablespoons plain flour | 1½ tablespoons all-purpose flour |
| 450 ml/¾ pint hot beef stock | 2 cups hot beef stock |
| 1 tablespoon tomato purée | 1 tablespoon tomato paste |
| 1 tablespoon chutney | 1 tablespoon chutney |
| 1 × 350 g/12 oz can corned beef, cut into large cubes | 1 × 12 oz can luncheon meat, cut into large cubes |
| desiccated coconut or chopped fresh parsley to garnish | dried shredded coconut or chopped fresh parsley for garnish |

Setting to use: HIGH

Place the celery, if used, onion, garlic and curry paste in a large bowl. Cook, covered, for 5 minutes. Stir halfway through cooking.

Stir in the flour. Gradually blend in the stock, tomato purée

(paste) and chutney. Cook, uncovered, for 4 minutes. Stir halfway through cooking.

Stir in the meat. Cook, uncovered, for 8 minutes. Stir halfway through cooking.

Spoon onto a warm serving dish. Sprinkle with coconut or chopped parsley and serve.

# === Strawberry Creams ===

Place the strawberries in a medium bowl. Cook, covered, for 4 minutes.

Spoon the berries into a serving bowl or divide between four small dishes. Retain a few whole berries for decoration.

Place the blancmange (pudding) powder and sugar in a large jug. Mix in a little of the milk to make a smooth paste, then gradually add the rest of the milk.

Cook, uncovered, for 5 minutes or until thick. Stir every minute to avoid lumps.

Whisk in the beaten egg. Pour over the strawberries and decorate with the reserved strawberries. Serve at once.

**METRIC/IMPERIAL**
250 g/8 oz frozen stawberries
1 packet strawberry
    blancmange powder
2 tablespoons caster sugar
300 ml/½ pint evaporated
    milk and 300 ml/½ pint
    fresh milk, or 600 ml/1 pint
    fresh milk
1 egg, lightly beaten

Setting to use: **HIGH**

**AMERICAN**
½ lb [2½-3 cups] frozen
    strawberries
1 package strawberry-flavored
    pudding powder
2 tablespoons sugar
1 cup evaporated milk and
    1 cup fresh milk, or 2 cups
    fresh milk
1 egg, lightly beaten

▽ *Economical family lunch: clockwise from front: egg mayonnaise; spiced-up beef on brown rice; strawberry creams*

33

# Mexican Meal

## guacamole with crudité
## chilli con carne
## rice
## tossed green salad
## orange semolina pudding

### Serves 4

*Although these recipes are not truly traditional they do have a Mexican feel. The guacamole can be served with hot corn chips or fried tortillas instead of the crudité.*

**WINE NOTE** If you like your chilli con carne to be very hot then lager is probably the best accompaniment; if however you serve a milder version try serving any of the Bulgarian red wines.

**ACTION PLAN**
1. Make the orange pudding and chill.
2. Prepare the vegetable crudité, cover and refrigerate.
3. Make the avocado dip, cover tightly.
4. Cook the chilli con carne in the microwave.
5. Meanwhile cook the rice on the conventional hob, following package instructions.

## Guacamole

| METRIC/IMPERIAL | AMERICAN |
|---|---|
| 2 large ripe avocados, halved and stoned | 2 large ripe avocados, halved and seeded |
| 1 tablespoon chopped fresh chives or grated onion | 1 tablespoon chopped fresh chives or grated onion |
| 1 clove garlic, crushed | 1 clove garlic, minced |
| 1 tablespoon oil | 1 tablespoon oil |
| 1 tablespoon lemon juice | 1 tablespoon lemon juice |
| ¼ teaspoon Worcestershire sauce | ¼ teaspoon Worcestershire sauce |
| salt | salt |
| freshly ground black pepper | freshly ground black pepper |
| chopped fresh chives to garnish (optional) | chopped fresh chives for garnish (optional) |
| To serve: | To serve: |
| raw vegetable sticks | raw vegetable sticks |
| potato crisps or hot corn chips | potato crisps or hot corn chips |

Scoop and scrape the avocado flesh from the skins. Mash with the chives or onion, garlic, oil, lemon juice, Worcestershire sauce, and salt and pepper to taste.

Spoon into a small dish. Serve with sticks of raw vegetables, crisps or corn chips.

## Chilli Con Carne

| METRIC/IMPERIAL | AMERICAN |
|---|---|
| 1 medium onion, chopped | 1 medium onion, chopped |
| 1 clove garlic, crushed | 1 clove garlic, minced |
| 1 tablespoon tomato purée | 1 tablespoon tomato paste |
| 1½ teaspoons dried mixed herbs | 1½ teaspoons dried mixed herbs |
| ½-1 tablespoon chilli powder | ½-1 tablespoon chili powder |
| 1 × 450 g/16 oz can good quality minced beef in rich gravy | 1 × 450 g/16 oz can ground beef in rich gravy |
| 1 beef stock cube, crumbled | 1 beef bouillon cube, crumbled |
| 1 × 425 g/15 oz can red kidney beans, drained | 1 × 16 oz can red kidney beans, drained |
| salt | salt |
| freshly ground black pepper | freshly ground black pepper |
| rice to serve | rice to serve |

Setting to use: HIGH

Place the onion, garlic, tomato purée (paste), herbs and chilli powder in a large bowl. Cover and cook for 6 minutes. Stir halfway through cooking.

Stir in the canned beef in gravy, stock (bouillon) cube, kidney beans, and salt and pepper to taste. Cook, covered, for 7½ minutes. Stir halfway through cooking. Serve hot on a bed of rice.

## Orange Semolina Pudding

| METRIC/IMPERIAL | AMERICAN |
|---|---|
| 600 ml/1 pint milk | 2½ cups milk |
| 75 g/3 oz semolina | ¾ cup semolina |
| 25 g/1 oz caster sugar | 2 tablespoons sugar |
| 1 egg, lightly beaten | 1 egg, lightly beaten |
| grated rind of 1 large orange | grated rind of 1 large orange |
| 2 tablespoons double cream | 2 tablespoons heavy cream |
| 2 oranges, peeled, pips removed and cut into small pieces | 2 oranges, peeled, seeded and cut into small pieces |
| orange rind, shredded with a zester, to decorate | orange rind, shredded with a zester, to decorate |

Setting to use: HIGH

Place the milk in a very large bowl. Cook, uncovered, for 5 minutes or until boiling. Whisk in the semolina and sugar. Cook, lightly covered, for 4½ minutes. Whisk halfway through cooking. Check frequently to ensure the mixture does not boil over.

Beat in the egg and orange rind, then the cream. Divide the orange pieces between four dessert glasses. Pour over the semolina mixture. Refrigerate to chill.

Serve decorated with shredded orange rind.

▷ *Mexican meal: from front: guacamole with crudité; chilli con carne on rice; tossed green salad; orange semolina pudding*

# Filling Food

## vegetable soup
## curried kedgeree
## tomato salad
## baked stuffed apples

### Serves 4

*This is another economical lunch menu that is perfect family fare. If tomatoes are expensive serve a salad or green vegetable of your choice.*

**WINE NOTE** Spicy foods and eggs are never easy partners for wine, but a firm dry white like an *Alsace Pinot Blanc* will cope admirably.

**ACTION PLAN**
1. Hard-boil the eggs for the kedgeree on the conventional hob. Cool under running cold water.
2. Prepare the baked apples and set aside.
3. Start cooking the kedgeree. While the kedgeree is cooking heat the soup on the conventional hob.
4. Once the kedgeree is ready set it aside and put the apples in the microwave to cook.
5. Prepare tomato salad (see page 26).
6. Serve the soup. Reheat the kedgeree in the microwave before serving.

## Vegetable Soup

| METRIC/IMPERIAL | AMERICAN |
|---|---|
| 40 g/1½ oz butter | 3 tablespoons butter |
| 50 g/2 oz turnip, peeled and diced | ⅓ cup diced turnip |
| 1 carrot, peeled and diced | 1 carrot, peeled and finely diced |
| 1 leek, white part only, trimmed and finely sliced | 1 leek, white part only, trimmed and finely sliced |
| 1 stick celery, finely chopped | 1 stalk celery, finely chopped |
| 1 small onion, peeled and finely chopped | 1 small onion, peeled and finely chopped |
| 50 g/2 oz shredded cabbage | ⅔ cup shredded cabbage |
| ½ green pepper, cored, seeded and finely diced | ½ green pepper, cored, seeded and finely diced |
| 2 cloves garlic, peeled and crushed | 2 cloves garlic, peeled and crushed |
| 25 g/1 oz macaroni or rice | ¼ cup macaroni or rice |
| 750 g/1½ lb tomatoes, skinned and chopped or 1 × 540 g/ 1 lb 3 oz can tomatoes | 1½ lb tomatoes, skinned and chopped or 1 × 1¼ lb can tomatoes |
| 1 tablespoon tomato purée | 1 tablespoon tomato paste |
| 2 large sprigs chervil | 2 large sprigs chervil |

| | |
|---|---|
| 750 ml/1¼ pints hot beef stock | 3 cups hot beef stock |
| salt | salt |
| freshly ground black pepper | freshly ground black pepper |

Setting to use: HIGH

Place the butter, turnip, carrot, leek, celery, onion, cabbage, green pepper and garlic in a large bowl. Cook, covered, for 10 minutes. Stir halfway through cooking.

Stir in the macaroni or rice, tomatoes, tomato purée (paste), chervil, hot stock and salt and pepper to taste. Cook, covered, for 10 minutes. Stir halfway through cooking.

NOTE: This is a perfect standby soup. It can be put together using small quantities of whatever vegetables, rice or pasta you have in your storecupboard.

## Kedgeree

| METRIC/IMPERIAL | AMERICAN |
|---|---|
| 750 g/1½ lb haddock fillets | 1½ lb haddock fillets |
| 350 g/12 oz long-grain rice | 1¾ cups long-grain rice |
| 750 ml/1¼ pints hot chicken stock | 3 cups hot chicken stock |
| salt | salt |
| ¼ teaspoon oil | ¼ teaspoon oil |
| 1 tablespoon curry powder | 1 tablespoon curry powder |
| | ¼ cup butter, cut into cubes |

50 g/2 oz butter, cut into cubes
1 egg, beaten
2 hard-boiled eggs, chopped
50 g/2 oz cooked ham, diced
2 tablespoons chopped fresh
  parsley
2 teaspoons lemon juice
freshly ground black pepper
To garnish:
1 hard-boiled egg, yolk and
  white sieved separately
1 tablespoon finely chopped
  fresh parsley

1 egg, beaten
2 hard-cooked eggs, chopped
1/4 cup diced cooked ham
2 tablespoons chopped fresh
  parsley
2 teaspoons lemon juice
freshly ground black pepper
For garnish:
1 hard-cooked egg, yolk and
  white sieved separately
1 tablespoon finely chopped
  fresh parsley

Setting to use: HIGH

Place the haddock fillets in a shallow dish. Cook, covered, for 7 minutes. Turn the dish around halfway through cooking. Set aside, covered.

Place the rice, hot stock, a pinch of salt, the oil and curry powder in a large bowl. Cook, covered, for 12 minutes. Leave to stand, covered, for 8 minutes. Meanwhile, flake the fish.

Stir the butter and beaten egg into the rice. Add the fish, chopped eggs, ham, parsley, lemon juice and pepper to taste. Cook, covered, for 4 minutes. Stir halfway through cooking.

Serve garnished with alternate rows of sieved egg yolk, egg white and chopped parsley.

| METRIC/IMPERIAL | AMERICAN |
| --- | --- |
| 3 tablespoons mixed dried fruits | 3 tablespoons mixed dried fruits |
| 3 tablespoons apricot jam | 3 tablespoons apricot jam |
| 1 teaspoon ground cinnamon | 1 teaspoon ground cinnamon |
| 4 large cooking apples, total weight 1.25 kg/2¾lb | 4 large tart apples, total weight 2¾lb |

Setting to use: HIGH

Mix together the mixed fruit, jam and cinnamon.

Core the apples then make a cut around the middle of each apple.

Stand the apples in a shallow dish. Spoon the filling into the apple cavities. Cook for 7 minutes. Turn the dish round and cook for a further 7 minutes or until tender.

Let the apples stand for 4 minutes before serving.

▽ Filling food: from left: vegetable soup; curried kedgeree; tomato salad; baked stuffed apples

# Summer Celebration

## melon with ginger
## trout with horseradish
## buttered broccoli
## new potatoes
## minted sorbet

### Serves 4

*This cooling menu is perfect for a hot summer's day. Homemade sorbet is an excellent freezer standby. Alternatively buy a good quality orange or lemon sorbet to serve as dessert, sprinkle the scoops with a little chopped mint before serving.*

**WINE NOTE** Portuguese *Vinho Verde* will provide a good clean neutral background for the exciting flavours of ginger and horseradish found in this menu.

**ACTION PLAN**
1. Prepare the melon and chill.
2. While eating the first course cook the broccoli on the conventional hob and cook the trout in the microwave.
3. Take the sorbet from the freezer and if necessary, pop it into the microwave for a few seconds so that it is easier to serve.

## ═══ Melon with Ginger ═══

| METRIC/IMPERIAL | AMERICAN |
|---|---|
| *1 medium melon, quartered and seeded* | *1 medium melon, quartered and seeded* |
| *2 tablespoons caster sugar* | *2 tablespoons caster sugar* |
| *1-2 teaspoons ground ginger* | *1-2 teaspoons ground ginger* |
| *fresh fruit to garnish* | *fresh fruit for garnish* |

Setting to use: HIGH

Place a melon quarter on each of four serving dishes.

Mix together the sugar and ginger. Sprinkle the sugar mixture over the melon or hand separately. Garnish with a little fresh fruit.

If possible, chill before serving.

▷ *Summer celebration: clockwise from centre: melon with ginger; trout with horseradish; new potatoes; buttered broccoli; minted sorbet*

38

## Trout with Horseradish

| METRIC/IMPERIAL | AMERICAN |
|---|---|
| *4 frozen cleaned trout* | *4 frozen cleaned trout* |
| *50 g/2 oz butter* | *¼ cup butter* |
| *1 × 125 g/4 oz bottle creamed horseradish sauce to serve* | *1 × 4 oz bottle creamed horseradish sauce to serve* |
| To garnish: | For garnish: |
| *lemon slices* | *lemon slices* |
| *parsley sprigs* | *parsley sprigs* |

Setting to use: HIGH

Arrange the trout on a flat dish, and cook, covered, for 6 minutes.

Rearrange and place a piece of butter on each trout. Cook, covered, for a further 6 minutes. Let them stand for 5 minutes, covered

Arrange the trout on a serving dish. Garnish with lemon slices and parsley.

Serve with the horseradish sauce.

# Buttered Broccoli

| METRIC/IMPERIAL | AMERICAN |
|---|---|
| 500 g/1 lb fresh broccoli | 1 lb fresh broccoli |
| 3 tablespoons water | 3 tablespoons water |
| pinch of salt | pinch of salt |
| a knob of butter | 1 tablespoon butter |

Setting to use: HIGH

Halve the broccoli lengthways, then place in a large bowl with the water and salt. Arrange with the stalks upwards.

Cook, covered, for 7 minutes. Stand, covered, for 5 minutes then drain, and arrange in a warm serving dish and dot with the butter.

# Minted Sorbet

| METRIC/IMPERIAL | AMERICAN |
|---|---|
| 750 ml/1¼ pint water | 3 cups water |
| 2 rounded teaspoons powdered gelatine | 2 rounded teaspoons powdered gelatin |
| 150 g/5 oz granulated sugar | ²/₃ cup sugar |
| 150 ml/¼ pint apple juice | ²/₃ cup apple juice |
| 1-2 tablespoons freshly chopped mint | 1-2 tablespoons freshly chopped mint |
| 2 egg whites (large eggs) | 2 egg whites (large eggs) |
| sprigs of fresh mint to decorate | sprigs of fresh mint to decorate |

Setting to use: HIGH

Place 300 ml/½ pint (1¼ cups) water into a large jug. Stir in the gelatine and sugar. Cook uncovered for 4 minutes, stirring halfway through cooking.

Stir well until the sugar has completely dissolved. Stir in the remaining water, apple juice and chopped mint. Set aside and cool.

Pour the mixture into a metal container. Freeze until the edges of the mixture begin to set. Turn the mixture into a bowl. Whisk until thick. Whisk the egg whites until stiff and fold them into the mixture.

Pour the mixture into a large container. Freeze the sorbet until solid.

Remove from the freezer and refrigerate for 15 minutes before serving, decorate with sprigs of mint.

# Fish Fiesta

## mushrooms with garlic
## french bread
―――
## fish fillets with almonds
## mixed vegetables
―――
## spiced fruit cream
## langues de chat

### Serves 6

Serve warm crispy french bread with both the mushrooms and the fish fillets. To add interest serve it with butter to which you have beaten in freshly ground black pepper and grated lemon peel, a dash of anchovy essence (paste) or 1 tablespoon chopped fresh herbs.

**WINE NOTE** *White Rioja* is, in general, excellent value for money and it would make a perfect partner for both savoury courses of this meal.

**ACTION PLAN**
1. Make the fruit cream and chill.
2. Prepare and cook the fish rolls. Cover and set aside. Prepare the cream sauce, pour over the fish and set aside.
3. Cook the vegetables on the conventional hob while preparing and cooking the first course.
4. Pop the fish into the microwave to heat through while eating the first course.
5. Decorate the dessert before serving.

## ══ Mushrooms with Garlic ══

| METRIC/IMPERIAL | AMERICAN |
|---|---|
| 750 g/1½ lb button mushrooms | 1½ lb button mushrooms |
| 25 g/1 oz butter | 2 tablespoons butter |
| 1 small onion, finely grated | 1 small onion, finely grated |
| 2 cloves garlic, crushed | 2 cloves garlic, minced |
| 4 tomatoes, skinned and chopped | 4 tomatoes, skinned and chopped |
| 1 tablespoon tomato purée | 1 tablespoon tomato paste |
| 1 teaspoon chopped fresh mixed herbs | 1 teaspoon chopped fresh mixed herbs |
| salt | salt |
| freshly ground black pepper | freshly ground black pepper |
| chopped fresh parsley to garnish | chopped fresh parsley for garnish |

Setting to use: HIGH

Place the mushrooms in a large bowl. Cover and cook for 7 minutes. Stir halfway through cooking. Set aside, covered, while making the sauce.

Place the butter and onion in a large bowl. Cover and cook for 2 minutes. Stir in the garlic, tomatoes, tomato purée (paste), herbs, and salt and pepper to taste.

Drain the mushrooms and add to the sauce. Cover and cook for 3½ minutes. Stir halfway through cooking. Garnish with parsley and serve with French bread.

# Fish Fillets with Almonds

| METRIC/IMPERIAL | AMERICAN |
|---|---|
| 1 kg/2 lb plaice fillets | 2 lb flounder fillets |
| 25 g/1 oz button mushrooms, thinly sliced (optional) | ½ cup thinly sliced mushrooms (optional) |
| 1 medium onion, finely chopped | 1 medium onion, finely chopped |
| 1 clove garlic, crushed | 1 clove garlic, minced |
| 125 g/4 oz butter, cut into pieces | ½ cup butter, cut into pieces |
| 300 ml/½ pint dry white wine | 1¼ cups dry white wine |
| 300 ml/½ pint milk | 1¼ cups milk |
| 50 g/2 oz plain flour | ½ cup all-purpose flour |
| salt | salt |
| freshly ground black pepper | freshly ground black pepper |
| 1 tablespoon double cream | 1 tablespoon heavy cream |
| 75 g/3 oz flaked almonds, lightly toasted | ¾ cup slivered almonds, lightly toasted |

Setting to use: HIGH

Roll up the fillets and secure with wooden cocktail sticks if required. Set aside.

Place the mushrooms if using, onion, garlic, half of the butter and the wine in a shallow dish. Cook, covered, for 4 minutes or until the onion is tender. Stir halfway through cooking.

Place the fish rolls in the dish and baste with the wine sauce. Cook, covered, for 9 minutes. Rearrange halfway through cooking.

Drain off the liquid and reserve. Cover the fish and set aside.

Mix together the fish liquid and milk. Place the remaining butter in a large jug. Cook, uncovered, for 1 minute or until melted.

Blend in the flour, liquid, and salt and pepper to taste. Cook for 7 minutes or until thick. Stir after 4 minutes and every subsequent minute. Stir in the cream.

Arrange the fish rolls on a warm serving platter, removing cocktail sticks if used. Spoon over the sauce and scatter the almonds on top.

# Spiced Fruit Cream

| METRIC/IMPERIAL | AMERICAN |
|---|---|
| 1 × 825 g/1 lb 13oz can fruit in syrup, drained | 1 × 1¾ lb can fruit in syrup drained |
| ¼ teaspoon ground cinnamon or grated nutmeg | ¼ teaspoon ground cinnamon or grated nutmeg |
| 1 tablespoon brandy or sherry (optional) | 1 tablespoon brandy or sherry (optional) |
| **To decorate:** | **To decorate:** |
| chopped nuts | chopped nuts |
| slices of fresh or canned fruit | slices of fresh or canned fruit |

Setting to use: HIGH

Place the fruit, cinnamon and brandy, if used, in a blender or food processor. Purée until smooth.

Spoon into four serving glasses or wine glasses. Chill. Decorate and serve with fan waters, boudoir biscuits (lady fingers) or langues de chat.

NOTE: To make a creamier Fruit Fool like the one pictured on page 51, whip 250 ml/8 fl oz (1 cup) double (heavy) cream until stiff then fold in the puréed fruit mixture. Decorate with fresh fruit or swirls of cream.

△ Fish fiesta: from top right: mushrooms with garlic served with French bread; fish fillets with almonds: spiced fruit cream

# Sunday Lunch

quick'n'easy tomato soup
crispy rolls

turkey breasts with
rosemary
croquette potatoes

chocolate pudding
with cream or custard

### Serves 4

*This all-in-one turkey dish makes a change from
the usual Sunday roast. Use frozen croquettes
that can be fried or baked conventionally.*

**WINE NOTE** Turkey, like chicken, can be partnered by almost any wine; a young red *Bordeaux* (claret) would suit this warming, traditional meal.

**ACTION PLAN**
1. Cook the turkey dish.
2. Fry the croquette potatoes on the conventional hob. Reheat before serving.
3. Meanwhile, prepare the pudding for cooking. Heat the soup on the conventional hob and serve.
4. Reheat the main course. Cook the chocolate pudding while eating the main course.

## Quick 'n' Easy Tomato Soup

For speed use a good quality canned tomato soup but improve the flavour with any one of the following . . . .
*Tomato and Onion Soup:* Cook 1 finely diced onion in a little butter, add the soup and heat according to can instructions. Serve with a dash of dry sherry and swirl of cream.
*Tomato and Orange Soup:* Add the grated rind and juice of 1 orange, and 1 grated carrot. Heat through and serve with swirls of cream.
*Tomato and Basil Soup:* Add 2 tablespoons finely chopped basil and 1 grated carrot, serve topped with fresh basil sprigs.
*Tomato and Mushroom Soup:* Cook 50 g/2 oz (½ cup) sliced button mushrooms and add to the soup.

42

## Turkey Breasts with Rosemary

| METRIC/IMPERIAL | AMERICAN |
|---|---|
| 4 frozen turkey breast fillets, total weight about 350 g/ 12 oz | 4 frozen turkey breast tenderloin steaks, total weight about ¾ lb |
| 1 medium onion, peeled and chopped | 1 medium onion, peeled and chopped |
| 25 g/1 oz butter | 2 tablespoons butter |
| 2 tablespoons plain flour | 2 tablespoons all-purpose flour |
| 4 tablespoons milk | ¼ cup milk |
| 300 ml/½ pint hot chicken stock | 1¼ cups hot chicken stock |
| 125 g/4 oz frozen peas | 1 cup frozen peas |
| 125 g/4 oz frozen young whole carrots | 1½-2 cups frozen young whole carrots |
| 1 teaspoon chopped dried rosemary | 1 teaspoon chopped dried rosemary |
| salt | salt |
| freshly ground black pepper | freshly ground black pepper |

Setting to use: HIGH

Place the turkey in a shallow casserole. Cook, covered, for 3½ minutes. Remove, separate and cut into strips.

Place the onion and butter in a large bowl. Cover and cook for 6 minutes. Stir halfway through cooking.

Stir in the flour. Gradually add the milk, stock, peas, carrots, rosemary, turkey, and salt and pepper to taste. Cook, covered, for 12½ minutes. Stir after 4 and 8 minutes.

Let stand, covered, for 5 minutes before serving.

## Chocolate Pudding

| METRIC/IMPERIAL | AMERICAN |
|---|---|
| 125 g/4 oz butter | ½ cup butter |
| 125 g/4 oz caster sugar | ½ cup sugar |
| 2 large eggs | 2 large eggs |
| 25 g/1 oz cocoa powder | ¼ cup cocoa powder |
| 3 tablespoons hot water | 3 tablespoons hot water |
| 150 g/5 oz self-raising flour | 1¼ cups self-raising flour |

Setting to use: HIGH

Cream the butter and sugar together. Beat in the eggs.

Dissolve the cocoa powder in the hot water.

Fold the flour into the creamed mixture. Stir in the cocoa liquid. Spoon into a greased 900 ml/1½ pint pudding basin (1 quart steaming mold). Cover and cook for 4½-5 minutes.

Remove cover and let stand for 3 minutes. Turn out and serve at once, with cream, or custard or chocolate sauce.

NOTE: For additional flavour add the grated rind of an orange or 4 tablespoons chopped nuts.

▷ *Sunday lunch: from bottom right: quick 'n' easy tomato soup; served with crispy rolls; turkey breasts with rosemary; croquette potatoes; top: chocolate pudding with custard*

## Dinner for Friends

chilled courgette soup
french bread
___
spiced lamb
green peas
rice
___
queen of puddings

Serves 6

*Old fashioned desserts like this queen of puddings
are back in favour and its subtle flavour acts as a
perfect foil to the more spicy main course.*

WINE
NOTE
*Rosé d'Anjou* has a touch of sweetness to bring out the best in this main-course lamb dish and is suitable to serve throughout the meal.

ACTION
PLAN
1. Make the soup and chill.
2. Start preparing the spiced lamb, cook the onion, celery, garlic, butter and tomato for 6 minutes. Add remaining ingredients and set aside.
3. Make the queen of puddings but flash under a preheated grill just before serving.
4. Warm the French bread in the microwave.
5. Cook the vegetables on the conventional hob and return the spiced lamb to the microwave while eating the first course.

## Chilled Courgette Soup

| METRIC/IMPERIAL | AMERICAN |
|---|---|
| 500 g/1 lb courgettes, trimmed and finely sliced | 1 lb zucchini, trimmed and finely sliced |
| 1 large onion, finely grated | 1 large onion, finely grated |
| pinch of dried mint | pinch of dried mint |
| 150 ml/¼ pint boiling chicken stock | ⅔ cup boiling chicken stock |
| 25 g/1 oz cornflour | ¼ cup cornstarch |
| 450 ml/¾ pint milk | 2 cups milk |
| 150 ml/¼ pint cold water | ⅔ cup cold water |
| salt | salt |
| freshly ground black pepper | freshly ground black pepper |
| 150 ml/¼ pint single cream | ⅔ cup light cream |
| mint sprigs to garnish | mint sprigs for garnish |

44   Setting to use: HIGH

Place the courgettes (zucchini), onion, mint and hot stock in a large bowl. Cook, covered, for 12 minutes or until soft. Stir halfway through cooking. Set aside, covered.

Blend the cornflour (cornstarch) with the milk in a jug. Cook, uncovered, for 3 minutes. Stir every minute.

Place the vegetables, cornflour (cornstarch) sauce, water, salt and pepper in a blender or food processor. Purée until smooth. Stir in the cream. Adjust the seasoning.

Refrigerate until chilled. Serve garnished with mint sprigs.

## Spiced Lamb

| METRIC/IMPERIAL | AMERICAN |
|---|---|
| 1 medium onion, chopped | 1 medium onion, chopped |
| 1 stick celery, chopped | 1 stalk celery, chopped |
| 1 clove garlic, crushed | 1 clove garlic, minced |
| 25 g/1 oz butter | 2 tablespoons butter |
| 2 tablespoons tomato purée | 2 tablespoons tomato paste |
| 1½ tablespoons flour | 1½ tablespoons flour |
| 2 tomatoes, chopped | 2 tomatoes, chopped |
| 1 teaspoon dried mixed herbs | 1 teaspoon dried mixed herbs |
| 450 ml/¾ pint hot lamb or chicken stock | 2 cups hot lamb or chicken stock |

△ Dinner for friends: clockwise from right: chilled courgette soup; green peas: spiced lamb: queen of puddings

| | |
|---|---|
| 1 tablespoon soy sauce | 1 tablespoon soy sauce |
| 1 tablespoon Worcestershire sauce | 1 tablespoon Worcestershire sauce |
| 1 tablespoon soft dark brown sugar | 1 tablespoon soft dark brown sugar |
| 750 g/1½ lb cooked boneless lamb, finely chopped | 1½ lb cooked boneless lamb, finely chopped |

Setting to use: HIGH

Place the onion, celery, garlic, butter and tomato purée (paste) in a large bowl. Cook, covered, for 6 minutes. Stir halfway through cooking.

Stir in the flour. Gradually blend in the tomatoes, herbs, stock, soy sauce, Worcestershire sauce, sugar and lamb. Cook, covered, for 13 minutes. Stir halfway through cooking. Serve hot.

# Queen of Puddings

| METRIC/IMPERIAL | AMERICAN |
|---|---|
| 3 egg yolks | 3 egg yolks |
| 50 g/2 oz sugar | 50 g/2 oz sugar |
| 600 ml/1 pint milk | 2½ cups milk |
| 2 drops vanilla essence | 2 drops vanilla |
| 75 g/6 oz fresh white breadcrumbs | 3 cups fresh white bread crumbs |
| grated rind ½ lemon | grated rind ½ lemon |
| 2 tablespoons jam | 2 tablespoons jam |
| Topping: | Topping: |
| 175 g/6 oz caster sugar | ¾ cup superfine sugar |
| 3 egg whites | 3 egg whites |

Setting to use: HIGH/Conventional grill (broiler)

Place the egg yolks, sugar, milk and vanilla essence in a 1 litre/1¾ pint (4 cup) jug and whisk together. Cook for 4 minutes.

Place the breadcrumbs and grated lemon rind in a 1.2 l/2 pint (5 cup) casserole; stir in the milk mixture. Cook for 5½ minutes, stirring halfway through cooking. Set aside.

Place the jam in a dish and cook for 1 minute to soften. Gently spread the jam over the cooked breadcrumb mixture.

For the topping, whisk the egg whites until frothy, add half the sugar and continue whisking until stiff. Using a metal spoon fold in the remaining sugar then spread the meringue over the jam and swirl into decorative peaks.

Brown under a preheated grill (broiler) and serve.

45

# Autumn Lunch

## buttered corn-on-the-cob
## diced ham with barbecue sauce
## buttered noodles
## apple and lemon snow

### Serves 4

This economical menu should please all palates, and even those who turn their nose up at canned meat will enjoy the ham served in a spicy barbecue sauce. Toss the noodles in a little butter and chopped fresh parsley before serving.

**WINE NOTE** Hungarian *Bull's Blood* (Egri Bakavér) has the spicy flavour needed to stand up to the barbecue sauce.

**ACTION PLAN**
1. Make the apple and lemon snow and chill.
2. Make the ham dish and set aside.
3. Cook the corn-on-the-cob. Meanwhile, cook the noodles on the conventional hob. When 'al dente' – just tender – drain them and keep warm while serving the first course.
4. Reheat the ham dish in the microwave.

## Buttered Corn-on-the-Cob

| METRIC/IMPERIAL | AMERICAN |
|---|---|
| 4 frozen corn-on-the-cob | 4 frozen ears corn-on-the-cob |
| 50 g/2 oz butter or herb butter (See page 31) | 1/2 cup butter or herb butter (See page 31) |

Setting to use: HIGH

Wrap the corn in greaseproof (wax) paper, or place in a covered container. Cook for 12 minutes or until tender.

Place the corn on four individual dishes and top each with a piece of butter.

## Diced Ham with Barbecue Sauce

| METRIC/IMPERIAL | AMERICAN |
|---|---|
| 1 medium onion, chopped | 1 medium onion, chopped |
| 1 red or green pepper, cored, seeded and diced | 1 sweet red or green pepper, cored, seeded and diced |
| 1 clove garlic, crushed | 1 clove garlic, minced |
| 2 tablespons tomato purée | 2 tablespoons tomato paste |
| 2 tablespoons plain flour | 1 1/2 tablespoons all-purpose flour |
| 1 × 400 g/14 oz can tomatoes with juice, chopped | 1 × 400 g/16 oz can tomatoes with juice, chopped |
| 1 teaspoon dried mixed herbs | 1 teaspoon dried mixed herbs |
| scant 300 ml/1/2 pint hot ham or chicken stock | 1 cup hot ham or chicken stock |
| 1 tablespoon soy sauce | 1 tablespoon soy sauce |
| 3 tablespoons white wine vinegar | 3 tablespoons white wine vinegar |
| 3 tablespoons soft dark brown sugar | 3 tablespoons soft dark brown sugar |
| 1 × 500 g/1 lb can ham, jelly removed, diced | 1 × 1 lb can ham, jelly removed, diced |

▷ *Autumn lunch: anticlockwise from bottom left: buttered corn-on-the-cob; diced ham with barbecue sauce; buttered noodles; left: apple and lemon snow*

46

Setting to use: HIGH

Place the onion, red or green pepper, garlic and tomato purée (paste) in a large bowl. Cook, covered, for 6 minutes. Stir halfway through cooking.

Stir in the flour. Gradually blend in the tomatoes and juice, herbs, hot stock, soy sauce, vinegar, sugar and ham. Cook, covered, for 10 minutes. Stir halfway through cooking.

NOTE: Cooked chicken can be used in place of the canned ham.

# Apple and Lemon Snow

| METRIC/IMPERIAL | AMERICAN |
|---|---|
| 750 g/1½ lb cooking apples, peeled, cored and sliced | 1½ lb tart apples, peeled, cored and sliced |
| 3 tablespoons caster sugar | 3 tablespoons sugar |
| 3 tablespoons water | 3 tablespoons water |
| 1 tablespoon lemon juice | 1 tablespoon lemon juice |
| 2 eggs, separated | 2 eggs, separated |
| grated rind of 1 lemon | grated rind of 1 lemon |
| *few drops of green food colouring* | *few drops of green food coloring* |
| **To decorate:** | **To decorate:** |
| *glacé cherries* | *candied cherries* |
| *candied angelica* | *candied angelica* |

Setting to use: HIGH

Place the apples, sugar, water and lemon juice in a medium bowl. Cook, covered, for 5 minutes. Stir halfway through cooking. Drain.

Purée the apples with the egg yolks in a blender or food processor until smooth. Stir in the lemon rind and food colouring.

Whisk the egg whites until stiff. Gently fold into the apple mixture. Spoon into four glasses.

Decorate with cherries and angelica. Chill before serving, or serve warm.

NOTE: A variety of fruit can be used instead of the apples. Try fresh pears or puréed canned apricots. For a richer pudding, fold in 125 ml/4 fl oz (½ cup) whipped cream before adding the whisked egg whites.

# Summer Supper

## hot artichokes in sauce
## french bread
## spiced greek casserole
## lemon syllabub

### Serves 4

*This versatile menu can be served as a formal or casual lunch. On warmer days accompany the Greek casserole with a salad, but on colder days serve a variety of vegetables.*

**WINE NOTE** Resin-flavoured white *Retsina* makes an unusual, inexpensive and appropriate partner for this southern Mediterranean-style main course.

**ACTION PLAN**
1. Make the syllabub and chill.
2. Make the macaroni dish and set aside.
3. Prepare and serve the artichokes, meanwhile cook the vegetables on the conventional hob.
4. Reheat the spiced Greek casserole in the microwave before serving.

## Hot Artichokes in Sauce

| METRIC/IMPERIAL | AMERICAN |
|---|---|
| 1 × 400 g/14 oz can artichoke hearts, drained and chopped | 1 × 16 oz can artichoke hearts, drained and chopped |
| 4 tablespoons canned condensed cream of chicken soup | 1/4 cup canned condensed cream of chicken soup |
| 1/4 teaspoon curry powder | 1/4 teaspoon curry powder |
| salt | salt |
| freshly ground black pepper | freshly ground black pepper |
| To garnish: | For garnish: |
| parsley | parsley |
| lemon slices | lemon slices |

Setting to use: HIGH

Place the chopped artichokes in a large jug. Mix in the soup, curry powder, and salt and pepper to taste. Cook, uncovered, for 4 minutes. Stir halfway through cooking.
Serve garnished with parsley and lemon slices.

▷ *Summer supper: anticlockwise from bottom left: hot artichokes in sauce; spiced Greek casserole; lemon syllabub*

## Spiced Greek Casserole

| METRIC/IMPERIAL | AMERICAN |
|---|---|
| 250 g/8 oz quick-cooking macaroni | 1/2 lb quick-cooking elbow macaroni |
| 1/4 teaspoon oil | 1/4 teaspoon oil |
| 1.2 l/2 pints boiling water | 5 cups boiling water |
| salt | salt |
| 1 small green pepper, cored, seeded and finely diced | 1 small green pepper, cored, seeded and finely diced |
| 1 medium onion, finely chopped | 1 medium onion, finely chopped |
| 25 g/1 oz butter | 2 tablespoons butter |
| 2 tomatoes, skinned and chopped | 2 tomatoes, skinned and chopped |
| 1 tablespoon tomato purée | 1 tablespoon tomato paste |
| 1/2 teaspoon ground cinnamon | 1/2 teaspoon ground cinnamon |
| 1/2 teaspoon grated nutmeg | 1/2 teaspoon grated nutmeg |

2 cloves garlic, crushed
freshly ground black pepper
500 g/1 lb minced beef
4 tablespoons grated cheese
watercress to garnish

2 cloves garlic, minced
freshly ground black pepper
1 lb ground beef
1/4 cup grated cheese
watercress for garnish

Setting to use: HIGH

Place the macaroni, oil, boiling water and a pinch of salt in a very large bowl. Ensure that the macaroni is completely immersed. Cook, covered, for 8 minutes. Set aside.

Place the green pepper, onion, butter, tomatoes, tomato purée (paste), cinnamon, nutmeg, garlic, and salt and pepper to taste in a very large bowl. Cook, covered, for 7 minutes. Stir halfway through cooking.

Stir the meat into the vegetables. Cook, covered, for 8 minutes. Stir halfway through cooking.

Drain the macaroni. Toss together macaroni and meat sauce. Spoon into a shallow warm serving dish and sprinkle with grated cheese. Garnish with watercress.

## Lemon Syllabub

METRIC/IMPERIAL
finely grated rind and juice of
 1 lemon
3 tablespoons caster sugar
120 ml/4 fl oz medium or
 sweet white wine or sweet
 sherry
300 ml/1/2 pint double cream
curls of lemon rind (using a
 zester) to decorate

AMERICAN
finely grated rind and juice of
 1 lemon
3 tablespoons sugar
1/2 cup medium or sweet white
 wine or cream sherry
1 1/4 cups heavy cream
curls of lemon rind (using a
 zester) to decorate

Whisk together the lemon rind and juice, sugar and wine or sherry. Strain, if desired, to remove the rind. Gradually add the cream, whisking all the time until the mixture is firm and peaky.

Spoon the syllabub into four wine glasses. Decorate with curls of lemon rind. Chill before serving if possible.

49

# Family Celebration

## salmon with lemon mayonnaise
## kidney ragoût
## brown rice
## raspberry cream cheese dessert

### Serves 4

*Although this menu has a touch of class it is low on cost and high on nutrients, making it perfect for a family celebration. It is important not to overcook the kidneys otherwise they will toughen and develop a strong flavour.*

WINE NOTE — A red *Côtes-du-Rhône* makes a satisfying accompaniment to kidneys served in most forms, and especially in a casserole.

ACTION PLAN
1. Prepare the salmon with lemon mayonnaise and set aside.
2. Cook the raspberries for the dessert then complete the recipe and refrigerate.
3. Cook the brown rice on the conventional hob, following package instructions.
4. Meanwhile cook the kidney ragoût in the microwave.

## Salmon with Lemon Mayonnaise

| METRIC/IMPERIAL | AMERICAN |
|---|---|
| 1 × 450 g/1 lb can pink salmon, drained and flaked | 1 × 1 lb can salmon, drained and flaked |
| 1½-2 tablespoons lemon juice | 1½-2 tablespoons lemon juice |
| salt | salt |
| freshly ground black pepper | freshly ground black pepper |
| 4-6 tablespoons mayonnaise | 4-6 tablespoons mayonnaise |
| grated rind of ½ lemon | grated rind of ½ lemon |
| To garnish: | For garnish: |
| paprika or cayenne pepper | paprika or cayenne pepper |
| sliced stuffed olives and/or twists of lemon | sliced stuffed olives and/or twists of lemon |

Mix the salmon with 1 tablespoon of the lemon juice, and salt and pepper to taste. Divide between four scallop shells or small serving plates.

Blend together the mayonnaise, lemon rind, and remaining lemon juice to taste. Do not add too much lemon juice or the mayonnaise will be thin.

Spoon the mayonnaise over the salmon. Sprinkle with paprika or cayenne pepper and garnish with sliced stuffed olives and/or twists of lemon.

## Kidney Ragoût

| METRIC/IMPERIAL | AMERICAN |
|---|---|
| 1 teaspoon chopped fresh rosemary | 1 teaspoon chopped fresh rosemary |
| 1 medium onion, chopped | 1 medium onion, chopped |
| ½ red pepper, cored, seeded and diced | ½ sweet red pepper, cored, seeded and diced |
| 1 courgette, trimmed and sliced | 1 zucchini, trimmed and sliced |
| 25 g/1 oz butter | 2 tablespoons butter |
| 1 clove garlic, crushed | 1 clove garlic, minced |
| 25 g/1 oz cornflour | ¼ cup cornstarch |
| 150 ml/¼ pint red wine | ⅔ cup red wine |
| scant 300 ml/½ pint hot beef stock | 1¼ cups hot beef stock |
| 12 lambs' kidneys, cored and halved | 12 lambs' kidneys, cored and halved |
| 50 g/2 oz fresh or drained canned mushrooms, coarsely chopped | ½ cup coarsely chopped fresh or canned mushrooms |
| 1 tablespoon tomato purée | 1 tablespoon tomato paste |
| salt | salt |
| freshly ground black pepper | freshly ground black pepper |
| fresh rosemary to garnish | fresh rosemary for garnish |

Setting to use: HIGH

Place the rosemary, onion, red pepper, courgette (zucchini), butter and garlic in a large bowl. Cook, covered, for 5½ minutes. Stir halfway through cooking.

Stir in the cornflour (cornstarch). Gradually blend in the wine, hot stock, kidneys, mushrooms, tomato purée (paste) and salt and pepper to taste. Cook, covered, for 12 minutes. Stir after 4 and 8 minutes. Remove the cover after 10 minutes of cooking.

Spoon into a warm serving dish and garnish with fresh rosemary.

## Raspberry Cream Cheese Dessert

| METRIC/IMPERIAL | AMERICAN |
|---|---|
| 175 g/6 oz frozen raspberries or other soft fruit | 1½ cups frozen raspberries or other soft fruit |
| 175 g/6 oz full fat soft cheese | ¾ cup cream cheese |
| ½-1 tablespoon icing sugar | ½-1 tablespoon confectioners' sugar |
| 150 ml/¼ pint double cream | ⅔ cup heavy cream |
| extra raspberries to decorate | extra raspberries to decorate |
| langues du chat or boudoir biscuits to serve (optional) | langues du chat or ladyfingers to serve (optional) |

Setting to use: HIGH

Place the raspberries in a shallow dish. Cook, uncovered for 1½ minutes.

Beat the cheese until soft. Beat in the raspberries and ½ tablespoon sugar. Taste and add more sugar if required.

Whip the cream until stiff. Gently fold the raspberry mixture into the cream.

Spoon into four glasses. Decorate with extra raspberries and chill if possible.

Serve with langues du chat, boudoir biscuits (ladyfingers) or wafers if using.

NOTE: For a special treat to finish the family celebration add a dash of a liqueur such as framboise to this desert. Cointreau would be a good alternative if the dessert was made with strawberries.

Any soft fruit can be used to make this delicious dessert. Simply clean and trim them and they're ready to use.

△ *Family celebration: from left: salmon with lemon mayonnaise; kidney ragoût; brown rice; raspberry cream cheese dessert*

51

# Winter Lunch

## hot tuna with capers
## brown bread
## beef and vegetable casserole
## green beans
## fruit crumble with custard

### Serves 4

*This warming lunch menu for the family is put together in minutes using mainly canned foods.*

**WINE NOTE** Full-bodied red wines are perfect to serve with beef. This rustic casserole deserves an equally rustic wine, try one from the French countryside, perhaps a *Cahors* or *Madiran*.

**ACTION PLAN**
1. Prepare and cook the beef and vegetable casserole. Set aside.
2. Make the fruit crumble and cook it in the microwave.
3. Make the tuna and caper mixture and spoon it into ramekin dishes while browning the crumble under a preheated grill (broiler).
4. Cook the green beans.
5. Reheat the beef and vegetable casserole in the microwave while serving the first course.
6. Make or heat the custard before serving the pudding.

## Hot Tuna with Capers

| METRIC/IMPERIAL | AMERICAN |
| --- | --- |
| 25 g/1 oz butter | 2 tablespoons butter |
| 25 g/1 oz plain flour | 1/4 cup all-purpose flour |
| 300 ml/1/2 pint milk | 1 1/4 cups milk |
| 1/2 teaspoon anchovy essence | 1/4 teaspoon anchovy paste |
| 1 × 200 g/7 oz can tuna fish, drained and flaked | 1 × 7 oz can tuna fish, drained and flaked |
| freshly ground black pepper | freshly ground black pepper |
| 1 tablespoon capers, drained | 1 tablespoon capers, drained |
| parsley sprigs or capers to garnish | parsley sprigs or capers for garnish |

Setting to use: HIGH

Place the butter in a large jug. Cook, uncovered, for 1 minute or until melted. Stir in the flour. Gradually blend in the milk and anchovy essence [paste]. Cook, uncovered, for 3 minutes. Stir every minute.

Stir in the tuna fish, pepper to taste and capers. Cook, uncovered, for 2 minutes. Stir the mixture halfway through cooking.

Spoon into four warm ramekins or one warm serving dish. Garnish with sprigs of parsley or capers.

## Beef and Vegetable Casserole

| METRIC/IMPERIAL | AMERICAN |
| --- | --- |
| 250 g/8 oz potatoes, peeled and cubed | 1/2 lb potatoes, peeled and cubed |
| 1 medium onion, sliced | 1 medium onion, sliced |
| 2 carrots, peeled and sliced | 2 carrots, peeled and sliced |
| 2 courgettes, trimmed and sliced | 2 zucchini, trimmed and sliced |
| 9 tablespoons water | 9 tablespoons water |
| 2 tablespoons tomato purée | 2 tablespoons tomato paste |
| 1 1/2 teaspoons dried mixed herbs | 1 1/2 teaspoons dried mixed herbs |
| 1 clove garlic, crushed (optional) | 1 clove garlic, minced (optional) |
| 1 beef stock cube, crumbled | 1 beef bouillon cube, crumbled |

| | |
|---|---|
| ¹/₄ teaspoon gravy browning or malt extract | ¹/₄ teaspoon gravy browning agent or malt extract |
| 1 × 439 g/15¹/₂ can chunky steak in rich gravy | 1 × 16 oz can chunky steak in rich gravy |
| salt | salt |
| freshly ground black pepper | freshly ground black pepper |
| chopped fresh parsley to garnish | chopped fresh parsley for garnish |

Setting to use: HIGH

Place the potatoes, onion, carrot, courgette (zucchini) and 3 tablespoons water in a large bowl. Cover and cook for 10 minutes. Stir halfway through cooking.

Stir in the tomato purée (paste), herbs, garlic if used, stock (bouillon) cube, remaining water, the gravy browning, canned steak with gravy, and salt and pepper to taste. Cook, covered, for 6 minutes.

Serve garnished with chopped parsley.

NOTE: A 1 × 250 g/8 oz can of potatoes can be used in place of fresh. Drain them and add them to the casserole with the canned steak with gravy.

Any selection of canned or frozen vegetables can be used in place of the fresh vegetables listed and the mixed herbs can be replaced with a herb of your choice.

## Fruit Crumble

| METRIC/IMPERIAL | AMERICAN |
|---|---|
| 1 × 400g/14 oz can fruit pie filling, or frozen fruit sweetened to taste | 1 × 16 oz can fruit pie filling, or frozen fruit sweetened to taste |
| 150 g/6 oz plain flour | 1¹/₂ cups all-purpose flour |
| 75g/3 oz soft brown sugar | ¹/₂ cup dark brown sugar |
| 75 g/3 oz butter | 6 tablespoons butter |

Setting to use: HIGH

Place the fruit pie filling or frozen fruit in a 1 1/2 pint (1 quart) dish. If using frozen fruit, cover and cook for 4 to 5 minutes.

Rub together the flour, sugar and butter until the mixture resembles fine breadcrumbs.

Sprinkle the crumble over the fruit. Cook, uncovered, for 6 minutes. Let it stand for 3 minutes before serving, with cream or canned or homemade custard.

If desired, and a flameproof dish is used, the crumble can be browned under a preheated conventional grill [broiler]. 53

# Formal Entertaining

These delicious menus are suitable to serve at any formal occasion.
The beautifully illustrated 'Final Touch' and 'Table Dressing' ideas
that are scattered throughout this chapter show the host or hostess
how to add the finishing touches to both the table and the food.

# For All Seasons

artichoke mousse
french bread

---

orange-stuffed veal
mange-tout with
garlic butter
new potatoes

---

rich chocolate ice cream

Serves 6

*The blend of colours and flavours makes this meal
suitable to serve at any time of year*

**WINE NOTE** Try one of France's best rosés, like *Tavel* or *Lirac*, with the mousse, and follow this with a *Tokay d'Alsace* to partner the stuffed veal dish. The ice cream will be best enjoyed on its own as it has a numbing effect on the palate.

**ACTION PLAN**

*On the day before or in the morning:*
1. Make the artichoke mousse and refrigerate.
2. Prepare the stuffing for the veal and refrigerate.
3. Make the ice cream and freeze.

*Later in the day:*
1. Prepare the garnishes for the various dishes, and garnish the artichoke mousse.
2. Stuff the veal ready for cooking and refrigerate.
3. Scrub the potatoes for cooking.

*Before serving:*
1. Start cooking the veal 1 hour before serving.
2. Cook the potatoes and the buttered mange-tout (snow peas) conventionally, (or if preferred in the microwave while the veal is standing).
3. Make the sauce for the veal in the microwave while you are dishing up the veal and vegetables.
4. Soften the ice cream briefly in the microwave before serving, if necessary.

▷ *A meal for all seasons: clockwise from back: orange-stuffed veal; mange-tout with garlic; new potatoes; rich chocolate ice cream*

## Artichoke Mousse

| METRIC/IMPERIAL | AMERICAN |
|---|---|
| 150 ml/¼ pint chicken stock | ⅔ cup chicken stock |
| 15 g/½ oz powdered gelatine | 2 tablespoons unflavored gelatin |
| 15 g/½ oz butter | 1 tablespoon butter |
| 15 g/½ oz plain flour | 2 tablespoons all-purpose flour |
| 1 × 400 g/14 oz can artichoke hearts | 1 × 14 oz can artichoke hearts |
| 1 teaspoon lemon juice | 1 teaspoon lemon juice |
| 2 large eggs, separated | 2 large eggs, separated |
| salt | salt |
| freshly ground black pepper | |

*150 ml/¼ pint double cream,*
*    whipped*
To garnish:
*parsley sprigs*
*lemon twists*

*freshly ground black pepper*
*⅔ cup heavy cream, whipped*
For garnish:
*parsley sprigs*
*lemon twists*

Setting to use: HIGH

Place the stock in a jug. Cook, uncovered, for 1 minute or until hot.

Sprinkle in the gelatine and stir briskly until the gelatine has dissolved. Set aside.

Place the butter in a medium bowl and cook, uncovered, for 15 seconds or until melted. Stir in the flour, then gradually blend in the liquid from the can of artichoke hearts and the lemon juice. Cook, uncovered, for 2 minutes. Stir after 1 and 1½ minutes.

Whisk the egg yolks into the sauce. Chop the artichokes and stir these in. Cook, uncovered for 1 minute. Pour the sauce into a blender and add stock, gelatine and salt and pepper to taste. Purée until smooth. Pour into a bowl and chill until almost set.

Fold the whipped cream into the artichoke mixture. Whisk the egg whites until stiff and fold in gently. Spoon into a 750 ml/1¼ pint (3 cup) soufflé dish. Chill until set.

Serve garnished with sprigs of parsley and lemon twists.

## Orange-stuffed Veal

| METRIC/IMPERIAL | AMERICAN |
|---|---|
| *40 g/1½ oz fresh white breadcrumbs* | *¾ cup soft white bread crumbs* |
| *50 g/2 oz sultanas* | *⅓ cup golden raisins* |
| *grated rind of 2 oranges* | *grated rind of 2 oranges* |
| *1 small onion, grated* | *1 small onion, grated* |
| *1 tablespoon marmalade* | *1 tablespoon marmalade* |
| *1 teaspoon dried rosemary* | *1 teaspoon dried rosemary* |
| *salt* | *salt* |
| *freshly ground black pepper* | *freshly ground black pepper* |
| *1 egg, lightly beaten* | *1 egg, lightly beaten* |
| *1 × 1.5 kg/3 lb boned shoulder joint of veal* | *1 × 3 lb boneless veal shoulder roast* |
| Sauce: | Sauce: |
| *25 g/1 oz cornflour* | *¼ cup cornstarch* |
| *2 tablespoons fresh orange juice* | *2 tablespoons fresh orange juice* |
| *1 tablespoon brandy* | *1 tablespoon brandy* |
| *about 450 ml/¾ pint cold chicken stock* | *about 2 cups cold chicken stock* |
| *grated rind of 1 orange* | *grated rind of 1 orange* |
| To garnish: | For garnish: |
| *orange slices* | *orange slices* |
| *watercress* | *watercress* |

Setting to use: HIGH/Conventional Oven

Make the stuffing, mix together the breadcrumbs, sultanas (raisins), orange rind, onion, marmalade, rosemary and salt and pepper to taste. Add sufficient egg to bind the ingredients together.

Untie and open the veal. Cut along the meat if there is insufficient space for the stuffing.

Stuff the cavity or spread the stuffing over the meat. Reroll and tie securely with string.

Place the veal on a trivet in a shallow, non-metallic, ovenproof container. Cook, uncovered for 24 minutes. Turn over halfway through cooking.

Pour off the juices from the dish and set aside. Transfer the meat to a conventional oven which has been preheated to 220°C/425°F/Gas Mark 7. Cook for 15 minutes. Alternatively, wrap the meat tightly in foil and leave to rest at room temperature for 20 minutes before serving.

To make the sauce, mix together the cornflour (cornstarch), orange juice and brandy in a large jug. Stir in the juices from the veal and add sufficient stock to make 600 ml/1 pint (2½ cups). Add the orange rind. Cook, uncovered, for 3 minutes or until thick. Stir every minute. Add salt and pepper to taste.

Remove the string from the veal and place the meat on a warm serving platter.

Garnish with orange slices and watercress, and serve with the sauce.

**NOTE:** To calculate microwave cooking times for a larger piece of veal, when the veal has been stuffed, weigh it and calculate microwave cooking time – 8 minutes to each 500 g/1 lb. The conventional oven cooking time or the resting time remains unaltered.

For Lemon-stuffed Veal, use the grated rind of 2 lemons in place of the orange rind in the stuffing, and use lemon juice and the grated rind of 1 lemon in the sauce. Garnish the veal with lemon slices and watercress or sprigs of fresh parsley and serve as above.

## Mange-Tout with Garlic Butter

| METRIC/IMPERIAL | AMERICAN |
|---|---|
| *350 g/12 oz mange-tout, trimmed and any strings removed* | *¾ lb snow or sugar peas, trimmed and any strings removed* |
| *3 tablespoons water* | *3 tablespoons water* |
| *pinch of salt* | *pinch of salt* |
| *25 g/1 oz garlic butter, cut into pieces (see page 87)* | *2 tablespoons garlic butter, cut into pieces (see page 87)* |

Setting to use: HIGH

Place the mange-tout (snow peas) in a large bowl. Add the water and salt. Cook, covered, for 8 minutes. Stir halfway through cooking.

Let them stand, covered, for 5 minutes. Drain. Toss the mange-tout (snow peas) with the garlic butter until melted.

## New Potatoes

| METRIC/IMPERIAL | AMERICAN |
|---|---|
| *3 tablespoons salted water* | *3 tablespoons salted water* |
| *500 g/1 lb new potatoes, scrubbed* | *1 lb new potatoes, scrubbed* |
| *1 sprig fresh mint* | *1 sprig fresh mint* |
| *50 g/2 oz butter, cut into pieces* | *¼ cup butter, cut into pieces* |

Setting to use: HIGH

Place the salted water in a large bowl. Add the potatoes and mint. Cook, covered, for 9 minutes. Stir halfway through cooking. Let them stand, covered, for 5 minutes.

Drain the potatoes and toss in the butter.

## Rich Chocolate Ice Cream

| METRIC/IMPERIAL | AMERICAN |
|---|---|
| *150 g/5 oz plain or milk chocolate, broken into pieces* | *5 squares semisweet or sweet chocolate, broken into pieces* |
| *4 eggs, separated* | *4 eggs, separated* |
| *125 g/4 oz caster sugar* | *½ cup sugar* |
| *300 ml/½ pint double cream* | *1¼ cups heavy cream* |
| To decorate: | To decorate: |
| *chocolate curls* | *chocolate curls* |
| *fan wafers* | *fan wafers* |
| *cigarettes Russe* | *cigarettes Russe* |

Setting to use: HIGH

Place the chocolate in a very large jug. Cook, uncovered, for 2½ minutes or until melted. Beat in the egg yolks. Set aside.

In a large bowl, whisk the egg whites until stiff. Gradually whisk in the sugar a teaspoon at a time. Set aside.

In another large bowl, whip the cream until stiff. Whisk in the chocolate mixture a little at a time. Fold the chocolate mixture into the egg whites.

Spoon into a 1.75 l/⅓ pint (2 quart) freezerproof container and freeze for at least 5 hours. It is not necessary to stir the ice cream during the freezing process.

To serve, place scoops of ice cream in individual dishes. Decorate with curls of chocolate and cigarettes Russe and serve immediately.

# Plan Ahead

## marinated trout fillets
## .tossed green salad

## normandy-style veal casserole
## braised rice

## chocolate cups with fruit cream

### Serves 4

*All the dishes in this menu can be prepared a day or so in advance, leaving you free to enjoy the occasion.*

**WINE NOTE**

Try a dry *Sauvignon Blanc* wine from Touraine or elsewhere with the trout fillets and follow this with a red *Bordeaux* (claret) for the veal. The chocolate flavour of the dessert will prove too strong for most wines, so complete the meal with a spirit to serve as a digestif.

**ACTION PLAN**

*On the day before:*
1. Prepare the trout and leave to marinate.
2. Make the chocolate cups and refrigerate.
3. Make the veal casserole, cool and refrigerate overnight.

*In the morning:*
1. Fill the chocolate cups and chill to set.
2. Prepare the ingredients for the salad.

*Before serving:*
1. Start cooking the rice in the microwave 25 minutes before required.
2. Reheat the veal on top of the conventional hob approximately 20 minutes before required or reheat in the microwave after cooking the rice.
3. Toss the salad just before serving.
4. Decorate the chocolate cups just before serving the trout.

▽ *Plan ahead: clockwise from left: Normandy-style veal casserole; braised rice; chocolate cups with fruit cream*

△ Plan ahead: marinated trout fillets with French bread and tossed green salad

# Normandy-Style Veal Casserole

| METRIC/IMPERIAL | AMERICAN |
|---|---|
| 25 g/1 oz butter | 2 tablespoons butter |
| 1 onion, chopped | 1 onion, chopped |
| 250 g/8 oz carrots, sliced | 1 cup sliced carrots |
| 2 cloves garlic, crushed | 2 cloves garlic, minced |
| 1 teaspoon chopped fresh parsley | 1 teaspoon chopped fresh parsley |
| 1 teaspoon chopped fresh thyme | 1 teaspoon chopped fresh thyme |
| 125 g/4 oz button mushrooms, sliced | 1 cup sliced button mushrooms |
| 1 courgette, trimmed and sliced | 1 zucchini, trimmed and sliced |
| 850 g/1¾ lb pie veal, cubed | 1¾ lb veal for stew, cubed |
| 25 g/1 oz cornflour | ¼ cup cornstarch |
| 150 ml/¼ pint dry cider | ⅔ cup hard cider |
| 150 ml/¼ pint hot veal stock | ⅔ cup hot veal stock |
| 1 bouquet garni | 1 bouquet garni |
| salt | salt |
| freshly ground black pepper | freshly ground black pepper |

Setting to use: HIGH/DEFROST (30%)

Place the butter, onion, carrots, garlic, parsley and thyme in a large bowl. Cook, covered, for 7 minutes. Stir in the mushrooms, courgette (zucchini) and veal. Cook, covered, for 10 minutes.

Blend the cornflour (cornstarch) with the cider. Add to the veal mixture with the stock, bouquet garni, and salt and pepper to taste. Cook, covered, for 6 minutes or until the liquid is boiling.

Reduce the power to DEFROST (30%). Cook, covered, for 45 minutes or until tender. Stir the casserole several times during cooking.

Let it stand, covered, for 10 minutes, then discard the bouquet garni before serving.

NOTE: For a more provincial flavour use a dry white wine in place of the cider.

# PLAN AHEAD
# Marinated Trout Fillets

| METRIC/IMPERIAL | AMERICAN |
|---|---|
| 4 medium trout, cleaned and filleted | 4 medium trout, cleaned and filleted |
| 1 large onion, peeled and thinly sliced | 1 large onion, peeled and thinly sliced |
| 150 ml/¼ pint cold water | ⅔ cup cold water |
| 150 ml/¼ pint white wine vinegar | ⅔ cup white wine vinegar |
| ¼ teaspoon ground mace | ¼ teaspoon ground mace |
| pinch of salt | pinch of salt |
| 12 black peppercorns | 12 black peppercorns |
| 4 bay leaves | 4 bay leaves |

Setting to use: HIGH

Roll up each trout fillet with the skin outside and place in a shallow dish. Arrange the onion over the trout.

Mix together the water, vinegar, mace, salt, peppercorns and bay leaves. Pour over the trout and onions. Cook, covered, for 9 minutes. Turn around halfway through cooking.

Let cool, then marinate in the refrigerator for at least 24 hours.

Serve the trout fillets with brown bread and a tossed green salad.

NOTE: Herring or mackerel fillets can be used in place of trout fillets.

# Braised Rice

| METRIC/IMPERIAL | AMERICAN |
|---|---|
| ¼ teaspoon oil | ¼ teaspoon oil |
| 2 tablespoons finely chopped onion | 2 tablespoons finely chopped onion |
| 250 g/8 oz long-grain rice | 1 cup long-grain rice |
| 750 ml/1¼ pints boiling chicken or veal stock | 3 cups boiling chicken or veal stock |
| pinch of salt | pinch of salt |
| To garnish: | For garnish: |
| paprika | paprika |
| 1 tablespoon chopped fresh parsley | 1 tablespoon chopped fresh parsley |

Setting to use: HIGH

Place the oil and onion in a large bowl. Cook, covered, for 2 minutes.

Stir in the rice, boiling stock and salt. Cook, covered, for 14 minutes. Stir halfway through cooking.

Let it stand, covered, for 10 minutes.

Fluff up the rice with a fork and serve garnished with paprika and chopped parsley.

# Chocolate Cups with Fruit Cream

METRIC/IMPERIAL
200 g/7 oz plain chocolate,
    broken into pieces
150 ml/¼ pint fruit purée
125 g/4 oz full fat soft cheese
150 ml/¼ pint double cream,
    stiffly whipped
To decorate:
150 ml/¼ pint stiffly whipped
    cream
grated chocolate

Setting to use: HIGH

AMERICAN
7 squares semisweet
    chocolate, broken to pieces
⅔ cup fruit purée
½ cup cream cheese
⅔ cup heavy cream, stiffly
    whipped
To decorate:
⅔ cup stiffly whipped
    cream
grated chocolate

Place the chocolate in a medium bowl. Cook, uncovered, for 3 minutes. Stir after 2½ minutes. Divide the melted chocolate between 8 small paper cake (cup cake) cases. Use doubled paper cases to give extra support. Using a teaspoon, spread the chocolate evenly over the bottom and up the sides of the cases.

Invert and leave to harden. When hard, gently peel off the paper cases.

Beat together the fruit purée and cheese until smooth. Fold in the whipped cream.

Spoon the mixture into the chocolate cases. Chill until set.

Serve decorated with rosettes of whipped cream and grated chocolate.

NOTE: For a marbled effect beat half the fruit purée into the cheese then fold in the whipped cream. Stir in the remaining purée until well streaked. Spoon into cases and chill.

## SHOW-OFF SALADS

Salads benefit from good presentation, just as much as the main dish does.

### Variety is...

Forget that tired combination of lettuce, tomato and cucumber served with mayonnaise. With the wide variety of imported vegetables (and fruit – many fruits make delicious additions to salads) available you can really go to town on combining unusual textures and colours.

Visit your local vegetable shop or market and take a really good look at the wonderful shapes, sizes and colours of vegetables ranging from white Chinese cabbage; dark green spinach and watercress, pale green but curly endive; crunchy cabbage; shiny peppers and, of course, the dazzling yellow of sweetcorn. Radishes tomatoes and carrots present lovely rich tones, and 'red' cabbage gives you a vibrant purple veined with white. To offset these rich colours add a variety of white vegetables and don't forget the pulses like lentils and kidney beans.

Move away from the usual wooden or white china salad bowl. Try using a glass container which gives you more scope to show off the different components of the salad to best advantage.

### Small beginnings

Try serving individual portions of salad, and for a striking effect, layer vegetables that are strong in colour in individual glass bowls so that your guests see stripes of colour encircling the bowl.
For example a layer of spinach, followed by sliced mushrooms, sweetcorn, then a layer of sliced tomato and topped with mustard and cress to complete the scheme. Once you are more confident move on to a large glass bowl and let your imagination loose on bigger things.

### Undress it

Never dress a green salad in advance. The vegetables will become limp and the vinaigrette dressing will form an unattractive greasy film on the sides of the bowl. Toss the salad in a well-seasoned dressing just before serving, preferably at the table or serve a selection of dressings for guests to dress their own.

# Back To Basics

## hot leek and potato soup

## steak and kidney pudding
## sugared carrots
## creamed potatoes

## crème caramel

### Serves 6

*A collection of old favourites that complement each other and produce a classic menu to entertain family or friends on winter evenings.*

**WINE NOTE** The soup is best taken on its own as a warming start to the meal, while Californian, South African or Australian *Cabernet Sauvignon* wine will work gloriously well with the main course. Try a Hungarian *Tokay Aszu* wine with the dessert for a lingering finish to this winter menu.

**ACTION PLAN**

*On the day before:*
1. Marinate the steak for the meat pudding.

*In the morning:*
1. Make the soup and keep, covered, in the refrigerator.
2. Make the pastry for the pudding. Cook the steak and kidney filling. Refrigerate.
3. Prepare the vegetables for cooking, pack the carrots in plastic bags and refrigerate, keep the potatoes in water to prevent discoloration.
4. Make the crème caramel.

*Before serving:*
1. Unmould the crème caramel and decorate with cream if liked.
2. Assemble the meat pudding and start cooking 30 minutes before serving. Keep hot in pan of boiling water on the conventional hob.
3. Cook the potatoes in the microwave or conventionally and cream them. Set aside. Reheat in the microwave just before serving.
4. Reheat the soup on the conventional hob for 10 to 15 minutes before required, or in the microwave if space permits.
5. Cook the carrots in the microwave as the first course is served, alternatively cook them conventionally.

# Hot Leek and Potato Soup

| METRIC/IMPERIAL | AMERICAN |
|---|---|
| 350 g/12 oz potatoes, peeled and thinly sliced | ¾ lb potatoes, peeled and thinly sliced |
| 750 g/1½lb white part of leeks, trimmed and thinly sliced | 1½lb white part of leeks, trimmed and thinly sliced |
| 50 g/2 oz butter, cut into small pieces | ¼ cup butter, cut into small pieces |
| | ¼ cup water |

4 tablespoons water
900 ml/1½ pints hot chicken
    stock
salt
freshly ground black pepper
croûtons to garnish

1 quart hot chicken stock
salt
freshly ground black pepper
croûtons for garnish

Setting to use: HIGH

Place the potatoes, leeks, butter and water in a large bowl. Cook, covered, for 9 minutes. Stir the soup halfway through cooking.

Add half the stock, and salt and pepper to taste. Cook, covered, for 6½ minutes.

Add the remaining stock. Pour the soup into a blender or food processor and purée until smooth. Pass through a sieve. Cook for 2 minutes to reheat.

Serve garnished with croûtons.

NOTE: This soup is also delicious cold. Make as above then refrigerate the soup until well chilled. Thin the soup with a little single (light) cream if necessary and serve it garnished with chopped chives.

▽ *Back to basics: clockwise from centre front: sugared carrots; creamed potatoes; steak and kidney pudding; hot leek and potato soup; crème caramel*

# Steak and Kidney Pudding

| METRIC/IMPERIAL | AMERICAN |
| --- | --- |
| 500 g/1 lb braising steak, trimmed and cut into cubes | 1 lb chuck steak, trimmed and cut into cubes |
| scant 150 ml/¼ pint brown ale | ⅔ cup dark beer |
| 1 onion, chopped | 1 onion, chopped |
| 1 teaspoon chopped fresh parsley | 1 teaspoon chopped fresh parsley |
| ½ teaspoon chopped fresh rosemary | ½ teaspoon chopped fresh rosemary |
| 25 g/1 oz plain flour | ¼ cup all-purpose flour |
| 6 lambs' kidneys, skinned, cored and sliced | 6 lambs' kidneys, skinned, cored and sliced |
| salt | salt |
| freshly ground black pepper | freshly ground black pepper |
| 50 g/2 oz mushrooms, sliced | ½ cup sliced mushrooms |
| **Pastry:** | **Pastry:** |
| 250 g/8 oz self-raising flour | 2 cups self-rising flour |
| ½ teaspoon salt | ½ teaspoon salt |
| 125 g/4 oz shredded suet | ¾ cup shredded beef suet |
| 175-200 ml/6-7 fl oz water | 1 cup water |

Setting to use: HIGH/DEFROST (30%)

Place the steak in a medium bowl. Pour over the beer and marinate for 24 hours. Stir once or twice during the time. Drain the meat, retaining the liquid.

Place the onion, parsley and rosemary in a very large bowl. Cook, covered, for 4 minutes. Stir in the flour, kidneys, steak, salt and pepper to taste and finally the marinade. Cook, covered, for 10 minutes. Stir halfway through cooking.

Reduce the power to DEFROST (30%) and cook, covered for 35 minutes. Stir once or twice during cooking. Stir in the mushrooms and cook for a further 10 minutes.

Meanwhile, make the pastry, Mix together the flour, salt and suet. Bind with the water. Roll out two-thirds of the pastry and use to line a greased 1.2 l/2 pint pudding basin (5 cup steaming mold). Roll out the remainder of the pastry to form a lid.

Spoon the cooked meat mixture into the pastry-lined basin. Dampen the top edges with a little water and put on the pastry lid, ensuring the edges are well sealed. Cover loosely with plastic wrap to allow for the rise of the pastry. Increase the power to HIGH (100%) and cook for 9 minutes.

Serve with a napkin wrapped around the basin.

# Sugared Carrots

| METRIC/IMPERIAL | AMERICAN |
| --- | --- |
| 50 g/2 oz butter, cut into pieces | ¼ cup butter, cut into pieces |
| 25 g/1 oz soft dark brown sugar | 2½ tablespoons dark brown sugar |
| 500 g/l lb carrots, sliced lengthwise | 1 lb carrots, sliced lengthwise |
| 1 tablespoon chopped fresh parsley to garnish | 1 tablespoon chopped fresh parsley for garnish |

Setting to use: HIGH

Place the butter and sugar in a medium bowl. Cook, uncovered, for 1 minute.

Stir in the carrots. Cook, covered, for 8 minutes. Let them stand, covered, for 3 minutes.

Transfer to a warm serving dish and garnish with chopped fresh parsley.

# Creamed Potatoes

| METRIC/IMPERIAL | AMERICAN |
| --- | --- |
| 3 tablespoons water | 3 tablespoons water |
| pinch of salt | pinch of salt |
| 750 g/1½ lb potatoes, peeled and halved | 1½ lb potatoes, peeled and halved |
| 25 g/1 oz butter, cut in pieces | 2 tablespoons butter, cut in pieces |
| 2 tablespoons milk | 2 tablespoons milk |
| 1 tablespoon cream | 1 tablespoon cream |
| pinch grated nutmeg | pinch of grated nutmeg |
| salt | salt |
| freshly ground white pepper | freshly ground white pepper |
| parsley sprigs to garnish | parsley sprigs to garnish |

Setting to use: HIGH

Place the water and salt in a large bowl. Add the potatoes. Cook, covered, for 9 minutes. Stir halfway through cooking. Let them stand, covered, for 9 minutes.

Drain the potatoes and pass through a sieve or potato ricer. Set aside.

Place the butter and milk in a small bowl. Cook, uncovered, for 1 minute. Beat the butter, milk, cream, nutmeg, and salt and pepper to taste into the potatoes. Reheat if necessary.

Pile into a warm serving dish and garnish with the sprigs of parsley.

# Crème Caramel

| METRIC/IMPERIAL | AMERICAN |
| --- | --- |
| **Caramel:** | **Caramel:** |
| 125 g/4 oz granulated sugar | ½ cup sugar |
| 4 tablespoons water | ¼ cup water |
| **Custard:** | **Custard:** |
| 600 ml/1 pint milk less 2 tablespoons | 2⅓ cups milk |
| 4 eggs, lightly beaten | 4 eggs, lightly beaten |
| 25 g/1 oz caster sugar | 2 tablespoons sugar |
| 2 tablespoons double cream | 2 tablespoons heavy cream |

Setting to use: HIGH/DEFROST (30%)

Place the sugar and water in a small bowl. Cook, uncovered, for 2½ minutes. Stir until the sugar has dissolved, then cook, uncovered, for 5 minutes longer or until the caramel is a golden colour.

Divide the caramel between 6 custard cups or small bowls, and swirl around to coat the bottom and sides evenly. Set aside.

To make the custard, place the milk in a large jug. Cook, uncovered, for 4 minutes. Whisk in the eggs, sugar and cream. Strain into the custard cups.

Arrange the cups in a circle in the microwave. Reduce the power to DEFROST (30%) and cook, uncovered, for 14 to 17 minutes or until just set. Rearrange halfway through cooking.

Set aside to cool, then chill. Unmould onto individual serving plates to serve.

**NOTE:** The actual cooking time will vary depending upon the temperature of the heated milk. Therefore, check after 14 minutes and remove any custards as soon as they are cooked.

# Cold Creation

## asparagus with tarragon butter

## chicken galantine
## tossed green salad
## pasta salad

## caramelized oranges

### Serves 4

*This is a menu to serve when the weather turns warmer and when the first tender young asparagus arrives in the shops.*

WINE NOTE

White burgundy (*Bourgogne Blanc*) will be perfect with this starter, and it would be just as good to serve with the Chicken Galantine. For a special treat, look for the words *Premier Cru* or *Grand Cru* on the bottle. These terms, indicating wine from the best vineyards of the region, should guarantee an excellent bottle.

Oranges are a difficult ingredient to match with wine, so try serving an orange-based liqueur (like *Grand Marnier*) afterwards with coffee in place of serving wine with the dessert.

ACTION PLAN

*On the day before:*
1. Prepare the chicken galantine and leave to press in the refrigerator.

*In the morning:*
1. Coat the galantine with sauce, then add garnish and aspic. Refrigerate.
2. Make the caramelized oranges and refrigerate. (Decorate just before serving.)

*Later in the day:*
1. Prepare the asparagus for cooking.
2. Prepare the pasta salad, but do not add the avocado. Keep cool. Prepare the greens for the salad and refrigerate.

*Before serving:*
1. Start cooking the asparagus 15 minutes before serving.
2. Add the avocado to the pasta salad and toss. Toss the green salad with its vinaigrette dressing just before serving.

▽ *Cold creation: clockwise from bottom left: tossed green salad; chicken galatine; pasta salad; asparagus with tarragon butter*

65

# FLOWER POWER

*The decorative techniques used in aspic work can be used on other dishes so they are well worth perfecting.*

Floral designs are traditionally used to decorate chicken galantines and other cold meats that are glazed in chaud-froid sauce then coated with aspic (see below). To achieve this professional look it is necessary to invest in a set of tiny metal aspic cutters. The set will provide you with a number of cutters of various shapes and is available from kitchenware shops.

Select brightly coloured vegetables – thin strips from red, green or yellow peppers; skin from a cucumber; strips of carrot, or pieces of orange or lemon peel that have been removed with a vegetable parer. Finely sliced radishes and the leaves of fresh tarragon can also be used.

Blanch these vegetable or fruit strips in boiling water for one minute then drain and dry them. (The blanching softens the strips enabling the shapes to sit easily on the curved surface of the meat.)

Using the aspic cutters, cut the desired shapes from the vegetable and fruit strips. Create your design on a work surface, then when you are happy with it, carefully transfer it to the food. Hold this decorative garnish in place by spooning over a thin layer of aspic jelly. Leave to set before serving.

# Asparagus with Tarragon Butter

| METRIC/IMPERIAL | AMERICAN |
|---|---|
| 500 g/1 lb asparagus, scraped and trimmed | 1 lb asparagus, scraped and trimmed |
| 3 tablespoons water | 3 tablespoons water |
| 125 g/4 oz butter | 1/2 cup butter |
| 1 teaspoon chopped fresh tarragon | 1 teaspoon chopped fresh tarragon |

Setting to use: HIGH

Arrange the asparagus in a shallow oblong dish with the tips facing the centre. Add the water. Cook, covered, for 10 minutes. Rearrange the asparagus halfway through cooking. Set aside, covered, while preparing the butter.

Place the butter and tarragon in a small bowl. Cook, uncovered, for 3 minutes or until melted and hot.

Drain the asparagus and arrange on a warmed serving dish. Pour over the tarragon butter.

# Chicken Galantine

| METRIC/IMPERIAL | AMERICAN |
|---|---|
| 350 g/12 oz pork sausagemeat | 3/4 lb bulk pork sausage meat |
| 25 g/1 oz desiccated coconut | 1/3 cup shredded dried coconut |
| 50 g/2 oz fresh breadcrumbs | 1 cup soft white bread crumbs |
| 1 1/2 teaspoons chopped fresh parsley | 1 1/2 teaspoons chopped fresh parsley |
| 1 1/2 teaspoons chopped fresh thyme | 1 1/2 teaspoons chopped fresh thyme |
| 2 teaspoons chopped fresh chives | 2 teaspoons chopped fresh chives |
| salt | salt |
| freshly ground black pepper | freshly ground black pepper |
| 1 × 2kg/4 lb chicken, boned | 1 × 4 lb chicken, boned |

| Chaudfroid sauce: | Chaudfroid sauce: |
|---|---|
| 1 piece of carrot | 1 piece of carrot |
| 1 celery stick, halved | 1 celery stalk, halved |
| 1 small onion, quartered | 1 small onion, quartered |
| 8 black peppercorns | 8 black peppercorns |
| 600 ml/1 pint milk | 2 1/2 cups milk |
| 600 ml/1 pint cold water | 2 1/2 cups cold water |
| 25 g/1 oz aspic jelly powder | 1 envelope aspic-flavored gelatin |
| 50 g/2 oz butter | 1/4 cup butter |
| 50 g/2 oz plain flour | 1/2 cup all-purpose flour |
| 1 teaspoon powdered gelatine | 1 teaspoon unflavored gelatin |
| 4 tablespoons double cream | 1/4 cup heavy cream |
| salt | salt |
| freshly ground black pepper | freshly ground black pepper |
| **To garnish:** | **For garnish:** |
| thin strips of cucumber skin to resemble flower stems | thin strips of cucumber skin to resemble flower stems |
| pieces of tomato skin, cut into petal shapes | pieces of tomato skin, cut into petal shapes |
| strips of cucumber skin, cut into leaf shapes | strips of cucumber skin, cut into leaf shapes |

Setting to use: HIGH

Work together the sausagemeat, coconut, breadcrumbs, parsley, thyme, chives, and salt and pepper to taste. Spread the chicken out skin side down and smooth out the flesh. Make an oblong of the sausagemeat filling and place it across the middle of the chicken. Fold up the chicken from each side over the filling, ensuring that the roll is not too long to fit in the microwave cooker. Secure with a few stitches using a trussing needle and thread and tie the roll securely.

Place the chicken roll, join side down, in a shallow dish. Cook, uncovered, for 21 minutes. Remove from the cooker, wrap in foil and let it stand for 20 minutes.

Remove the foil and pat off excess moisture with kitchen paper towels. Place the galantine between two plates with a 2 kg/4 lb weight on top. Leave to press for approximately 12 hours in the refrigerator.

To make the sauce, place the carrot, celery, onion, peppercorns and milk in a large jug. Cook, uncovered, for 4 minutes. Leave to infuse for 15 minutes, then strain. Set aside.

Place 300 ml/½ pint (1¼ cups) of the cold water in a jug and cook for 3½ minutes. Stir in the aspic jelly powder (aspic-flavored gelatin) until dissolved. Stir in the remaining water. Stand the jug in a bowl of hot water.

Place the butter in another large jug and cook for 1 minute or until the butter has melted. Blend in the flour and slowly stir in the flavoured milk. Cook for 2½ minutes, stirring every minute.

Stir the gelatine into 150 ml/¼ pint (⅔ cup) of the aspic until dissolved. Beat into the sauce with the cream, and salt and pepper to taste. Press the sauce through a fine sieve to obtain a high gloss. Set the remaining aspic aside.

Place the galantine on a wire rack. Remove the string. Coat the galantine with the sauce using a large spoon and applying slowly.

Allow the sauce to set slightly, then garnish the galantine with the vegetable skins. Gently coat the garnish and the galantine with several layers of aspic. Chill to set.

# Pasta Salad

| METRIC/IMPERIAL | AMERICAN |
|---|---|
| 175 g/6 oz pasta spirals | 1½ cups pasta spirals |
| 1 l/1¾ pints boiling water | 1 quart boiling water |
| 1 tablespoon vegetable oil | 1 tablespoon vegetable oil |
| salt | salt |
| freshly ground black pepper | freshly ground black pepper |
| ¼ teaspoon dry mustard | ¼ teaspoon dry mustard |
| 3 tablespoons olive oil | 3 tablespoons olive oil |
| 1 tablespoon wine vinegar | 1 tablespoon wine vinegar |
| 1 stick celery, finely chopped | 1 stalk celery, finely chopped |
| 1 carrot finely grated | 1 carrot, finely grated |
| ½ green pepper, cored, seeded and diced | ½ green pepper, cored, seeded and diced |
| ½ red pepper, cored, seeded and diced | ½ sweet red pepper, cored seeded and diced |
| 2 cloves garlic, crushed | 2 cloves garlic, minced |
| 1 teaspoon chopped fresh herbs of your choice | 1 teaspoon chopped fresh herbs of your choice |
| 1 tablespoon toasted almonds | 1 tablespoon toasted almonds |
| 2 avocados, peeled, stoned and cut into pieces | 2 avocados, peeled, seeded and cut into pieces |

Setting to use: HIGH

Place the pasta, boiling water and vegetable oil in a large bowl. Cook, covered, for 8 minutes.

Check during cooking to be sure that the pasta remains immersed in the water. Leave to stand, covered for 10 minutes, then drain. Rinse the pasta under cold running water. Drain thoroughly and set aside.

Place the salt, pepper and mustard in a mixing bowl. Add the olive oil and mix together. Whisk in the vinegar.

Add the celery, carrot, peppers, garlic, herbs and almonds. Toss in the pasta. Gently fold in the avocado pieces just before serving.

# Caramelized Oranges

| METRIC/IMPERIAL | AMERICAN |
|---|---|
| finely grated rind of 3 oranges | finely grated rind of 3 oranges |
| 175 g/6 oz sugar | ¾ cup sugar |
| 175 ml/6 fl oz water | ¾ cup water |
| 6 oranges, peeled, and pips removed | 6 oranges, peeled, and seeds removed |
| 2 tablespoons brandy | 2 tablespoons brandy |
| orange peel strips to decorate | orange peel strips to decorate |

Setting to use: HIGH

Place the orange rind, sugar and water in a medium bowl. Cook, uncovered, for 4 minutes or until boiling. Stir well to dissolve the sugar. Cook for 6 minutes. Allow to cool.

Slice the oranges and arrange in a shallow dish. Stir the brandy onto the sauce and pour over the oranges. Refrigerate until well chilled. Serve sprinkled with orange peel strips.

▽ Cold creation: caramelized oranges

# Cool It

## chilled avocado soup
## smoked salmon mousse
## potato salad
## tossed green salad
## summer fruit salad

### Serves 4

*Prepare this up-market menu a day in advance to leave yourself free of preparation worries. It is the perfect meal to serve on a hot summer's day when the cold dishes will be much appreciated.*

WINE NOTE
Simply serve the best German *Kabinett* or *Spätlese* wine you can manage with the first two courses of this light summer meal. The fruit salad needs no accompaniment.

ACTION PLAN

*On the day before or in the morning:*
1. Make the avocado soup and refrigerate.
2. Make the salmon mousse and refrigerate.
3. Make the potato salad and refrigerate.
4. Make the fruit salad and refrigerate.

*Later in the day:*
1. Prepare the salad greens and a vinaigrette dressing (see page 19) but do not combine.

*Before serving:*
1. Unmould the salmon mousse and garnish.
2. Remove the avocado stones (seeds) from the soup just before serving.
3. Toss the green salad in a little vinaigrette dressing just before serving.

## Chilled Avocado Soup

| METRIC/IMPERIAL | AMERICAN |
|---|---|
| 4 large ripe avocados, peeled, stoned and chopped | 4 large ripe avocados, peeled, seeded and chopped |
| 750 ml/1¼ pints milk | 3 cups milk |
| 2 large green peppers, cored, seeded and finely chopped | 2 large green peppers, cored, seeded and finely chopped |
| 1 small onion, finely chopped | 1 small onion, finely chopped |
| salt | salt |
| freshly ground black pepper | freshly ground black pepper |
| 150 ml/¼ pint double cream | ⅔ cup heavy cream |
| a little mild paprika to garnish | a little mild paprika for garnish |

68

Setting to use: HIGH

Combine the avocados with 300 ml/½ pint (1¼ cups) of milk in a blender or food processor. Purée until smooth. Set aside.

Place the peppers and onion in a large bowl. Cook, covered for 7 minutes or until tender. Stir halfway through cooking. Stir in the avocado purée, remaining milk, and salt and pepper to taste. Cook, covered, for 6 minutes.

Purée the soup until smooth. Stir in the cream. Place two avocado stones (seeds) in the soup to prevent discoloration. Refrigerate until chilled.

Remove the avocado stones (seeds) and serve the soup garnished with a sprinkling of paprika.

## Smoked Salmon Mousse

| METRIC/IMPERIAL | AMERICAN |
|---|---|
| 25 g/1 oz butter | 2 tablespoons butter |
| 25 g/1 oz plain flour | ¼ cup all-purpose flour |
| 300 ml/½ pint cold chicken stock | 1¼ cups cold chicken stock |
| ¼ teaspoon ground cumin | ¼ teaspoon ground cumin |
| 4 tablespoons dry white wine | ¼ cup dry white wine |
| 15 g/½ oz powdered gelatine | 1½ tablespoons unflavored gelatin |
| 300 ml/½ pint mayonnaise | 1¼ cups mayonnaise |
| 2 teaspoons anchovy essence | ½ teaspoon anchovy paste |
| 400 g/14 oz smoked salmon, chopped | 14 oz smoked salmon, chopped |
| salt | salt |
| freshly ground black pepper | freshly ground black pepper |
| 150 ml/¼ pint double cream, whipped | ⅔ cup heavy cream, whipped |
| To garnish: | For garnish: |
| lemon slices | lemon slices |
| fresh parsley | fresh parsley |

Setting to use: HIGH

Place the butter in a large jug. Cook, uncovered, for 1 minute or until melted. Stir in the flour. Gradually stir in the stock. Add the cumin. Cook for 3½ minutes. Stir the sauce every minute.

Place the wine in a small bowl. Stir in the gelatine and cook for 4 seconds. Briskly stir until the gelatine has dissolved.

Beat the gelatine mixture into the sauce. Put to one side and allow the mixture to cool.

Fold the mayonnaise, anchovy essence (paste), salmon, salt and pepper to taste and the cream into the sauce. Spoon the mixture into a 1.2 l/2 pint (5 cup) mould. Chill the mousse until set.

Unmould the mousse and garnish with lemon slices and a sprig of fresh parsley.

NOTE: For a Smoked Meat Mousse, use 400 g/14 oz diced smoked ham or beef in place of the smoked salmon and add 2 teaspoons of drained capers instead of the cumin. Omit the anchovy essence (paste).

▷ *Cool it: clockwise from top left: chilled avocado soup; tossed green salad; smoked salmon mousse; potato salad; centre: summer fruit salad*

# SMALL BUT IMPRESSIVE

*Individual servings of starters and puddings need not look lost.*

Have you ever slaved over the preparation of a pâté, mousse or fool but at the end of it all discovered that it is difficult to present the completed dish attractively. The secret of successful presentation is to use 'props' to support and enhance the look of small portions. Garnishes also have a big part to play.

## For starters

There is nothing worse than a neutral coloured portion served on a neutral-coloured plate. Capitalize on shapes: for a shellfish starter use a shell-shaped white dish and highlight its shape by standing it on another dish of a different shape.

## Don't be fooled

Puddings presented in stemmed glasses can look lost. Stand the glasses on plates of a strongly contrasting colour, sharpen up the pink of a raspberry fool by serving it on navy blue or black plates. Place these on larger dishes – white or a toning pale colour so that it frames the smaller plate. Or use doilies to add the feminine touch, and for additional interest arrange the decoration on the plate rather than on the pudding.

## Shape up

Repetition of shapes attracts attention and creates visual interest. A slice of meat loaf can look uninteresting, even though it will taste superb.

Place the same slice on a square serving plate with a light garnish and it will look far more appealing.

---

# Potato Salad

| METRIC/IMPERIAL | AMERICAN |
|---|---|
| 3 tablespoons water | 3 tablespoons water |
| salt | salt |
| 750 g/1½ lb potatoes, peeled and cut into 1 cm/½ inch cubes | 1½ lb potatoes, peeled and cut into ½ inch cubes |
| 1 tablespoon wine vinegar | 1 tablespoon wine vinegar |
| freshly ground black pepper | freshly ground black pepper |
| 3 tablespoons olive oil | 3 tablespoons olive oil |
| 1 tablespoon grated onion | 1 tablespoon grated onion |
| 1 tablespoon chopped fresh chives to garnish | 1 tablespoon chopped fresh chives for garnish |

Setting to use: HIGH

Place the water, a pinch of salt and the potatoes in a large bowl. Cook, covered, for 9 minutes. Stir halfway through cooking. Let stand, covered, for 10 minutes.

Place the vinegar and salt and pepper to taste in a small bowl. Stir briskly to dissolve the salt. Gradually beat in the oil and onion.

Drain the potatoes and while still warm, gently toss in the dressing. Set aside to cool.

Garnish with chopped chives.

NOTE: For additional flavour add a little diced, crisply fried bacon; 2 to 4 tablespoons chopped walnuts, hazelnuts or toasted flaked almonds. Any chopped fresh herb can be used in place of the chives, stir into the potato salad while it is still warm if liked.

# Summer Fruit Salad

| METRIC/IMPERIAL | AMERICAN |
|---|---|
| 1 tablespoon lemon juice | 1 tablespoon lemon juice |
| 125 g/4 oz caster sugar | ½ cup sugar |
| 150 ml/¼ pint water | ⅔ cup water |
| 1 orange, peeled, segmented and pips removed | 1 orange, peeled, sectioned and seeded |
| 1 kiwifruit, peeled and sliced | 1 kiwifruit, peeled and sliced |
| 1 dessert apple, peeled, cored and sliced | 1 apple, peeled, cored and sliced |
| 1 pear, peeled, cored and sliced | 1 pear, peeled, cored and sliced |
| 6 strawberries, hulled and halved | 6 strawberries, hulled and halved |
| 8 sweet cherries, stoned | 8 sweet cherries, pitted |
| 75 g/3 oz grapes, peeled, halved and pips removed | ¾ cup grapes, peeled, halved and seeded |
| ¼ melon, peeled, seeded and diced | ¼ melon, peeled, seeded and diced |
| 2 tablespoons sweet sherry | 2 tablespoons cream sherry |

Setting to use: HIGH

Place the lemon juice, sugar and water in a large jug. Cook, covered, for 5 minutes.

Stir well to ensure the sugar has dissolved. Cool and refrigerate until cold.

Arrange the prepared fruit in a bowl. Stir the sherry into the cold syrup and pour over the fruit. Chill before serving if desired.

# Intimate French Affair

snails with garlic butter
French bread

rabbit in vermouth
braised celery
crumbed cauliflower
brown rice

apricot cream

### Serves 2

This meal, which has a definite French flavour, is
ideal for those more intimate occasions.

A *Chablis* or White Burgundy (*Bourgogne Blanc*) is ideal
with the snails, while a white *Côtes-du-Rhône* should
complement the vermouth in the rabbit's sauce.
*Montbazillac* with the apricot cream provides a
memorable end to the meal.

WINE
NOTE

*On the day before or in the morning:*
1. Prepare the garlic butter for the snails and refrigerate.
2. Make the apricot cream and refrigerate.

*Later in the day:*
1. Stuff the shells with snails and garlic butter, ready for cooking.
2. Prepare the ingredients for the rabbit.
3. Prepare the vegetables for cooking.
4. Decorate the apricot cream and refrigerate.
5. Prepare the breadcrumb mixture for the cauliflower.

*Before serving:*
1. Start cooking the rabbit 20 minutes before required. Keep hot or reheat just before serving.
2. Cook the snails just before serving. Meanwhile, purée the sauce for the rabbit.
3. Cook the vegetables while eating the first course, braise the celery in the microwave and cook the cauliflower and rice on the conventional hob or cook both in the microwave and reheat just before serving.
4. Pop the fried breadcrumbs in the microwave for a few moments before sprinkling over the cauliflower.

ACTION
PLAN

▽ *An intimate French affair: snails with garlic butter served with French bread*

## Snails with Garlic Butter

| METRIC/IMPERIAL | AMERICAN |
|---|---|
| 45 g/1½ oz butter | 3 tablespoons butter |
| 1 teaspoon finely grated onion | 1 teaspoon finely grated onion |
| 2 cloves garlic, crushed | 2 cloves garlic, minced |
| pinch of salt | pinch of salt |
| pinch of grated nutmeg | pinch of grated nutmeg |
| 1 teaspoon chopped fresh parsley | 1 teaspoon chopped fresh parsley |
| freshly ground black pepper | freshly ground black pepper |
| 12 canned snails with shells | 12 canned snails with shells |

Setting to use: HIGH

Cream together the butter, onion, garlic, salt, nutmeg, parsley and pepper to taste. Push some of the butter mixture into each shell.

Place the snails in the shells and cover with the remaining butter.

Arrange the shells, with the open ends uppermost, in a circle on a plate covered with coarse salt to hold them steady.

Cook, uncovered, for 1½ to 2 minutes. Serve hot with plenty of brown bread fingers or French bread so that your guests can use it to soak up the butter.

NOTE: Canned snails can also be served in a tomato sauce. Simply prepare a fresh tomato sauce (see page 93), add the canned snails and heat through for a few minutes.

△ *An intimate French affair: clockwise from top right: crumbed cauliflower; rabbit in vermouth; braised celery; apricot cream*

# *Rabbit in Vermouth*

| METRIC/IMPERIAL | AMERICAN |
|---|---|
| 1 onion, finely chopped | 1 onion, finely chopped |
| 1 celery stick, finely sliced | 1 celery stalk, finely sliced |
| 6 tomatoes, skinned and chopped | 6 tomatoes, skinned and chopped |
| 2 tablespoons tomato purée | 2 tablespoons tomato paste |
| 2 cloves garlic, crushed | 2 cloves garlic, minced |
| 1 teaspoon chopped fresh sage | 1 teaspoon chopped fresh sage |
| 1 teaspoon chopped fresh parsley | 1 teaspoon chopped fresh parsley |
| 4 rabbit joints | 4 rabbit pieces |
| 50 g/2 oz butter, cut into pieces | 1/4 cup butter, cut into pieces |
| 50 g/2 oz cornflour | 1/2 cup cornstarch |
| 150 ml/1/4 pint milk | 2/3 cup milk |
| 300 ml/1/4 pint hot chicken stock | 1 1/4 cups hot chicken stock |
| 150 ml/1/4 pint dry vermouth | 2/3 cup dry vermouth |
| salt | salt |
| freshly ground black pepper | freshly ground black pepper |
| sage leaves to garnish | sage leaves for garnish |

Setting to use: HIGH

Place the onion, celery, tomatoes, tomato purée (paste), garlic and herbs in a large bowl. Cook, covered, for 6 minutes. Place the rabbit around the sides of the bowl. Cover and cook for 6 minutes. Rearrange halfway through cooking.

Remove the rabbit and keep hot. Stir the butter into the sauce until melted. Blend the cornflour (cornstarch) with the milk until smooth. Stir into the sauce with the stock and vermouth. Cook for 4 minutes, stirring every minute.

Purée the sauce in a blender or food processor. Add salt and pepper to taste.

Arrange the rabbit on a warm, non-metallic serving platter and spoon over the sauce. Cover and cook for 5 minutes. Stand, covered for 4 minutes before serving, garnished, with sage leaves.

# Braised Celery

| METRIC/IMPERIAL | AMERICAN |
|---|---|
| 500 g/1 lb head celery, trimmed and sticks halved | 1 lb bunch celery, trimmed and stalks removed |
| 1 carrot, peeled and grated | 1 carrot, peeled and grated |
| 1 onion, thinly sliced | 1 onion, thinly sliced |
| 3 tablespoons water mixed with a pinch of salt | 3 tablespoons water mixed with a pinch of salt |
| 150 ml/1/4 pint hot chicken stock | 2/3 cup hot chicken stock |
| 25 g/1 oz butter, cut into pieces | 2 tablespoons butter, cut into pieces |
| freshly ground black pepper | freshly ground black pepper |

Setting to use: **HIGH**

Place half the celery in a casserole dish. Spread over the carrot and onion and cover with the remaining celery. Pour over the salted water. Cook, covered, for 8½ minutes. Rearrange halfway through cooking.

Mix together the hot stock, butter and pepper to taste. Pour over the celery. Cook, covered, for 4 minutes. Let it stand, covered, for 4 minutes before serving.

# Crumbed Cauliflower

| METRIC/IMPERIAL | AMERICAN |
|---|---|
| 1 small cauliflower, trimmed weight 500 g/1 lb | 1 cauliflower, trimmed weight 1 lb |
| 50 g/2 oz butter | 1/4 cup butter |
| 50 g/2 oz brown breadcrumbs | 2/3 cup brown breadcrumbs |
| 1 tablespoon chopped fresh tarragon | 1 tablespoon chopped fresh tarragon |
| 1 tablespoon lemon juice | 1 tablespoon lemon juice |
| salt | salt |
| freshly ground black pepper | freshly ground black pepper |
| 2 hard-boiled eggs, yolks and whites sieved separately, to garnish | 2 hard-cooked eggs, yolks and whites sieved separately, for garnish |

Setting to use: **HIGH/Conventional Hob**

Make an incision in the base of the cauliflower stalk. Place in a medium bowl.

Cover and cook for 10 minutes. Turn over halfway through cooking.

Meanwhile, place the butter in a frying pan. Using the conventional hob, melt the butter and fry the crumbs until brown. Stir in the tarragon, lemon juice, salt and pepper.

Drain the cauliflower and place in a warm serving dish. Sprinkle with the breadcrumb mixture. Garnish with a pattern of sieved egg yolk and white.

# Apricot Cream

| METRIC/IMPERIAL | AMERICAN |
|---|---|
| 500 g/1 lb apricots, stoned and quartered | 1 lb apricots, pitted and quartered |
| 3 tablespoons water | 3 tablespoons water |
| 75 g/3 oz caster sugar | 1/3 cup sugar |
| 20 g/3/4 oz powdered gelatine | 1 envelope unflavored gelatin |
| 300 ml/1/2 pint double cream, stiffly whipped | 1 1/4 cups heavy cream, stiffly whipped |
| **To decorate:** | **To decorate:** |
| whipped cream (optional) | whipped cream (optional) |
| thin slices of fresh apricot | thin slices of fresh apricot |

Setting to use: **HIGH**

Place the apricots (reserve two for decoration), water and sugar in a medium bowl. Cook, covered, for 5 minutes. Stir halfway through cooking.

Pour the mixture into a blender or food processor and sprinkle in the gelatine. Purée until smooth and the gelatine has dissolved. Set aside to cool.

Gently fold the whipped cream into the purée and pour into a glass serving dish. Chill until set. Serve decorated with whipped cream and thin slices of fresh apricot.

NOTE: This pudding serves 2 to 4. If you don't want any leftovers divide the mixture into four individual serving dishes and pop two into the freezer. Thaw, uncovered, and decorate just before serving.

## CLEVER CROUTONS

*Croûtons add crunch to a soup but they need not just be predictable cubes of toasted or fried bread. Garnishes and the extra little touches can add a great deal to the overall appeal.*

### Birthday croûtons
*If you are giving a birthday dinner, cut small bread croûtons into the initials of your birthday guest. Cut as many as you require, from slices of white or brown bread, toast, fry or dry them in the microwave and serve them in the soup.*

### Super shapes
*Use aspic cutters to cut a selection of tiny shapes – stars, triangles, half moons, ovals, rounds and hearts. Pile them into a shallow dish and pass them round separately. Alternatively cut the bread into larger shapes for your guests to nibble.*

### Cheat's choice
*For the hostess in a real hurry, keep some Italian bread sticks handy – they look attractive and take no time to prepare! Either stand them in a tall glass tumbler on the table, or place a couple on each side plate before the guests sit down at the table.*

73

# Game For Guests

globe artichokes
with hollandaise sauce
___

roast pheasants with
cranberry sauce
potato balls
brussels sprouts
with cream
___

coffee chocolate dessert

### Serves 4

*A sophisticated menu to impress your guests on
an early autumn evening.*

**WINE NOTE** A *Riesling* wine from Alsace makes a suitably distinguished accompaniment to this fine starter while a top red Rhône wine, like *Hermitage or Côte Rôtie*, would do the same for the game course. The dessert would be best unaccompanied or taken with a glass of *Cognac*.

**ACTION PLAN**

*On the day before or in the morning:*
1. Make the cranberry purée.
2. Make the coffee chocolate dessert and refrigerate.

*Later in the day:*
1. Prepare the vegetables for cooking. Keep the potatoes covered with water to prevent discoloration.
2. Decorate the coffee chocolate dessert.

*Before serving:*
1. Start cooking the artichokes 1 hour before serving. When ready, remove from the microwave and keep hot or set aside and reheat in the microwave just before serving.
2. Start cooking the pheasants 45 minutes before required while preparing the Hollandaise sauce.
3. Cook the vegetables while eating the first course, use a conventional hob, if it is more convenient.
4. After the first course, complete the pheasants under the grill (broiler) and heat the cranberry sauce.

▷ *Game for guests: anticlockwise from top right: globe artichokes with hollandaise sauce; potato balls; Brussels sprouts with cream; roast pheasants with cranberry sauce; coffee chocolate dessert*

# Globe Artichokes with Hollandaise Sauce

| METRIC/IMPERIAL | AMERICAN |
|---|---|
| 4 globe artichokes | 4 globe artichokes |
| 300 ml/½ pint water | 1¼ cups water |
| 1 tablespoon lemon juice | 1 tablespoon lemon juice |
| ¼ teaspoon salt | ¼ teaspoon salt |
| Hollandaise sauce: | Hollandaise sauce: |
| 2 small egg yolks | 2 small egg yolks |
| 1 tablespoon lemon juice | 1 tablespoon lemon juice |
| 125 g/4 oz butter, cut into 8 pieces | ½ cup butter, cut into 8 pieces |
| pinch of cayenne pepper | pinch of cayenne |
| ½ teaspoon dry mustard | ½ teaspoon dry mustard |

Setting to use: HIGH

Trim the point from the outer leaves of the artichokes. Cut or snap off the stalks. Rinse the artichokes in a large bowl of cold water and drain upside down.

Place the water, lemon juice and salt in a large shallow container. Cook, covered, for 4 minutes or until boiling. Stand the artichokes in the dish and cover with plastic wrap. Cook, covered, for 20 minutes or until the bases are tender. Rearrange halfway through cooking. Set aside, covered, while making the sauce.

For the sauce, place the egg yolks and lemon juice in a small bowl. Mix together lightly. Cook, uncovered, for 30 seconds then beat hard until smooth.

Beat the butter, one piece at a time, into the sauce. Finally beat in the cayenne pepper and mustard.

Serve the artichokes immediately with the sauce.

# Roast Pheasants with Cranberry Sauce

| METRIC/IMPERIAL | AMERICAN |
|---|---|
| 175 g/6 oz fresh cranberries | 1½ cups fresh cranberries |
| 125 g/4 oz caster sugar | ½ cup sugar |
| 50 g/2 oz butter | ¼ cup butter |
| 2 × 1 kg/2 lb pheasants | 2 × 2 lb pheasants |
| 8 rashers streaky bacon, stretched | 8 slices bacon, stretched |
| 1 teaspoon cornflour | 1 teaspoon cornstarch |
| 3 tablespoons sweet sherry | 3 tablespoons cream sherry |
| grated rind of 1 orange | grated rind of 1 orange |
| **To garnish:** | **For garnish:** |
| pheasant tail feathers | pheasant tail feathers |
| watercress | watercress |

Setting to use: HIGH/DEFROST (30%)
Conventional Grill (Broiler)

Place the cranberries and sugar in a small bowl. Cook, covered, for 4 minutes.

Reduce the power to DEFROST (30%) and continue cooking the cranberries for 10 minutes. Stir thoroughly halfway through cooking.

Place the cranberry mixture in a blender or food processor and purée until smooth. Set aside.

Place half of the butter inside each pheasant. Cover the thin ends of the legs with foil. Wrap the bacon around each bird and secure with wooden cocktail sticks. Truss the birds with string.

Place the birds, breast side down, in a shallow casserole dish. Cook, covered for 10 minutes on FULL power. Turn over and cook, covered, for 9 minutes.

Remove the bacon, cocktail sticks and foil. Place the birds under a preheated conventional grill (broiler), breast side up, to crisp and brown the skin.

Meanwhile, blend together the cornflour (cornstarch), sherry and orange rind. Stir into the cranberry purée. Pour into a large jug. Cook on full power for 3 minutes. Stir every minute.

Arrange the birds on a warm serving platter. Spoon over the cranberry sauce. Garnish with the pheasant tail feathers and watercress.

NOTE: The roast pheasant can be served with bread sauce rather than cranberry sauce.

# SAY IT WITH FLOWERS

*The flowers you use to decorate your table need not be an
extravagant affair that stands in the middle of the table.*

*Before you decide which flowers will look the best with your linen
and general decor, consider the size of floral arrangement you can
have. Don't have a huge arrangement on a small round table —
your guests will feel crowded. Similarly, a very small single
arrangement will be lost on a grander table.*

## On the flat
Try a flattish arrangement as your centrepiece. It will not obstruct
your guests' view across the table and it also minimises the chance
of someone knocking over the arrangement.

If you don't have a suitable vase use a large shallow ashtray or
dessert bowl. Lay the stems of foliage across the bottom so that the
leaves frame the edge. Then fill in the spaces with big flattish
blooms such as cabbage roses, chrysanthemums or daisies.

## A little charmer
Tiny, individual floral arrangements can be just as good-looking
as a large one. All you need are humble egg cups or butter pat
holders that you may already have in your cupboard.

Fill them with a careful arrangement of rockery plants that
have miniature single flowers on individual stems, or those with
multi-floret heads, like Alysum or London Pride. Place each
arrangement centrally or to the left hand side of the place setting.

## On the water front
If you are in a hurry and have very few flowers available, try
floating flower heads in water. They could be the individual florets
from a geranium head, carnations, or any flower with a flat base
that will lie comfortably on the surface of water. Remove the stalks
completely, and float in a shallow container, like a glass bowl or
glass ashtray.

# Brussels Sprouts with Cream

**METRIC/IMPERIAL**
3 tablespoons water
pinch of salt
750 g/1½ lb Brussels sprouts,
 trimmed and a cross slit
 into the base of each stem
6 tablespoons double cream

**AMERICAN**
3 tablespoons water
pinch of salt
1½ lb Brussels sprouts,
 trimmed and a cross slit
 into the base of each stem
6 tablespoons heavy cream

Setting to use: HIGH

Place the water, salt and sprouts in a large bowl. Cook,
covered, for 12 minutes. Stir halfway through cooking. Let
them stand, covered, for 5 minutes.

Drain the sprouts and toss in the cream. Cook, uncovered,
for 45 seconds to warm the cream. Do not allow to boil.

# Potato Balls

**METRIC/IMPERIAL**
1 kg/2 lb potatoes, peeled
3 tablespoons water
salt
25 g/1 oz butter, cut into small
 pieces
1 tablespoon chopped fresh
 parsley (optional)

**AMERICAN**
2 lb potatoes, peeled
3 tablespoons water
salt
2 tablespoons butter, cut into
 small pieces
1 tablespoon chopped fresh
 parsley (optional)

Setting to use: HIGH

Cut the potatoes into marble-sized balls using a special
vegetable cutter or melon baller. Discard the potato trim-
mings (or reserve for use in a soup).

Place the potato balls, water and salt in a large bowl. Cook,
covered, for 8 minutes. Gently stir halfway through cooking.
Let them stand, covered, for 5 minutes.

Drain the potato balls and toss with the butter and
chopped parsley if using.

# Coffee Chocolate Dessert

**METRIC/IMPERIAL**
35 g/1¼ oz cornflour
25 g/1 oz caster sugar
1 rounded teaspoon instant
 coffee powder
450 ml/¾ pint milk
25 g/1 oz milk chocolate,
 broken into pieces
150 ml/¼ pint single cream
To decorate:
whipped cream
chocolate curls

**AMERICAN**
5 tablespoons cornstarch
2 tablespoons sugar
1 heaping teaspoon instant
 coffee powder
2 cups milk
1 heaping teaspoon instant
 coffee powder
⅔ cup light cream
To decorate:
whipped cream
chocolate curls

Setting to use: HIGH

Mix together the cornflour (cornstarch), sugar and coffee in
a large jug. Blend in the milk until smooth. Cook, uncovered,
for 4 minutes or until thick. Stir every minute. Set aside.

Place the chocolate in a small bowl. Cook, uncovered, for
1½ minutes or until melted. Pour the cornflour (cornstarch)
mixture onto the chocolate and beat well.

Stir in the single (light) cream. Spoon into four glass
dishes. Refrigerate until set.

Serve decorated with rosettes of whipped cream and
chocolate curls.

# Fuel Food

## consommé with peas

## lamb chops
## in spicy sauce
## boiled potatoes
## caraway cabbage

## blackberry suet pudding
## cream

### Serves 4

*This autumnal menu is perfect to serve those guests who you know have a hearty appetite.*

The delicate flavour of this soup is best appreciated without wine, while a Portuguese *Dão* will provide a rich, solid background for the main course. Suet pudding is not often eaten with wine but *Moscatel de Valencia* partners it with remarkable success.

*On the day before or in the morning:*
1. Coat the chops with the spice mixture and refrigerate.
2. Make the soup and refrigerate.

*Later in the day:*
1. Prepare the vegetables for cooking. Keep the potatoes covered with water to prevent discoloration.
2. Make the pastry for the fruit pudding.

*Before serving:*
1. Assemble the fruit pudding ingredients, ready for cooking.
2. Start cooking the chops 15 minutes before required.
3. Reheat the soup on the conventional hob 10 to 15 minutes before required, if the microwave is needed for other purposes.
4. Put the vegetables (see page 58) to cook in the microwave or on the conventional hob just before serving the soup.
5. Assemble and start cooking the fruit pudding after clearing the table of the first course or 10 minutes before serving.

▽ *Fuel food: clockwise from left: consommé with peas; caraway cabbage; boiled potatoes; lamb chops in spicy sauce*

77

△ Fuel food: blackberry suet pudding

# Lamb Chops in Spicy Sauce

| METRIC/IMPERIAL | AMERICAN |
|---|---|
| 3 tablespoons tomato purée | 3 tablespoons tomato paste |
| 3 tablespoons olive oil | 3 tablespoons olive oil |
| 3 tablespoons lemon juice | 3 tablespoons lemon juice |
| 1 teaspoon chilli powder | 1 teaspoon chili powder |
| 1 teaspoon ground ginger | 1 teaspoon ground ginger |
| 1 teaspoon ground coriander | 1 teaspoon ground coriander |
| 2 cloves garlic, crushed | 2 cloves garlic, minced |
| 1 teaspoon chopped fresh parsley | 1 teaspoon chopped fresh parsley |
| salt | salt |
| freshly ground black pepper | freshly ground black pepper |
| 8 lamb cutlets, total weight about 750 g/1½ lb | 8 lamb rib chops, total weight about 1½ lb |
| To garnish: | For garnish: |
| lemon slices (optional) | lemon slices (optional) |
| watercress | watercress |

Setting to use: HIGH

Mix together the tomato purée (paste), oil, juice, chilli powder, ginger, coriander, garlic, parsley, and salt and pepper to taste.

Coat each chop on both sides with the spice mixture and place in a shallow dish. Cover and refrigerate the chops for at least 7 hours.

Preheat a large microwave browning dish for 8 minutes, or following the cooker manufacturer's instructions.

Drain the chops, reserving any spice mixture in the dish. Arrange the chops in the preheated browning dish and press down to sear. Turn the chops over and cook, uncovered, for 6 minutes. Turn over and rearrange halfway through cooking.

Place the chops on a warm serving platter. Heat the reserved spice mixture in the microwave for a few seconds then pour it over the chops. Garnish with slices of lemon, if using, and sprigs of watercress.

NOTE: Pork can be used in place of the lamb, select lean chops or spareribs.

FUEL FOOD

# Consommé with Peas

| METRIC/IMPERIAL | AMERICAN |
|---|---|
| 350 g/12 oz lean minced beef | ¾ lb lean ground round steak |
| 2 egg whites, lightly whisked | 2 egg whites, lightly whisked |
| ¼ teaspoon salt | ¼ teaspoon salt |
| ½ teaspoon beef extract | ½ teaspoon beef extract |
| 1.2 1/2 pints hot beef stock | 5 cups hot beef stock |
| 5 tablespoons dry sherry | 5 tablespoons dry sherry |
| 3 tablespoons cooked peas to garnish | 3 tablespoons cooked peas for garnish |

Setting to use: HIGH/DEFROST (30%)

Place the meat, egg whites, salt and beef extract in a large bowl. Whisking all the time, pour on the hot stock. Cook, covered for 5 minutes or until boiling.

Reduce the power to DEFROST (30%). Cook, uncovered, for 45 minutes.

Strain carefully through a scalded jelly cloth, or use a piece of muslin, or cheesecloth. Stir in the sherry. Cook, uncovered, for 4 minutes to reheat.

Place the cooked peas in the bottom of a warmed tureen. Pour over the consommé.

NOTE: If speed is of the essence use canned consommé. Heat through and stir in the sherry just before serving with the green pea garnish.

# Caraway Cabbage

| METRIC/IMPERIAL | AMERICAN |
|---|---|
| 3 tablespoons water | 3 tablespoons water |
| salt | salt |
| 350 g/12 oz cabbage, stalk removed and finely shredded | ¾ lb cabbage, stalk removed and finely shredded |
| 40 g/1½ oz butter, cut into pieces | 3 tablespoons butter, cut into pieces |
| 1 tablespoon caraway seeds | 1 tablespoon caraway seeds |
| freshly ground black pepper | freshly ground black pepper |

Setting to use: HIGH

Place the water, a pinch of salt and the cabbage in a large bowl. Cook, covered, for 8 minutes. Stir halfway through cooking.

Drain the cabbage and stir in the butter until melted. Add the caraway, salt and pepper to taste, and serve hot.

NOTE: The caraway seed can be omitted but for additional flavour add 2 tablespoons crumbled crispy bacon, 2 tablespoons browned flaked almonds or grated rind of ½ lemon.

# Blackberry Suet Pudding

| METRIC/IMPERIAL | AMERICAN |
| --- | --- |
| 250 g/8 oz self-raising flour | 2 cups self-rising flour |
| 125 g/4 oz shredded suet | ¾ cup shredded suet |
| 125/4 oz granulated sugar | ½ cup granulated sugar |
| 120 ml/4 fl oz water | ½ cup water |
| 250 g/8 oz blackberries, puréed | 1 cup puréed blackberries |
| 50 g/2 oz soft dark brown sugar | ⅓ cup dark brown sugar |
| 1 rounded teaspoon cornflour | 1 heaping teaspoon cornstarch |
| 2 tablespoons orange juice | 2 tablespoons orange juice |

Setting to use: HIGH

Mix together the flour, suet and granulated sugar. Stir in the water to bind the pastry. Divide the pastry into five portions, each one larger than the last. Roll each out into a round.

Stir half of the blackberries and the brown sugar together. Place the smallest round of pastry in the bottom of a well-greased 1.2 1/2 pint pudding basin (5 cup steaming mold). Cover with 1 tablespoon of the blackberries. Continue until all the pastry rounds have been layered in the basin with the blackberries. Finish with the largest pastry round.

Loosely cover the basin with plastic wrap to allow for rising. Cook for 7½ minutes. Let it stand for 3 to 4 minutes before loosening the pudding with a knife and turning out. Keep hot.

Sieve the remaining cooked blackberries. Mix with the cornflour (cornstarch) and orange juice in a small jug. Cook, uncovered, for 2 minutes. Stir every minute.

Spoon the sauce over the pudding and serve immediately with cream or custard sauce.

NOTE: This pudding is best served hot as it tends to toughen on cooling. Any puréed fresh fruit can be used, try apples, plums, apricots or loganberries.

# THE CENTRAL THEME

*Break away from using flowers as your table decoration.*

Flowers are pretty, but certainly not essential for an attractive looking table. There are many alternatives to traditional floral arrangements, all that is required is a little imagination.

## Floral flambé
Floating candles create an impressive centrepiece that is quick to create. They are readily available in the shops and will be a great talking point. Arrange them in a shallow dish of water perhaps with a few rose petals or tiny flower heads. The flickering light from the gently moving candles is reflected in the water and looks very pretty.

## Glittering occasion
For a special occasion, birthday or anniversary try something glittery. Tiny gold and silver stars on the tablecloth will twinkle away throughout the meal. Throw them in the centre of the table – they will work their own way to the edge.

## Something fruity
Beautifully arranged fruit is always pleasing to the eye so why not try this as an alternative centrepiece. Select fruit that is in prime condition. Wash it thoroughly under cold running water then dry gently with absorbent kitchen paper. Some fruits like apples look even better if they are polished up while you dry them to give them a real shine. Then using a platter, shallow dish or compote dish, build up a pyramid of fruits in contrasting shapes and colours. Take care that the arrangement does not grow too high, or the whole lot may collapse half-way through the meal.

## Ribbons and bows
Use dried flowers and gift wrapping ribbon in complementary colours to create a pretty pyramid. Using florist foam arrange the dried flowers in a well shaped mount and place on a plate covered with a doily. Cut the ribbon into various lengths and pull each length across the blunt edge of a pair of scissors and intertwine the resulting curled ribbons around the flowers. You can split the ribbon into thinner widths and tease some of these thinner ribbons into casual curls so that they trail along the table, like party streamers.

Continue this idea through to the rest of the table. Tie matching bows around traditionally rolled napkins and curl the long ends. You could also slip a dried flower through the bow.

# Vegetarian Feast

### bean salad

### vegetable lasagne
### italian salad
### herb bread

### brandied berries

## Serves 4

*This light summery meal is perfect to serve to those friends who don't eat meat, fish or dairy produce.*

**WINE NOTE** Either red or white wine might accompany this vegetable lasagne: choose from among the good, inexpensive range of wines produced by Yugoslavia or Rumania. A white port to serve with the dessert makes for an unusual end to the meal.

**ACTION PLAN**

*In the morning or afternoon:*
1. Make the bean salad and the dressing but do not combine. Refrigerate.
2. Prepare the vegetable mixture for the lasagne.
3. Prepare the Italian salad and refrigerate.
4. Assemble the brandied berries and refrigerate.
5. Prepare the herb bread.

*Before serving:*
1. Cook the vegetable lasagne 30 minutes before required. Keep it warm.
2. Toss the bean salad in the dressing and serve while heating the herb bread in the microwave.
3. Brown the lasagne under the grill if using cheese.
4. Toss the Italian salad in the dressing just before serving.

# Herb Bread

| METRIC/IMPERIAL | AMERICAN |
|---|---|
| 1 vienna loaf | 1 small long loaf |
| 125 g/4 oz 100% vegetable margarine, softened | ½ cup 100% vegetable margarine, softened |
| 2 teaspoons dried mixed herbs or 1 tablespoon fresh | 2 teaspoons dried mixed herbs or 1 tablespoon fresh |
| 2 cloves garlic, crushed | 2 cloves garlic, crushed |
| freshly ground black pepper | freshly ground black pepper |

Setting to use: HIGH

Slice the bread diagonally at 1 cm/½ inch intervals but do not cut through the base of the loaf.

Beat together the margarine, herbs, garlic and black pepper and spread on both sides of the bread slices. Spread any leftover margarine mixture along the top and sides of the loaf of bread.

*▷ Vegetarian feast: clockwise from left: bean salad; Italian salad; vegetable lasagne; herb bread*

Wrap the loaf in greaseproof paper or plastic wrap and cook for 1 minute 10 seconds. Unwrap and serve immediately.

NOTE: For a crisper top, place the buttered loaf under a pre-heated hot grill (broiler) for a few seconds immediately before serving.

# Bean Salad

| METRIC/IMPERIAL | AMERICAN |
|---|---|
| 1 medium onion, sliced | 1 medium onion, sliced |
| 2 tomatoes, skinned and sliced | 2 tomatoes, skinned and sliced |
| 1 × 425 g/15 oz can red beans, drained | 1 × 15 oz can red kidney beans, drained |
| 1 tablespoon tomato purée | 1 tablespoon tomato paste |
| 1 stick celery, washed and sliced | 1 stalk celery, washed and sliced |
| 1 clove garlic, crushed | 1 clove garlic, crushed |
| 1 tablespoon freshly chopped parsley | 1 tablespoon freshly chopped parsley |
| salt | salt |
| freshly ground black pepper | freshly ground black pepper |
| 4 to 5 tablespoon vinaigrette dressing (see page 19) | 4 to 5 tablespoons vinaigrette dressing (see page 19) |

Setting to use: **HIGH**

Place the onion in a medium bowl. Cook, covered, for 3½ minutes or until tender. Set aside to cool.

Gently stir together the onion, tomatoes, tomato purée (paste), beans, celery, garlic, parsley and salt and pepper to taste.

Just before serving, gently toss the salad in the vinaigrette dressing.

VEGETARIAN FEAST

81

# WHITE IS RIGHT

The dinner service you buy will be with you for a long time – so choose with care.

China must be versatile. Many people choose a particular service because it looks good in the shop – without food on it. It is easy to be charmed by a particular pattern, but if it is strong in colour or design, it could be very restricting later on; and you may tire of that particular look. An added advantage of buying classic white china is that it is more likely to be available for a number of years, thus enabling additions and replacements to be bought in the event of any breakages.

## A neutral ally

Although it may be hard to envisage, the simpler and plainer your basic dinner set, the better. Otherwise the food you prepare could be fighting a constant battle with its background setting. Bear in mind that some colours look positively unattractive as a background to certain foods. So it really makes sense to go for classic simplicity – plain white.

If the basic set is white it is easy to add to your repertoire by getting additional specialist plates, such as corn-on-the-cob dishes, avocado dishes, etc, as these are always available in white.

## Must it be dead plain?

Possessing a white chine dinner service does not mean that it cannot have a decoration of some sort. It can have an embossed finish, a contrasting moulded border, a thin rim of colour, gold or silver, or it can have an unobtrusive coloured border pattern around the edge.

Make sure, too, that you have enough of each type of plate. There is nothing worse than giving a dinner party and having to wash up the plates you've just been using, so that they are ready for the next course.

## Over the top?

One idea that looks truly stupendous is to have your entire table – china, linens and cutlery – all in white. The effect can be dazzling, especially for a summer lunch party. Any table decoration will look spectacular against the white backdrop. The only discernible difference is in the various textures of lace, plain cotton and white ceramic cutlery handles. This way your food and wine will always reign supreme.

# Vegetable Lasagne

| METRIC/IMPERIAL | AMERICAN |
|---|---|
| 175 g/6 oz green lasagne | 6 oz green lasagne |
| ½ teaspoon vegetable oil | ½ teaspoon vegetable oil |
| ¼ teaspoon salt | ¼ teaspoon salt |
| 900 ml/1½ pints boiling water | 3¾ cups boiling water |
| 2 cloves garlic, crushed | 2 cloves garlic, crushed |
| ½ red pepper, seeded and sliced | ½ red pepper, seeded and sliced |
| 1 medium onion, chopped | 1 medium onion, chopped |
| 2 courgettes, trimmed and sliced | 2 zucchini, trimmed and sliced |
| 1 teaspoon mixed herbs | 1 teaspoon mixed herbs |
| 50 g/2 oz mushrooms, chopped | ½ cup chopped mushrooms |
| 2 tablespoons vegetable oil | 2 tablespoons vegetable oil |
| 40 g/1½ oz plain flour | 6 tablespoons all-purpose flour |
| 300 ml/½ pint water | 1¼ cups water |
| 1 × 400 g/14 oz can tomatoes in juice, chopped | 1 × 14 oz can tomatoes in juice, chopped |
| salt | salt |
| freshly ground black pepper | freshly ground black pepper |
| 50 g/2 oz cheddar cheese, finely grated (optional) | ½ cup finely grated cheddar cheese (optional) |

Setting to use: HIGH

Place the lasagne in a shallow oblong dish approximately 33 × 19 × 5 cm (13 × 8 × 2 inches). Mix together the oil, salt and boiling water. Pour over the lasagne and ensure the pasta is completely covered. Cook, covered, for 9 minutes. Check occasionally that the pasta is still covered with water. Set aside, covered, for 10 minutes.

Place the garlic, pepper and onion in a medium bowl. Cook, covered, for 4½ minutes. Mix in the courgette (zucchini), herbs and mushrooms and the 2 tablespoons oil. Cook, covered, for 3 minutes.

Stir in the flour. Gradually blend in the water, tomatoes and juice and salt and pepper to taste. Cook, uncovered, for 5 minutes. Stir every minute to avoid lumps.

Place a layer of the drained lasagne over the base of a heatproof casserole dish. Pour over half of the vegetable sauce. Cover with the remaining lasagne and then the remaining sauce.

If serving with cheese, sprinkle the cheese over the lasagne and cook under a preheated grill until the cheese is brown and bubbling. Serve at once.

# Italian Salad

| METRIC/IMPERIAL | AMERICAN |
|---|---|
| ½ curly endive, separated into leaves | ½ head chicory, separated into leaves |
| 1 head chicory, sliced into rings | 1 head endive, sliced into rings |
| 1 bulb fennel, sliced into rings | 1 bulb fennel, sliced into rings |
| 1 small head radiccio, separated into leaves | 1 small head red chicory, separated into leaves |
| 8 radishes, sliced if large | 8 radishes, sliced if large |
| 4 tablespoons vinaigrette dressing (see page 19) | ¼ cup vinaigrette dressing, (see page 19) |
| salt | salt |
| freshly ground black pepper | freshly ground black pepper |
| sprig of fennel | sprig of fennel |

Put all the ingredients in a salad bowl, toss well, then taste and adjust the seasoning. Garnish with fennel.

# Brandied Berries

| METRIC IMPERIAL | AMERICAN |
|---|---|
| 250 g/8 oz redcurrants, tops removed | ½ lb redcurrants, tops removed |
| 250 g/8 oz raspberries | ½ lb raspberries |
| 4 tablespoons brandy | 4 tablespoons brandy |
| caster sugar to taste | superfine sugar to taste |
| **To decorate:** | **To decorate:** |
| 1 egg white, lightly beaten | 1 egg white, lightly beaten |
| caster sugar | superfine caster sugar |
| mint leaves | mint leaves |

First of all, prepare the glasses. Dip the rims of four wine glasses into the beaten egg white and then in the sugar to give a frosted effect.

Arrange alternate layers of fruit in the glasses. Pour over the brandy. Sprinkle with caster sugar to taste and refrigerate for 2 to 3 hours.

Decorate each glass of brandied berries with a mint leaf.

NOTE: To give your guests an unexpected treat, replace the brandy with Framboise or Kirsch liqueur. And for an alternative decoration frost a small bunch of redcurrants to hang on the rim of the glass. Simply brush the currants with beaten egg white, dip in sugar to coat and then leave to dry on greaseproof (waxed) paper. This method can also be used on flowers and leaves for extra special decorations.

▽ Vegetarian feast: brandied berries

# Classic Cuisine

## fresh tomato soup
## lamb guard of honour
## carrots tossed in parsley
## green beans in sour cream
## new potatoes
## mango soufflés

### Serves 6

*This impressive main course is perfect for more special occasions. It is best served in summer when ingredients are at their best.*

WINE NOTE

A *Sercial Madeira* will, like sherry, serve well as an aperitif and first course soup accompaniment, while a red *Rioja Reserva* will appease the guard of honour. Mango soufflé is too much of a challenge for wine, though a glass of *Rum* might be welcome afterwards.

ACTION PLAN

*On the day before or in the morning:*
1. Make the soup but do not add the cream. Refrigerate.
2. Prepare the stuffing for the lamb roast.
3. Prepare the vegetables for cooking and refrigerate. Make the buttered crumbs for the beans.
4. Make the soufflés and refrigerate.

*Later in the day:*
1. Stuff the lamb roast, ready for cooking.
2. Decorate the soufflés. Refrigerate.

*Before serving:*
1. Start cooking the lamb 1 hour before required.
2. While the lamb is resting, cook the vegetables in the microwave cooker or cook conventionally.
3. Reheat the soup and add garnish just before serving.

---

1 teaspoon caster sugar / 1 teaspoon sugar
300 ml/½ pint milk / 1¼ cups milk
1 bay leaf / 1 bay leaf
1 bouquet garni / 1 bouquet garni
450 ml/¾ pint hot chicken stock / 2 cups hot chicken stock
To garnish: / For garnish:
4 tablespoons double cream / ¼ cup heavy cream
fresh basil / fresh basil

Setting to use: HIGH

Place the butter and onion in a large bowl. Cook, covered, for 4 minutes. Stir in the flour, tomato purée (paste), tomatoes, thyme, oregano and sugar. Slowly stir in the milk. Add the bay leaf and bouquet garni. Cook, covered, for 10 minutes. Stir halfway through cooking.

Remove and discard the bay leaf and bouquet garni. Add the stock. Purée the soup in a blender or food processor or until smooth, then pass through a sieve.

Reheat, uncovered, for 3½ minutes. Serve garnished with swirls of cream and basil.

# Lamb Guard of Honour

| METRIC/IMPERIAL | AMERICAN |
| --- | --- |
| 25 g/1 oz butter | 2 tablespoons butter |
| 1 small onion, finely chopped | 1 small onion, finely chopped |
| grated rind of 1 orange | grated rind of 1 orange |
| 1 clove garlic, crushed | 1 clove garlic, minced |
| ½ teaspoon ground coriander | ½ teaspoon ground coriander |
| 75 g/3 oz fresh white breadcrumbs | 1½ cups soft white breadcrumbs |
| 1 tablespoon orange juice | 1 tablespoon orange juice |
| salt | salt |
| freshly ground black pepper | freshly ground black pepper |
| 1 egg, lightly beaten | 1 egg, lightly beaten |
| 1 lamb guard of honour, prepared weight 750 g/ 1½ lb, consisting of 12 chops | 1 lamb guard of honour, prepared weight 1½ lb, consisting of 12 chops |
| fresh cherries to garnish | fresh cherries for garnish |

Setting to use: HIGH

Place the butter, onion, orange rind, garlic and coriander in a small bowl. Cook, covered, for 3½ minutes. Stir in the breadcrumbs, orange juice, and salt and pepper to taste. Add sufficient egg to bind the mixture.

Stuff the lamb roast with the orange mixture and place in a shallow dish. Cook, uncovered, for 22 minutes. Turn around halfway through cooking.

Wrap tightly in foil and leave to rest for 15 minutes. Serve garnished with cherries.

# Fresh Tomato Soup

| METRIC/IMPERIAL | AMERICAN |
| --- | --- |
| 25 g/1 oz butter | 2 tablespoons butter |
| 1 large onion, chopped | 1 large onion, chopped |
| 40 g/1½ oz plain flour | ⅓ cup all-purpose flour |
| 2 tablespoons tomato purée | 2 tablespoons tomato paste |
| 750 g/1½ lb ripe tomatoes, quartered | 1½ lb ripe tomatoes, quartered |
| 1 sprig fresh thyme | 1 sprig fresh thyme |
| 1 teaspoon chopped fresh oregano | 1 teaspoon chopped fresh oregano |

# Green Beans in Sour Cream

| METRIC/IMPERIAL | AMERICAN |
| --- | --- |
| 500 g/1 lb green beans, trimmed and cut into 2.5 cm/1 inch pieces | 1 lb green beans, trimmed, strings removed and cut into 1 inch pieces |
| 3 tablespoons water | 3 tablespoons water |
| 150 ml/¼ pint soured cream | ⅔ cup sour cream |
| ¼ teaspoon grated nutmeg | ¼ teaspoon grated nutmeg |
| salt | salt |
| freshly ground black pepper | freshly ground black pepper |

| | | | | |
|---|---|---|---|---|

40 g/1½ oz butter
40 g/1½ oz coarse fresh white
   breadcrumbs

3 tablespoons butter
¾ cup coarse soft white bread
   crumbs

Setting to use: HIGH/Conventional Hob

Place the beans and water in a medium bowl. Cover and cook for 7 minutes. Stir halfway through cooking.

Drain the beans and stir in the sour cream, nutmeg, and salt and pepper to taste. Cook for 3 minutes. Stir after 2 minutes. Do not allow the cream to boil.

Meanwhile, place the butter in a frying pan (skillet). Using the conventional hob melt the butter and fry the breadcrumbs until golden brown.

Drain the beans and sprinkle with the crumbs to serve.

# Mango Soufflés

METRIC/IMPERIAL
6 tablespoons water
2 tablespoons powdered
   gelatine
300 ml/½ pint mango purée
1½ tablespoons white wine

AMERICAN
6 tablespoons water
1½ tablespoons unflavored
   gelatin
1½ cups mango purée
1½ tablespoons white wine

125 g/4 oz caster sugar
300 ml/½ pint double cream.
   stiffly whipped
6 egg whites
**To decorate:**
whipped cream
fresh mango slices

½ cup sugar
1¼ cups heavy cream. stiffly
   whipped
6 egg whites
**To decorate:**
whipped cream
fresh mango slices

Setting to use: HIGH

Place the water and gelatine in a small jug. Cook, uncovered, for 30 seconds. Stir to ensure the gelatine has dissolved. Beat into the mango purée, then stir in the wine and sugar. Set aside to cool.

Gently fold the cream into the mango purée. Whisk the egg whites until stiff and fold them in.

Tie a band of greaseproof (wax) paper around six ramekin or individual soufflé dishes, rising approximately 1 cm/½ inch above the rim of the dishes. Gently spoon the mango mixture into the dishes. Chill until set.

With the help of a wet knife, gently remove the paper collars. Decorate with whipped cream and mango.

▽ Classic cuisine: clockwise from bottom left: fresh tomato soup; green beans in sour cream; carrots tossed in parsley; lamb guard of honour; right: mango soufflé

# Makes a Change

baked avocado
___
turkey rolls with
garlic butter
brown rice
courgettes medley
___
pears with chocolate
sauce

### Serves 4

*This menu consists of variations on classic recipes which will both surprise and impress your guests.*

**WINE NOTE** A dry *Muscat d'Alsace* will make an exciting partner for the avocado, while an Italian *Barbaresco* is excellent with the main course turkey dish. Chocolate is another difficult partner for wine, though *Muscat de Beaumes de Venise* could be enjoyed with the pudding.

**ACTION PLAN**

*In the morning:*
1. Prepare the stuffing for the avocados. Refrigerate.
2. Prepare the turkey rolls for cooking. Refrigerate.
3. Prepare the vegetables for cooking. Refrigerate.
4. Cook the pears and refrigerate, tightly covered.

*Later in the day:*
1. Stuff the avocados, ready for cooking, and cover tightly.

*Before serving:*
1. Cook the vegetables and keep hot.
2. Cook the avocados just before serving.
3. Cook the turkey rolls while eating the first course.
4. Make the chocolate sauce just before serving.

## Baked Avocado

| METRIC/IMPERIAL | AMERICAN |
|---|---|
| 65 g/1½ oz butter | 3 tablespoons butter |
| 50 g/2 oz fresh brown breadcrumbs | 1 cup soft brown bread crumbs |
| 125 g/4 oz finely chopped smoked meat | 4 cup finely chopped smoked meat |
| 6 tablespoons double cream | 6 tablespoons heavy cream |
| ½ teaspoon chopped fresh parsley | ½ teaspoon chopped fresh parsley |
| salt | salt |
| freshly ground black pepper | freshly ground black pepper |
| 2 large avocados | 2 large avocados |
| 1 tablespoon lemon juice | 1 tablespoon lemon juice |
| To garnish: | For garnish: |
| 2 tablespoons double cream | 2 tablespoons heavy cream |
| lemon slices | lemon slices |

Setting to use: HIGH

Place the butter in a medium bowl. Cook, uncovered, for 30 seconds or until melted. Stir in the breadcrumbs and smoked meat.

Add sufficient cream to bind the mixture, the parsley, and salt and pepper to taste. Cook for 1½ minutes.

Cut the avocados in half, remove the stones (seeds) and sprinkle the flesh with lemon juice. Pile the smoked meat mixture in the hollow in each avocado half. Arrange on a plate and cook, uncovered, for 3½ minutes.

Garnish with a drizzle of cream and lemon slices.

# Turkey Rolls with Garlic Butter

△ *Makes a change: from right: courgettes medley; turkey rolls with garlic butter on brown rice; baked avocado; pears with chocolate sauce*

**METRIC/IMPERIAL**
4 turkey breast fillets, total
  weight about 625 g/1¼ lb
125 g/4 oz butter
2 cloves garlic, crushed
8 rashers streaky bacon, rind
  removed and stretched
brown rice to serve
parsley sprigs to garnish

**AMERICAN**
4 turkey breast tenderloin
  steaks, total weight 1¼ lb
½ cup butter
2 cloves garlic, minced
8 slices bacon, derinded
  and stretched
brown rice to serve
parsley sprigs for garnish

Setting to use: HIGH

Place the turkey slices between pieces of greaseproof (wax) paper and beat them until thin.

Cream together the butter and garlic. Divide into four portions and spread over the centre of each turkey slice.

Turn the edges to neaten, then roll up the turkey to make parcels.

Roll two slices of bacon around each roll and secure with wooden cocktail sticks if necessary.

Arrange the turkey rolls in a circle in a shallow dish. Cook, covered, for 3 minutes. Rearrange and cook, covered, for a further 3 minutes.

Let them stand for 3 minutes, then transfer the turkey rolls to a bed of brown rice. Garnish with sprigs of parsley. Serve the garlic butter left in the dish separately.

NOTE: 4 tablespoons of chopped fresh parsley or 2 teaspoons of fresh tarragon can be used to flavour the butter instead of the crushed garlic.

87

# Courgettes Medley

| METRIC/IMPERIAL | AMERICAN |
|---|---|
| 1 medium onion, sliced | 1 medium onion, sliced |
| 2 cloves garlic, crushed | 2 cloves garlic, minced |
| 25 g/1 oz butter, cut into pieces | 2 tablespoons butter, cut into pieces |
| 350 g/12 oz courgettes, trimmed and sliced | ¾ lb zucchini, trimmed and sliced |
| 250 g/8 oz tomatoes, skinned and chopped | ½ lb tomatoes, skinned and chopped |
| 1 tablespoon tomato purée | 1 tablespoon tomato paste |
| 1 teaspoon chopped fresh parsley | 1 teaspoon chopped fresh parsley |
| salt | salt |
| freshly ground black pepper | freshly ground black pepper |

Setting to use: **HIGH**

Place the onion, garlic and butter in a large bowl. Cook, covered, for 3 minutes.

Stir the courgettes (zucchini), tomatoes, tomato purée (paste), parsley and salt and pepper to taste into the onion mixture. Cook, covered, for 8 minutes. Stir halfway through cooking.

NOTE: You can vary the vegetables used in this recipe. Replace the courgettes (zucchini) with aubergine (egg plant) slices or replace half the courgettes (zucchini) with matchsticklike strips of carrot.

# Pears with Chocolate Sauce

| METRIC/IMPERIAL | AMERICAN |
|---|---|
| 4 pears, total weight 500 g/ 1 lb, peeled but with stalks left on | 4 pears, total weight 1 lb, peeled but with stalks left on |
| 125 g/4 oz plain chocolate, broken into pieces | 4 squares semisweet chocolate, broken into pieces |
| 25 g/1 oz caster sugar | 2 tablespoons sugar |
| 1 to 2 tablespoons sweet sherry | 1 to 2 tablespoons cream sherry |
| candied angelica cut into the shape of leaves to decorate (optional) | candied angelica cut into the shape of leaves to decorate (optional) |

Setting to use: **HIGH**

Stand the pears in a circle on a plate. Cook, uncovered, for 5 minutes. Set aside to cool.

Place the chocolate in a small bowl. Cook, uncovered, for 2 minutes or until melted. Stir in the sugar and sufficient sherry to make a coating sauce.

Arrange the pears on a serving dish or in individual glasses. Pour over the chocolate sauce. Decorate with two leaves of angelica on the top of each pear if liked.

NOTE: A potato peeler is easier to use than a knife when peeling the pears as this results in a better shape.

## FEATHERED FOR FRIENDS

*Feathered cream enhances the look of any dish.*

### Simple soups

Recipes suggest you add a swirl of cream to the soup just before serving it. Make this swirl look a little more delicate by creating a feathered effect. Simply pour a little cream into the soup, then when it rises to the surface, draw the point of a skewer across the cream using a zig-zag motion. Add a herb sprig and serve.

### Something sweet

The same decorative effect can be used to enhance the look of creamy fools. Trickle a little melted chocolate or jam onto the pudding then quickly draw a skewer through it. Alternatively, sprinkle a layer of muscovado sugar and set aside for two hours until the sugar is moist then swirl the sugar through the mixture.

### All in a row

For a more uniform feathered pattern on cream-covered cakes, smooth whipped cream over the surface of the cake then trickle lines of heated redcurrant jelly across the surface, about 25mm/1 inch apart. Using a skewer, quickly draw the point across the rows of jelly in either one direction only or in alternate directions.

# Winter Warmer

celery soup
___

roast pork with walnut
and apple stuffing
roast potatoes
courgette slices
creamed swede
___

cheesecake

### Serves 6

This menu makes good use of the season's ingredients

WINE
NOTE

Try a lively young *Chianti* with both the first and main course. Look for a sweet (*doux* or *moelleux*) *Vouvray* to match the cheesecake.

ACTION
PLAN

*On the day before or in the morning:*
1. Make the celery soup, but do not add the cream.
2. Prepare the stuffing for the pork and refrigerate.
3. Make the cheesecake and refrigerate.

*Later in the day:*
1. Stuff the pork, ready for cooking.
2. Prepare the vegetables for cooking and keep covered with cold water to prevent discoloration.
3. Decorate the cheesecake and refrigerate.

*Before serving:*
1. Roast potatoes in the conventional oven 1 hour before required.
2. Start cooking the pork 50 minutes before required.
3. While the pork is resting, cook the swede (rutabaga). Purée and keep hot.
4. Reheat the soup and stir in the cream just before serving.
5. Cook the courgettes (zucchini) slices while eating the first course.

▽ *Winter warmer: clockwise from right: celery soup; roast pork with walnut and apple stuffing; courgette slices; creamed swede; cheesecake*

# Celery Soup

| METRIC/IMPERIAL | AMERICAN |
|---|---|
| 500 g/1 lb celery, finely chopped | 1 lb celery, finely chopped |
| 1 onion, chopped | 1 onion, chopped |
| 25 g/1 oz butter | 2 tablespoons butter |
| 1 tablespoon plain flour | 1 tablespoon all-purpose flour |
| 600 ml/1 pint milk | 2½ cups milk |
| 600 ml/1 pint hot chicken stock | 2½ cups hot chicken stock |
| ¼ teaspoon celery salt | ¼ teaspoon celery salt |
| freshly ground black pepper | freshly ground black pepper |
| 3 tablespoons double cream | 3 tablespoons heavy cream |
| chopped celery leaves to garnish | chopped celery leaves for garnish |

Setting to use: HIGH

Place the celery, onion and butter in a large bowl. Cook, covered for 10 minutes. Stir halfway through cooking.

Stir in the flour. Slowly blend in the milk, half the chicken stock, the celery, and salt and pepper to taste. Cook, covered, for 8 minutes. Stir halfway through cooking.

Add remaining stock and purée in blender or food processor until smooth.

Cook, uncovered, for 2 minutes to reheat. Slowly stir in the cream. Serve garnished with chopped celery leaves.

# Roast Pork with Walnut and Apple Stuffing

| METRIC/IMPERIAL | AMERICAN |
|---|---|
| 3 spring onions, trimmed and chopped | 3 scallions, trimmed and chopped |
| 50 g/2 oz walnuts, chopped | ½ cup chopped walnuts |
| 50 g/2 oz butter | ¼ cup butter |
| 1 small apple, peeled, cored and chopped | 1 small apple, peeled, cored and chopped |
| 2 teaspoons dried marjoram | 2 teaspoons dried marjoram |
| salt | salt |
| freshly ground black pepper | freshly ground black pepper |
| 50 g/2 oz fresh white breadcrumbs | 1 cup soft white bread crumbs |
| 1 × 1.5 kg/3¼ lb boned fillet end leg of pork | 1 × 3¼ lb boneless pork leg roast |
| bunches of watercress to garnish | bunches of watercress for garnish |

Setting to use: HIGH/Conventional Oven

Place the onions, walnuts, butter, apple, marjoram, and salt and pepper to taste in a medium bowl. Cook, covered, for 4 minutes. Stir halfway through cooking. Stir in the bread-crumbs.

Place the pork flat on a board and slit open the meat from end to end with a sharp knife. Fill the cut and pocket left by the bone with the stuffing. Draw the meat over the stuffing and tie the roast into shape with string.

Place the roast in a shallow, non-metallic ovenproof, shallow container. Cook, uncovered, for 25 minutes. Turn around halfway through cooking.

Pour off the juices to make a gravy. Transfer the pork to a conventional oven which has been preheated to 160°C/325°F/Gas Mark 3 and cook for 20 minutes. Alternatively, wrap the meat tightly in foil and let rest for 20 minutes before carving.

Remove the string and place the pork on a warm serving platter Garnish with bunches of watercress and serve with the gravy.

NOTE: If possible, weigh the stuffed pork to calculate microwave cooking time: 8 minutes to each 500 g/1 lb. The conventional cooking time or the resting time remains unaltered.

# Creamed Swede

| METRIC/IMPERIAL | AMERICAN |
|---|---|
| 750 g/1½ lb swede, peeled and diced | 1½ lb rutabaga, peeled and diced |
| 3 tablespoons water | 3 tablespoons water |
| 15 g/½ oz butter | 1 tablespoon butter |
| 1½ tablespoons double cream | 1½ tablespoons heavy cream |
| salt | salt |
| freshly ground black pepper | freshly ground black pepper |
| parsley sprig to garnish | parsley sprig for garnish |

Setting to use: HIGH

Place the diced swede (rutabaga) and water in a large bowl. Cook, covered, for 9 minutes. Stir halfway through cooking.

Place the swede (rutabaga), water, butter, cream, and salt and pepper to taste in a blender or food processor and purée until smooth.

Reheat if necessary. Place in a warm serving dish and garnish with a sprig of parsley.

# Cheesecake

| METRIC/IMPERIAL | AMERICAN |
|---|---|
| 50 g/2 oz butter | ¼ cup butter |
| 2 teaspoons golden syrup | 2 teaspoons light corn syrup |
| 125 g/4 oz malted milk biscuits, finely crushed | 1 cup finely crushed graham crackers |
| 250 g/8 oz curd cheese | ½ cup cream cheese |
| 125 g/4 oz full fat soft cheese | 1½ cups cottage cheese, sieved |
| 125 g/4 oz cottage cheese, sieved | 1 envelope gelatin |
| 15 g/½ oz gelatine | 2 tablespoons rum |
| 2 tablespoons rum | ¼ cup sugar |
| 50 g/2 oz sugar | 2 large eggs, lightly beaten |
| 2 large eggs, lightly beaten | 3 tablespoons golden raisins |
| 25 g/1 oz sultanas | 2 tablespoons sour cream |
| 2 tablespoons soured cream | |
| **To decorate:** | **To decorate:** |
| whipped cream | whipped cream |
| sultanas | golden raisins |

Setting to use: HIGH

Place the butter and syrup in a small jug. Cook, uncovered, for 1 minute or until melted. Mix with the biscuits (crackers) and spread over the bottom of a 21 cm/8½ inch loose-bottomed fluted flan or quiche pan. Using the back of a spoon, press down the crust and smooth it over.

Beat together the cheeses in a very large jug. Cook, uncovered, for 1½ minutes. Stir after 1 minute. Sprinkle the gelatine over the rum, then dissolve over a low heat. Beat in the softened gelatine, sugar and eggs. Cook, uncovered, for 3 minutes. Beat every minute.

Stir in the sultanas (golden raisins). Cook for a further 30 seconds. Stir in the sour cream. Spread over the crust in the pan. Chill until set.

Decorate with rosettes of whipped cream and a few sultanas (golden raisins).

# LIGHTING-UP TIME

*Candlelight creates a wonderfully relaxed atmosphere.*

The lighting in your dining room is important to the overall feel of the meal. Harsh lighting is unkind and not condusive to a relaxed atmosphere. So, say goodbye to the bright lights. Turn off the central ceiling light, and turn to other sources such as standard lamps, wall lights or table lamps. With this lower lighting level, candles come into their own. It is not just the soft light they produce – rather like an open fire, there is something restful and pleasing about the flickering of a flame.

## The more the merrier

Elaborate candelabra which traditionally graced the formal baronial table can look incongruous in a modern setting. However, the idea of having more than two candles on the table is a good one. Be a little more adventurous. Go for groups of candles, which can look really quite spectacular.

## The long and short of it

Place a block of 'Oasis' that has been presoaked in water, on a dish, push in as many long thin candles as you think appropriate – don't go too mad, as they produce quite a heat in large numbers! Then take some pretty foliage from the garden – something with a good firm leaf, such as variegated Ivy – and cover up the 'Oasis' by pushing the leaves in at strategic points. You can decide on whether to use candles of only one colour, or perhaps pick out the colours in a patterned tablecloth.

## Outside in

For the reverse idea, group a set of slim candles around a simple central flower arrangement. Select a tumbler-shaped glass vase and fill it with flowers that will not hang over the sides – such as grasses, wheat, daisies or roses trimmed of their greenery. Be sure to cut off any greenery that overhangs the vase or the heat from the candles may set it alight.

These slim candles can be bought in sets and come complete with small ceramic holders to keep them stable. However, it is still a good idea to place the whole arrangement on a plate for safety.

## On several levels

If you are not particularly confident about something so creative, why not simply select candles of a different size and shape? Use all white candles (and so save money by using household type candles in the design) grouped together on a plate. Check whether they are non-drip – this makes them safer and less messy. Vary the height and texture – there are spiral candles, pearlised finishes and many other variations to choose from in the shops.

# Pick Of The Crop

## asparagus soup

## sole with tomato sauce
## creamed corn
## new potatoes

## raspberry meringue

### Serves 6

*The best of summer's fruit and vegetables are put to good effect in this colourful menu.*

**WINE NOTE** *Amontillado Sherry*, especially one labelled 'Very Old', would bring out the best in this fine soup, while a *Sancerre* or *Pouilly-Fumé* would both make excellent drinking with the main course sole. Meringues tend to overpower even the sweetest of wines, so are best enjoyed on their own.

**ACTION PLAN**

*In the morning:*
1. Make the asparagus soup but do not add the cream. Refrigerate.
2. Make the tomato sauce for the sole and refrigerate.
3. Make the meringue ring.

*Later in the day:*
1. Roll up the sole fillets, ready for cooking.
2. Whip the cream for the raspberry meringue. Refrigerate.

*Before serving:*
1. Reheat the soup and stir in the cream just before serving. Cook the potatoes.
2. Heat the creamed corn while eating the first course. Also warm the tomato sauce on the conventional hob.
3. After the first course, complete the fish dish.
4. Assemble the raspberry meringue just before serving.

# ═══ Asparagus Soup ═══

| METRIC/IMPERIAL | AMERICAN |
|---|---|
| 50 g/2 oz butter | 1/4 cup butter |
| 500 g/1 1lb asparagus, trimmed and sliced | 1 lb asparagus, trimmed and sliced |
| 1 onion, finely chopped | 1 onion, finely chopped |
| 50 g/2 oz cornflour | 1/2 cup cornstarch |
| 900 ml/1 1/2 pints milk | 1 quart milk |
| 1 bouquet garni | 1 bouquet garni |
| salt | salt |
| freshly ground white pepper | freshly ground white pepper |

| | |
|---|---|
| 150 ml/1/4 pint double cream cooked asparagus tips to garnish | 2/3 cup heavy cream cooked asparagus tips for garnish |

Setting to use: HIGH

Place the butter, asparagus and onion in a large bowl. Cook, covered for 9 minutes. Stir halfway through cooking.

Mix the cornflour (cornstarch) with a little of the milk to make a smooth paste. Stir in the remaining milk. Add to the asparagus. Add the bouquet garni, and salt and pepper to taste. Cook, covered, for 9 minutes. Stir after 2, 4 and 6 minutes.

Remove and discard the bouquet garni. Purée the soup in a blender or food processor until smooth. Stir in the cream. Reheat if necessary but do not boil. Garnish with cooked asparagus tips.

▽ *Pick of the crop: clockwise from right: asparagus soup; sole with tomato sauce; creamed corn; raspberry meringue*

# Fillets of Sole with Tomato Sauce

**METRIC/IMPERIAL**
*12 to 16 skinned sole fillets,
    total weight 750 g/1½ lb*
**Tomato Sauce:**
*20 g/¾ oz butter
3 shallots, finely chopped
1 clove garlic, crushed
1 teaspoon caster sugar
1 teaspoon chopped fresh
    basil
2 tablespoons tomato purée
20 g/¾ oz plain flour
350 g/12 oz tomatoes, skinned
    and chopped
scant 150 ml/¼ pint hot
    chicken stock*

**AMERICAN**
*12 to 16 skinned sole fillets,
    total weight 1½ lb*
**Tomato Sauce:**
*1½ tablespoons butter
3 shallots, finely chopped
1 clove garlic, minced
1 teaspoon sugar
1 teaspoon chopped fresh
    basil
2 tablespoons tomato paste
3 tablespoons all-purpose
    flour
¾ lb tomatoes, skinned and
    chopped
⅔ cup hot chicken stock*

*salt
freshly ground black pepper
1 tablespoon cream
fresh basil to garnish*

*salt
freshly ground black pepper
1 tablespoon cream
fresh basil for garnish*

Setting to use: **HIGH**

Roll up the fillets and arrange in one layer in a shallow dish. If required secure each with a wooden cocktail stick. Cover and cook for 3½ minutes. Rearrange and cook for a further 1 minute. Set aside, covered.

Place the butter, shallots, garlic, sugar, basil and tomato purée (paste) in a medium bowl. Cover and cook for 4½ minutes. Stir in the flour, tomatoes and hot stock. Cover and cook for 5 minutes. Stir after 2 and 4 minutes.

Sieve the sauce if liked and season to taste with salt and pepper. Stir in the cream.

Drain excess liquid from the sole if necessary, then pour over the sauce. Cook for 2 minutes to reheat. Serve garnished with fresh basil.

# BIG IS BEAUTIFUL

*Try a different and therefore more striking approach to serving vegetables.*

Hot vegetables take a fair amount of time and effort to prepare and it is quite an art fiddling the cooking times so that all the vegetables are ready to serve at the same time. After all this effort it is therefore a pity if the serving of them does not do justice to the vegetables themselves.

## Think ahead

Take time to work out which vegetables will complement the main dish. Select those vegetables that are in season and which are therefore in prime condition – this will make quite a difference to both the flavour and looks of the vegetable dishes.

Having made your final selection of vegetables, think about how you will serve them so that they look their best alongside the main dish.

## All together now

The impact of a bowl of boiled new potatoes with, say, separate dishes containing broccoli and carrots will not be enormous. However, if you combine these vegetables on one large platter they will take on an entirely new look. It is probably best to use a plain white platter allowing the vegetables to provide the pattern and colour.

## Build in blocks

A large platter leaves you plenty of scope for arrangement. Lay the vegetables in rows of contrasting colour, or arrange them in a circular design around a cauliflower or mound of new potatoes. Alternatively lay the vegetables out in individual portions next to one another – four baby carrots, next to five new potatoes with three spears of broccoli arranged in triangular shapes round the platter.

Don't get carried away with the number of vegetables used. Your guests can only eat so much.

---

# Creamed Corn

| METRIC/IMPERIAL | AMERICAN |
|---|---|
| 1 × 325 g/11 oz can sweetcorn kernels | 1 × 11 oz can whole kernel corn |
| 1 clove garlic, crushed | 1 clove garlic, crushed |
| 150 ml/¼ pint soured cream | ⅔ cup sour cream |
| chopped parsley, to garnish | chopped parsley, for garnish |

Setting to use: HIGH

Drain the sweetcorn and purée in a food processor for a few seconds with the crushed garlic. Stir in the soured cream. Cook for 2 to 3 minutes to heat. Garnish with chopped parsley.

# Raspberry Meringue

| METRIC/IMPERIAL | AMERICAN |
|---|---|
| 1 large egg white | 1 large egg white |
| 350 g/12 oz icing sugar, sifted | 3 cups confectioners' sugar, sifted |
| 350 g/12 oz raspberries or other fresh fruit | 2½ cups raspberries or other fresh fruit |
| 1 tablespoon brandy | 1 tablespoon brandy |
| 300 ml/½ pint double cream, stiffly whipped | 1¼ cups heavy cream, stiffly whipped |
| a few fresh raspberries to decorate | a few fresh raspberries to decorate |

Setting to use: HIGH

Whisk the egg white until stiff. Beat in the icing (confectioners') sugar a tablespoon at a time. When all the sugar has been incorporated, knead the mixture together by hand.

Roll the mixture into a long sausage shape about 45 cm/ 18 inches long.

Bring the two ends together to form a ring. Place on a non-metallic round serving plate. Cook, uncovered, for 2½ minutes. Set aside to cool.

Pile the raspberries in the centre of the meringue ring. Sprinkle with the brandy. Pipe rosettes of cream over the meringue. Decorate, if desired, with a few extra raspberries.

NOTE: The meringue is very sweet and crumbly and should be cooked on the serving dish to avoid it breaking.

# Extra Special

### country pâté
### melba toast

---

### fruit-stuffed duck
### duchesse potatoes
### broccoli with lemon butter

---

### charlotte russe

#### Serves 4

*A rich winter menu that highlights the excellent marriage of rich duck with fruit stuffing.*

WINE NOTE

A *Chablis* will accompany both the pâté and duck well (*Chablis Premier Cru* or *Grand Cru* would be better still), while a golden *Sauternes* would be ideal with the creamy dessert.

ACTION PLAN

*On the day before or in the morning:*
1. Make the pâté.
2. Prepare the stuffing for the duck.
3. Make the charlotte russe.

*Later in the day:*
1. Turn out and garnish the pâté. Refrigerate.
2. Cook and pipe the duchesse potatoes onto a baking sheet, ready for cooking. Prepare the broccoli for cooking.
3. Stuff the duck, ready for cooking.

*Before serving:*
1. Start cooking the duck 1 hour before required.
2. Invert the charlotte russe onto a serving dish and refrigerate.
3. Bake the potatoes in the conventional oven 20 minutes before required.
4. Cook the broccoli while eating the first course.

▽ *Extra special: clockwise from right: country pâté with melba toast; fruit-stuffed duck; duchesse potatoes; broccoli with lemon butter*

# MY PLACE OR YOURS

Place names are useful for a formal dinner table and fun to use for a more informal evening meal. When giving a dinner party for a large number of guests it always helps if they can immediately see where to sit. Be creative with your place cards.

## Thank you fans

Fold an oblong of appropriately coloured paper into accordion pleats across the length to make a fan shape. Open it out and find the central pleat. Take the middle letter of the person's name and working outwards, write the individual letters in the name on each side of each pleat. Draw the pleats together again and secure tightly near the base with a bow in a matching or contrasting colour. These fans can be as big or small as you wish, as long as the guest can read the names.

## Keep it trad

Pretty up card-style place names with flowers or bows. Take an oblong of white card and bend the card in half lengthways as usual so that the card can stand up. Write the name of the guest on the bottom half and affix a dried flower or bow with glue. Fresh flowers can also be used, simply make a hole in the card and push through the flower stem, secure the stem on the reverse side with sticky tape.

As an alternative, take your card and bend it lengthways. Cut out a bold shape from stiff coloured paper (a heart is good for wedding anniversaries or Valentine's day parties) and write the name of the guest in the centre. Stick the bottom of the shape onto the front of the folded card so that the top half of the shape protrudes above the white card when in position.

# Country Pâté

| METRIC/IMPERIAL | AMERICAN |
|---|---|
| 6 rashers bacon, rinded | 6 slices bacon |
| 250 g/8 oz belly pork, rinded and boned | ½ lb fresh pork sides, boned |
| 250 g/8 oz calf's liver | ½ lb calf's liver |
| 1 onion, chopped | 1 onion, chopped |
| 2 cloves garlic, crushed | 2 cloves garlic, minced |
| 250 g/8 oz stewing beef | ½ lb beef chuck |
| 2 teaspoons anchovy essence | ½ teaspoon anchovy paste |
| ¼ teaspoon chopped fresh parsley | ¼ teaspoon chopped fresh parsley |
| ¼ teaspoon chopped fresh thyme | ¼ teaspoon chopped fresh thyme |
| ¼ teaspoon chopped fresh sage | ¼ teaspoon chopped fresh sage |
| ¼ teaspoon chopped fresh rosemary | ¼ teaspoon chopped fresh rosemary |
| 65 g/2½ oz fresh white breadcrumbs | 1¼ cups soft white bread crumbs |
| salt | salt |
| freshly ground black pepper | freshly ground black pepper |
| 2 large eggs, lighly beaten | 2 large eggs, lighly beaten |
| bay leaves to garnish | bay leaves for garnish |

Setting to use: HIGH

Line a 1.75 l/⅓ pint (7½ cup) soufflé dish with the bacon. Set aside.

Mince (grind) or process together the pork, liver, onion, garlic, beef, anchovy essence (paste), herbs, breadcrumbs, and salt and pepper to taste. Bind the mixture with the eggs.

Spread into the bacon-lined container. Cook, covered, for 15 minutes. Turn around halfway through cooking. Let stand, covered, for 10 minutes.

Remove the cover and replace it with greaseproof (wax) paper. Place a weighted plate on top. Leave to cool and set. Unmould for serving, garnished with bay leaves.

# Fruit-Stuffed Duck

| METRIC/IMPERIAL | AMERICAN |
|---|---|
| 175 g/6 oz fresh white breadcrumbs | 3 cups soft white bread crumbs |
| 350 g/12 oz dried prunes, soaked overnight, drained and stoned | 2 cups dried prunes, soaked overnight, drained and pitted |
| grated rind of 1 orange | grated rind of 1 orange |
| 1 orange, peeled, segmented and pips removed | 1 orange, peeled, segmented and seeds removed |
| 1 dessert apple, peeled, cored and chopped | 1 dessert apple, peeled, cored and chopped |
| salt | salt |
| freshly ground black pepper | freshly ground black pepper |
| 1 egg, lightly beaten | 1 egg, lightly beaten |
| 1 × 2.25 kg/5 lb duck, boned but in one piece (the butcher should be asked in advance to do this) | 1 × 5 lb duck, boned but in one piece (the butcher should be asked in advance to do this) |
| To garnish: | To garnish: |
| strips of orange peel | strips of orange peel |
| orange slices | orange slices |

Setting to use: HIGH

Mix together the breadcrumbs, prunes, orange rind, orange segments, apple, and salt and pepper to taste. Bind together with the egg.

Stuff the cavity of the duck. Close the end with string. Place the loose neck skin under the bird. Keeping the wings close to the bird, truss with string to make into the original shape of the bird.

Place the bird on a trivet, breast side down, in a shallow, non-metallic ovenproof dish. Cook, uncovered, for about 36 minutes (see Note below). Turn over after 10 minutes of cooking.

Drain off the juices, then transfer duck to a conventional oven which has been preheated to 200°C/400°F/Gas Mark 6.

Cook for 15 minutes, and let rest for 5 minutes before serving. Remove string and garnish with orange peel and orange slices.

NOTE: Stuff the duck, then weigh it to calculate the microwave cooking time. Allow 6 minutes per 500 g/1 lb. The conventional cooking time does not vary.

# Broccoli with Lemon Butter

| METRIC/IMPERIAL | AMERICAN |
|---|---|
| 3 tablespoons water | 3 tablespoons water |
| salt | salt |
| 500 g/1 lb broccoli, stalks halved lengthways | 1 lb broccoli, stalks halved lengthways |
| 125 g/40z butter, cut into pieces | 1/2 cup butter, cut into pieces |
| grated rind and juice of 1/2 lemon | grated rind and juice of 1/2 lemon |
| freshly ground black pepper | freshly ground black pepper |

Setting to use: HIGH

Place the water and a pinch of salt in a large bowl. Arrange the broccoli in the bowl with the stalks pointing upwards. Cook, covered, for 7 minutes. Let it stand, covered, for 5 minutes.

Meanwhile, place the butter, lemon rind and juice, and salt and pepper to taste in a small bowl.

Cook, uncovered, for 3 minutes or until the butter has melted and is hot.

Drain the broccoli and arrange in a warm serving dish. Pour over the hot butter sauce.

# Duchesse Potatoes

| METRIC/IMPERIAL | AMERICAN |
|---|---|
| 3 tablespoons water | 3 tablespoons water |
| salt | salt |
| 750 g/1 1/2 lb potatoes, peeled and halved | 1 1/2 lb potatoes, peeled and halved |
| 25 g/1 oz butter | 2 tablespoons butter |
| 1 small egg, lightly beaten | 1 small egg, lightly beaten |
| freshly ground black pepper | freshly ground black pepper |

Setting to use: HIGH/Conventional Oven

Place the water, a pinch of salt and the potatoes in a large bowl. Cover and cook for 9 minutes. Leave to stand, covered, for 8 to 10 minutes.

Drain the potatoes. Beat in the butter and sufficient egg to obtain a soft piping consistency. Add salt and pepper to taste.

Fill a forcing (pastry) bag fitted with a large star nozzle. Pipe rosettes of potato onto a greased baking tray. Brush with remaining beaten egg.

Cook in a preheat oven (220°C/425°F/Gas Mark 7) for 15 to 20 minutes or until golden.

# Charlotte Russe

| METRIC IMPERIAL | AMERICAN |
|---|---|
| 140 g/4 1/2 oz lemon jelly block, cut into pieces | 1 package lemon flavored gelatin |
| 300 ml/1/2 pint cold water | 1 cup cold water |
| pieces of glacé cherries and candied angelica. cut into flowers and stems or other shapes | pieces of candied cherries and angelica. cut into flowers and stems or other shapes |
| 16 Boudoir biscuits | 16 lady fingers |
| 300 ml/1/2 pint double cream | 1 1/2 cups heavy cream |
| 1/2 teaspoon vanilla essence | 1/2 teaspoon vanilla |
| 25 g/1 oz caster sugar | 2 tablespoons caster sugar |

EXTRA SPECIAL

Setting to use: HIGH

Place the jelly (gelatin) and half of the water in a large jug. Cook, uncovered, for 2 minutes or until the jelly (gelatin) has melted or dissolved. Stir well, then stir in the remaining water.

Pour a thin layer of jelly (gelatin) over the bottom of a 600 ml/1 pint (2 1/2 cup) soufflé dish or 12.5 cm/5 inch charlotte mould. Refrigerate to set. Keep the remaining jelly (gelatin) liquid.

Arrange the cherry and angelica shapes in a decorative pattern over the set jelly (gelatin). Gently spoon more jelly (gelatin) over the decoration – just sufficient to cover. Refrigerate until nearly set.

Cut the ends off the biscuits (cookies). Stand the biscuits (cookies) around the side of the dish, cut ends onto the jelly (gelatin) with the sugared side facing outwards. Press in the biscuits (cookies) as close together as possible.

Whip together the cream, vanilla and sugar until fairly stiff. Fold in the remaining jelly (gelatin). Spoon the cream mixture into the centre of the prepared dish. Refrigerate until set, then gently trim the biscuits (cookies) to the level of the cream filling.

To serve, dip the dish briefly into hot water, then unmould onto a serving dish.

▽ Extra special: charlotte russe

# Hot So Spicy

**hot crab with tarragon**

**curried beef**

**rice**

**selection of sambals**

**melon and mint sorbet**

### Serves 2

*The cuisines of hot countries are full of spicy foods and that is why curry has been selected for this summer menu. The refreshing melon ice is an excellent finishing touch.*

WINE NOTE
A dry *Muscat d'Alsace* will make an exciting partner for this seafood starter, while either the Australian or South African *Shiraz,* or a Californian *Zinfandel* would do justice to the main course dish. Iced desserts are best left unaccompanied as their coldness has a numbing effect on the palate.

ACTION PLAN

*On the day before:*
1. Make the melon and mint sorbet.
2. Marinate the beef for the curry.

*In the morning:*
1. Prepare the crab for cooking and refrigerate.
2. Cook the curry, allow to cool and refrigerate.

*Later in the day:*
1. Prepare the garnishes and decorations.
2. Prepare any side dishes for the curry.

*Before serving:*
1. Cook the rice, drain and set aside. Reheat for a few minutes before serving.
2. Cook the crab mixture, spoon into the shells and garnish just before serving.
3. Reheat the curry in the microwave while serving the crab.
4. Transfer the sorbet from the freezer to the refrigerator 15 minutes before serving.

▷ *Hot so spicy: clockwise from top left: hot crab with tarragon; curried beef; rice; melon and mint sorbet*

98

# Hot Crab with Tarragon

| METRIC/IMPERIAL | AMERICAN |
|---|---|
| 2 × 1 kg/2 lb cooked crabs | 2 × 2 lb cooked crabs |
| 125 g/4 oz butter | ½ cup butter |
| 2 teaspoons chopped fresh tarragon | 2 teaspoons chopped fresh tarragon |
| 3 cloves garlic, crushed | 3 cloves garlic, minced |
| 125 g/4 oz fresh white breadcrumbs | 2 cups soft white bread crumbs |
| 6 tablespoons double cream | 6 tablespoons heavy cream |
| salt | salt |
| freshly ground black pepper | freshly ground black pepper |
| To garnish: | For garnish: |
| 2 hard-boiled eggs, yolks and white sieved separately | 2 hard-cooked eggs, yolks and whites sieved separately |
| parsley | parsley |
| lemon and lime wedges | lemon and lime wedges |

Setting to use: HIGH

Twist the claws and legs off the crab and crack them with a heavy weight. Using a skewer, scrape out all the white meat and set it aside. Place the crabs on their backs and pull the

body in the centre away from the shell. Remove and discard the greyish white stomach sac and the grey feathered gills. Using a fork, scrape out the light and dark meat and mix with the meat from the claws. Scrub and rinse the shells.

Place the butter, tarragon and garlic in a large bowl. Cook, covered, for 3 minutes. Stir in the breadcrumbs, crab meat, cream, and salt and pepper to taste. Cook, covered, for 7 minutes. Stir halfway through cooking.

Spoon the mixture into the shells. Garnish with sieved egg yolk and white, sprigs of parsley and lemon and lime slices.

# Curried Beef

| METRIC/IMPERIAL | AMERICAN |
| --- | --- |
| 500 g/1 lb braising beef, cut into cubes | 1 lb beef chuck, cut into cubes |
| 2 tablespoons wine vinegar | 2 tablespoons wine vinegar |
| 150 ml/¼ pint red wine | ²/₃ cup red wine |
| 2 teaspoons brown sugar | 2 teaspoons dark brown sugar |
| ¼ teaspoon salt | ¼ teaspoon salt |
| 1 large onion, chopped | 1 large onion, chopped |
| 1 tablespoon chutney | 1 tablespoon chutney |
| 2 cloves garlic, crushed | 2 cloves garlic, minced |

| | |
| --- | --- |
| 1 cooking apple. peeled. cored and chopped | 1 tart apple. peeled. cored and chopped |
| ¼ teaspoon ground ginger | ¼ teaspoon ground ginger |
| 3 rounded teaspoons curry powder | 3 heaping teaspoons curry powder |
| 1 tablespoon tomato purée | 1 tablespoon tomato paste |
| 1 tablespoon desiccated coconut | 1 tablespoon dried shredded coconut |
| ¼ teaspoon grated nutmeg | ¼ teaspoon grated nutmeg |
| 1 tablespoon cornflour | 1 tablespoon cornstarch |
| strips of orange peel | strips of orange peel |

Setting to use: HIGH/DEFROST (30%)

Mix together the beef, vinegar, wine, sugar and salt in a large bowl. Leave to marinate for 24 hours, turning the meat occasionally.

Place the onion, chutney, garlic, apple, ginger, curry powder, tomato purée (paste), coconut and nutmeg in a large bowl. Cook, covered, for 8 minutes.

Mix a little of the marinade with the cornflour (cornstarch) to make a smooth paste. Stir into the vegetables with the beef and remaining marinade. Cook, covered, for 10 minutes

Stir and cover again. Reduce the power to DEFROST (30%) and cook for 40 minutes or until tender. Stir halfway through cooking. Remove the cover for the last 5 minutes. Sprinkle with orange peel strips and serve.

# SAY CHEESE

*Make the most of the decorative potential of the cheese course.*

Be imaginative with your selection of cheese. You don't need to buy up the local delicatessen – a good rule of thumb is to include one hard cheese, such as Cheddar; one cream cheese, like Boursin, and one blue or semi-soft cheese like Brie or Camembert.

## Extras for colour

Arrange the cheeses on a large platter or board and serve them with unusual garnishes. Choose salad vegetables and fruit that are in season – they will add colour to your arrangement as well as refreshing your guests' palates. A pretty cheese knife will add the finishing touch.

## Go crackers

The purists suggest that the cheese should only be served with fruit or vegetables but most people prefer to offer a selection of biscuits. With so many types around you can have as little or as much variety as you wish. Be careful though, to include different textures and shapes of biscuit for maximum decorative impact. A good basic selection would include a water-type biscuit, a digestive biscuit and a wheat or rye cracker.

# Sambals

Serve a selection of sambals or accompaniments with the curry . . .

chopped cucumber in natural yogurt, mixed with a little chopped fresh mint and crushed garlic; finely sliced onion and tomato; sliced banana dipped in lemon juice; a selection of chutneys and pickles; desiccated or shredded coconut sprinkled with a little chopped onion and chilli powder.

# Melon and Mint Sorbet

| METRIC/IMPERIAL | AMERICAN |
|---|---|
| 1 ripe melon, about 1 kg/2 lb. halved and seeded | 1 ripe melon, about 2 lb. halved and seeded |
| 3 tablespoons orange juice | 3 tablespoons orange juice |
| 125 g/4 oz sugar | ½ cup sugar |
| 2 rounded teaspoons powdered gelatine | 2 heaping teaspoons unflavored gelatin |
| 1 teaspoon chopped fresh mint | 1 teaspoon chopped fresh mint |
| 2 egg whites | 2 egg whites |
| fresh mint sprigs to decorate | fresh mint sprigs to decorate |

Setting to use: HIGH

Scoop the melon flesh out of the shells, keeping the shells intact. Set the shells aside. Put the melon flesh in a blender or food processor, add the orange juice and purée until smooth. Add enough water to the purée to make 900 ml/ 1½ pints (2 pints).

Place one-third of the purée in a large jug. Stir in the sugar and gelatine. Cook, uncovered, for 3½ minutes. Stir well to dissolve the sugar. Set aside to cool.

Stir in the mint and remaining purée. Pour into a metal container and freeze until the edges of the sorbet begin to set.

Turn the sorbet into a bowl and whisk until thick. Whisk the egg whites until stiff and whisk into the sorbet. Cover and freeze until firm, approximately 2½ hours.

Remove from freezer and place in refrigerator 15 minutes before serving in the melon halves. Serve decorated with sprigs of fresh mint.

# More Dash Than Cash

chicken noodle soup

pork steaks with orange
and wine sauce
mixed vegetables
with olives
braised brown rice

chocolate walnut crêpes

### Serves 4

*These recipes are low on cash but high in style,
yet this menu will impress even the most critical
of guests.*

Dry *Montilla* is an unexpectedly good match for the chicken noodle soup, while any light red wine from the Alto Adige region of Italy makes an attractively fruity match for the port steaks – try *Santa Maddalena* or *Lago di Caldaro*.

*On the day before or in the morning:*
1. Cook the crêpes, cool on a wire rack then cover and refrigerate.
2. Make the chicken noodle soup and refrigerate.

*Later in the day:*
1. Make and cook the pork dish, cover and refrigerate.
2. Fold the crêpes and arrange on a serving plate. Place the ingredients for the sauce in a jug ready to cook.

*Before serving:*
1. Cook the braised rice on the conventional hob.
2. Cook the mixed vegetables and while they are standing reheat the pork dish in the microwave.
3. Meanwhile reheat the soup on the conventional hob.
4. Reheat the crêpes and make the sauce while clearing the table after the main course.

▽ *More dash than cash: from right: chicken noodle soup; mixed vegetables with olives; braised brown rice; port steaks with orange*

# NOVEL NAPKINS
*Some unusual but simple ways to present table napkins*

## Ways with glasses
Here are three simple ideas for the napkin in the glass:
Use a napkin with contrast piping round the edge and open it

out flat. Starting with one corner, roll it up tightly across to the diagonally opposite corner. Bend the resulting 'rod' shape in half and push the bend into the bottom of the wine glass.

Another variation is the fan shape. Simply fold the napkin in accordion pleats and press lightly with an iron. Again, bend the flat bunch of pleats in the centre. Pin the top two edges together and push the bend into the bottom of the glass and pin these two edges together. Don't forget to mention the pins to your guests before they undo the napkins!

For the third version, fold the napkin over twice so that it forms a square. Then fold two opposite corners into the middle of the square so that the overall look is a kite shape with the free edges at the top of the kite. Put the bottom point of the 'kite' into the bottom of the glass. Allow the back points to stand up and pull the front two points down over the rim of the glass.

## Ring the changes
If you prefer a less contrived look, search the shops for interesting shaped napkin rings. Even silk flowers on simple plastic rings are inexpensive and contribute so much to the look of your table.

Contrast a plain tablecloth with a patterned napkin and pull the scheme together with the napkin ring.

## Patterned or plain
You may have some particularly beautiful, plain napkin rings, such as family silver, but don't let that stop you from experimenting. Napkins with scalloped edges in contrasting colour and prettily printed napkins with bold, geometric designs can be exploited to the full. Lay the napkin out flat and pull it through your plain ring by the centre. This will give a lovely free-flowing shape, and the border round the napkin will make its own pattern, showing the folds of the fabric. Very simple and visually arresting

# Chicken Noodle Soup

| METRIC/IMPERIAL | AMERICAN |
|---|---|
| 1 medium onion, finely chopped | 1 medium onion, finely chopped |
| 3 chicken stock cubes, crumbled | 3 chicken bouillon cubes, crumbled |
| 1 l/1¾ pints boiling water | 4 cups boiling water |
| 50 g/2 oz fine noodles | 1 cup fine noodles |
| ¼ teaspoon vegetable oil | ¼ teaspoon vegetable oil |
| 250 g/8 oz cooked chicken, finely chopped | 1 cup finely chopped cooked chicken |
| 1 tablespoon chopped fresh parsley | 1 tablespoon chopped fresh parsley |
| salt | salt |
| freshly ground black pepper | freshly ground black pepper |
| chopped fresh parsley to garnish | chopped fresh parsley for garnish |

Setting to use: HIGH

Place the onion in a large bowl. Cook, covered, for 3 minutes or until the onion is tender.

Stir in the stock cubes and boiling water. Add the noodles and oil. Cook, covered, for 6 minutes. Stir halfway through cooking.

Add the chopped chicken, parsley, salt and pepper and cook, covered, for a further 4 minutes. Serve sprinkled with a little extra parsley.

NOTE: 1 litre/1¾ pints (4 cups) homemade chicken stock can be used in place of the boiling water and stock cubes.

# Pork Steaks with Orange and Wine Sauce

| METRIC/IMPERIAL | AMERICAN |
|---|---|
| 1 medium onion, chopped | 1 medium onion, chopped |
| 150 ml/¼ pint unsweetened orange juice | ⅔ cup unsweetened orange juice |
| 150 ml/¼ pint medium or dry white wine | ⅔ cup medium or dry white wine |
| ½ pint/300 ml hot chicken stock | 1¼ cups hot chicken bouillon |
| 1 teaspoon dried chopped rosemary | 1 teaspoon dried chopped rosemary |
| rind of 1 orange removed with a zester | rind of 1 orange removed with a zester |
| salt | salt |
| freshly ground black pepper | freshly ground black pepper |
| 4 pork shoulder steaks total weight 625 g/1 lb 4 oz | 4 pork shoulder steaks total weight 1 lb 4 oz |
| 3 tablespoons cornflour | 3 tablespoons cornstarch |
| 1 orange, peeled and sliced | 1 orange, peeled and sliced |
| sprigs of fresh rosemary to garnish | sprigs of fresh rosemary for garnish |

Setting to use: HIGH and DEFROST (30%)

Place the onion in a large bowl. Cover and cook on HIGH for 3½ minutes or until tender. Stir in the orange juice, wine, hot stock and rosemary. Purée in a blender or food processor until smooth. Add the orange rind, salt and pepper. Set aside.

Arrange the pork steaks around the sides of the large bowl. Cover and cook on HIGH for 5½ minutes. Re-arrange halfway through cooking.

Place the steaks in the base of the bowl and pour over the sauce. Cook covered for 5 minutes or until the sauce is boiling. Reduce to DEFROST (30%) and cook for a further 20 minutes or until the meat is tender.

Remove the steaks from the sauce and place them in a warm shallow casserole dish. Keep warm.

Mix the cornflour with sufficient cold water to make a smooth paste. Add to the sauce. Increase the output (wattage) of the microwave to HIGH and cook the sauce, uncovered, for 3 minutes, stirring every minute. Add the orange slices. Cook for a further minute.

Pour the sauce over the steaks, arrange the orange slices on top and serve garnished with sprigs of rosemary.

# Braised Brown Rice

METRIC/IMPERIAL
50 g/2 oz butter
1 large onion, finely chopped
2 cloves garlic, crushed
salt
freshly ground black pepper
400 g/14 oz brown long-grain rice
900 ml/1½ pint hot chicken stock
150 ml/¼ pint dry white wine
chopped fresh parsley to garnish

AMERICAN:
¼ cup butter
1 large onion, finely chopped
2 cloves garlic, crushed
salt
freshly ground black pepper
2 cups brown long-grain rice
3¾ cups hot chicken stock
⅔ cup dry white wine
chopped fresh parsley for garnish

Setting to use: HIGH

Place the butter, onion and garlic, salt and pepper in a large bowl. Cover and cook for 8 minutes, stirring halfway through cooking.

Stir in the rice, hot chicken stock and wine. Cook, covered for a further 25 minutes. Set aside, covered, for 8-10 minutes. Sprinkle with chopped parsley and serve.

# Mixed Vegetables with Olives

METRIC/IMPERIAL
500 g/1 lb frozen mixed vegetables
2 tablespoons black olives, stoned and sliced

AMERICAN
1 lb frozen mixed vegetables
2 tablespoons pitted ripe olives, sliced

Setting to use: HIGH

Place the frozen vegetables in a medium bowl. Cook, covered for 9 minutes, stirring halfway through cooking. Stir in the sliced olives and let the vegetables stand covered for 5 minutes before serving.

▷ More dash than cash: chocolate walnut crêpes

# Chocolate Walnut Crêpes
MORE DASH THAN CASH

METRIC IMPERIAL
Crêpes:
1 egg
1 egg yolk
300 ml/½ pint milk
pinch of salt
125 g/4 oz plain flour
oil for frying
Sauce:
1 tablespoon cocoa powder
25 g/1 oz butter
1½ tablespoons golden syrup
8 pancakes (see above)
2 tablespoons chopped walnuts

AMERICAN
Crêpes:
1 egg
1 egg yolk
1¼ cups milk
pinch of salt
1 cup all-purpose flour
oil for frying
Sauce:
1 tablespoon unsweetened cocoa
2 tablespoons butter
1½ tablespoons corn syrup
8 pancakes (see above)
2 tablespoons chopped walnuts

Setting to use: HIGH/Conventional Hob

Place all the ingredients for the crêpes in a blender or food processor and blend until the mixture is smooth. Set aside for at least 30 minutes before using.

Using the conventional hob heat a little oil in a 15 cm/6" frying pan (skillet). Pour in sufficient crêpe mixture to just cover the base of the plan. Cook until golden brown on one side. Flip the crêpe over and cook until the second side is golden. Transfer to a plate, cover and keep warm. Continue until you have made eight crêpes.

For the sauce, place the cocoa powder (unsweetened cocoa), butter and syrup in a large jug. Cook, uncovered, for 1½ minutes or until the mixture is melted and hot.

Fold the crêpes in half, then half again to make a fan shape. Arrange on a serving dish. Heat uncovered for 1-1½ minutes.

Pour the sauce over the crêpes and sprinkle them with the chopped walnuts. Serve with cream or vanilla ice cream.

# Herbs and Spices

## tarragon pâté
## melba toast
## turkey casserole
## dolmas
## noodles with cream sauce
## or croquette potatoes
## ginger pineapple pudding

### Serves 4

*These recipes use fresh herbs and spices to give a delicious menu that can be served at any time of the year.*

WINE NOTE — For a palate-tingling start to the meal serve one of the many white *Vin de Savoie* wines with the pâté. One of the softer styles of claret, like *St-Emilion*, will bring out the best in the spicy turkey casserole.

ACTION PLAN

*On the day before or in the morning:*
1. Cook the turkey meat if necessary and refrigerate.
2. Make the tarragon pâté and refrigerate.
3. Prepare the filling for the dolmas, roll into shape and refrigerate.
4. Make the ginger pineapple pudding and refrigerate.

*Later in the day:*
1. Decorate the pudding.
2. Collect together the ingredients for the turkey casserole.

*Before serving:*
1. Garnish the pâté.
2. Cook the dolmas in the microwave while cooking the noodles conventionally.
3. Cook the turkey casserole in the microwave while serving the first course.

▷ *Herbs and spices: from bottom: tarragon pâté with melba toast: dolmas: turkey casserole: noodles with cream sauce: ginger pineapple pudding*

# Tarragon Pâté

| METRIC/IMPERIAL | AMERICAN |
|---|---|
| 1 small onion. finely chopped | 1 small onion. finely chopped |
| 1 clove garlic. crushed | 1 clove garlic. crushed |
| 4 tablespoons chicken stock | 4 tablespoons chicken stock |
| 350 g/12 oz calves' liver. cut into strips | 3/4 lb calves' liver. cut into strips |
| 50 g/2 oz butter | 1/4 cup butter |
| 1 tablespoon brandy | 1 tablespoon brandy |
| 1 tablespoon double cream | 1 tablespoon heavy cream |
| 1 teaspoon chopped fresh tarragon | 1 teaspoon chopped fresh tarragon |
| salt | salt |
| freshly ground black pepper | freshly ground black pepper |
| springs of tarragon to garnish | sprigs of tarragon for garnish |

Setting to use: HIGH

Place the onion, garlic and stock in a large bowl. Cook, covered, for 3 minutes. Stir in the liver and cook for 3½ minutes. Stir halfway through cooking.

Add the remaining ingredients, and salt and pepper to taste. Pour the mixture into four ramekin dishes. Refrigerate until firm.

Garnish with sprigs of tarragon just before serving. Serve with Melba toast.

NOTE: You can pour a little melted butter over the pâté about 1 hour before serving. Leave to set before garnishing.

# Turkey Casserole

| METRIC/IMPERIAL | AMERICAN |
|---|---|
| 1 clove garlic. crushed | 1 clove garlic. crushed |
| 25 g/1 oz butter | 2 tablespoons butter |
| 1 large onion. finely chopped | 1 large onion. finely chopped |
| 1/2 green pepper. seeded and finely chopped | 1/2 green pepper. seeded, and finely chopped |
| 1/2 red pepper. seeded and finely chopped | 1/2 red pepper, seeded and finely chopped |
| 1/2-1 teaspoon chilli powder | 1/2-1 teaspoon chili powder |
| 2 tablespoons tomato purée | 2 tablespoons tomato paste |
| 1 chicken stock cube, crumbled | 1 chicken bouillon cube, crumbled |
| 150 ml/1/4 pint water | 2/3 cup water |
| 125 g/4 oz sweetcorn kernels | 1/4 lb sweetcorn kernels |
| 125 g/4 oz button mushrooms | 1/4 lb button mushrooms |
| 1 teaspoon soy sauce | 1 teaspoon soy sauce |
| 1 teaspoon brown sugar | 1 teaspoon brown sugar |
| 500 g/1 lb cooked turkey, diced | 2 cups diced cooked turkey |
| salt | salt |
| freshly ground black pepper | freshly ground black pepper |
| natural yogurt to garnish | natural yogurt for garnish |

Setting to use: HIGH

Place the garlic, butter, onion, peppers, chilli powder and tomato purée (paste) in a large bowl. Cook, covered, for 7 minutes or until tender. Stir halfway through cooking.

Stir in the stock cube (bouillon cube), water, sweetcorn, mushrooms, soy sauce, brown sugar, turkey, salt and pepper. Cook, covered, for 8 minutes, stirring halfway through cooking.

Spoon onto a warm serving dish. Spoon over the yogurt. Serve at once.

NOTE: Chilli powders vary in their strength, so add a little at a time until the required degree of 'hotness' is obtained.

# Dolmas

| METRIC/IMPERIAL | AMERICAN |
|---|---|
| 8 large green cabbage leaves, stalk removed | 8 large green cabbage leaves, stalk removed |
| 1 medium onion, finely chopped | 1 medium onion, finely chopped |
| 250 g/8 oz tomatoes, skinned and chopped | 1/2 lb tomatoes, skinned and chopped |
| 15 g/1/2 oz butter | 1 tablespoon butter |
| 4 tablespoons plain flour | 4 tablespoons all-purpose flour |
| 300 ml/1/2 pint hot beef stock | 11/4 cups hot beef stock |
| 1/2 teaspoon Worcestershire sauce | 1/2 teaspoon Worcestershire sauce |
| 1/2 teaspoon dried oregano | 1/2 teaspoon dried oregano |
| salt | salt |
| freshly ground black pepper | freshly ground black pepper |
| 4 tablespoons cooked rice | 4 tablespoons cooked rice |

Setting to use: HIGH

Pour boiling water over the cabbage leaves and allow them to soften for a minute or so. Drain.

Place the onion, tomatoes and butter in a medium bowl. Cover and cook for 4 minutes.

Stir in the flour then add the stock, Worcestershire sauce, oregano, salt, pepper and rice. Stir well then cook, uncovered for 2 minutes.

Place a little of the vegetable mixture on to each cabbage leaf. Roll up the cabbage leaves to seal in the filling and tie each with string.

Arrange the dolmas in a shallow dish, cover and cook for 7 minutes, turning the dish round halfway through cooking. Leave the dolmas to stand for 5 minutes. Remove the string and serve.

# Noodles with Cream Sauce

| METRIC/IMPERIAL | AMERICAN |
|---|---|
| 250 g/8 oz spinach noodles | 1/2 lb spinach noodles |
| 1 teaspoon salt | 1 teaspoon salt |
| 1 tablespoon vegetable oil | 1 tablespoon vegetable oil |
| 1.75 l/3 pints boiling water | 33/4 pints boiling water |
| 124 g/4oz butter, diced | 1/2 cup diced butter |
| 75 ml/21/2 fl oz double cream | 1/3 cup heavy cream |
| freshly ground black pepper | freshly ground black pepper |
| 2 tablespoons grated Parmesan cheese | 2 tablespoons finely grated Parmesan cheese |

Setting to use: HIGH

Place the spinach noodles, salt, oil and boiling water in a very large bowl. Cover and cook for 9 minutes, checking occasionally to ensure that the noodles are totally covered with water. Set aside for 8 minutes.

Drain the noodles and toss in half the butter, the cream and the freshly ground black pepper. Transfer to a warm serving dish, top with the remaining butter and the grated Parmesan cheese.

NOTE: Herbs can make a delicious difference to these noodles. Toss some freshly chopped basil or parsley into the noodles with the butter.

For extra Italian flavouring, add a crushed clove of garlic when tossing in the butter and herbs.

# Croquette Potatoes

| METRIC/IMPERIAL | AMERICAN |
|---|---|
| 625 g/11/4 lb potatoes, peeled and chopped | 11/4 lb potatoes, peeled and chopped |
| 3 tablespoons water | 3 tablespoons water |
| salt | salt |
| 25 g/1 oz butter | 2 tablespoons butter |
| 1/2 tablespoon milk | 1/2 tablespoon milk |
| freshly ground black pepper | freshly ground black pepper |
| 1 egg, lightly beaten | 1 egg, lightly beaten |
| 75 g/3 oz toasted bread-crumbs | 11/2 cups toasted bread crumbs |

Setting to use: HIGH

Place the potatoes and water in a large bowl. Add a pinch of salt. Cook, covered for 9 minutes. Leave to stand, covered, for 5 minutes.

Beat the butter, milk and salt and pepper to taste into the potatoes. Roll the potato mixture into 16 cork shapes and refrigerate.

Dip the croquettes in the beaten egg and then roll in the breadcrumbs to coat.

Deep-fry until golden, drain on absorbent kitchen paper and serve.

# Ginger Pineapple Pudding

| METRIC/IMPERIAL | AMERICAN |
|---|---|
| 125 g/4 oz butter | 1/2 cup butter |
| 1 tablespoon golden syrup | 1 tablespoon corn syrup |
| 250 g/8 oz ginger biscuits, crushed | 1/2 lb ginger cookies, crushed |
| Filling: | Filling: |
| 4 tablespoons pineapple juice | 4 tablespoons pineapple juice |
| 15 g/1/2 oz powdered gelatine | 1 tablespoon powdered gelatin |
| 1 × 400 g/14 oz can crushed pineapple, drained | 1 × 14 oz can crushed pineapple, drained |
| 50 g/2 oz white marshmallows, chopped | 1 cup diced white marshmallows |
| 450 ml/3/4 pint whipping cream, whipped | 12/3 cups whipping cream, whipped |

Setting to use: HIGH

Place the butter and syrup in a medium bowl and cook for 13/4 minutes.

Stir in the crushed biscuits and mix well. Spoon into a 20 cm/8 in loose bottomed cake tin (spring-form pan) and press down well.

To make the filling, place the pineapple juice in a large jug and stir in the gelatine. Cook for 10 seconds then stir until the gelatine has dissolved.

Reserve a little pineapple for decoration. Place the remainder in a medium bowl with the marshmallows and cook for 1 minute or until the marshmallows have melted. Add the pineapple juice and gelatine mixture, whisking well.

Set the mixture aside until almost set then fold in two-thirds of the whipped cream. Spoon into the biscuit-lined cake tin smoothing the top. Chill until set. Decorate with the reserved pineapple and whipped cream before serving.

# Popular Choice

## potted shrimps

## beef olives
## buttered leeks
## beetroot with savoury cream
## new potatoes

## lemon meringue pie

### Serves 4

*These recipes have humble origins but they are all-time favourites that have stood the test of time.*

WINE NOTE

There are few better accompaniments for seafood than *Muscadet*, while a red burgundy (*Bourgogne Rouge*) would be superb with the beef olives, Lemon Meringue Pie is not well matched by wine.

ACTION PLAN

*In the morning:*
1. Make the potted shrimps, pour into ramekin dishes and refrigerate.
2. Prepare the beef olives for cooking.
3. Prepare the vegetables for cooking, cover tightly and refrigerate.
4. Prepare and cook the lemon meringue pie.

*Later in the day:*
1. Garnish the potted shrimps.

*Before serving:*
1. Cook the beetroot in the microwave, set aside then cook the leeks. Cook the potatoes conventionally.
2. Start cooking the beef olives 20 minutes before required.
3. Reheat the leeks and complete the beetroot dish just before serving.

▽ *Popular choice: from right: potted shrimps; buttered leeks; beef olives; beetroot with savoury cream; lemon meringue pie*

# Potted Shrimps

| METRIC/IMPERIAL | AMERICAN |
|---|---|
| 175 g/6 oz butter, cut into pieces | ³⁄₄ cup butter, cut into pieces |
| 350 g/12 oz peeled shrimps | ³⁄₄ lb shelled shrimp |
| pinch cayenne pepper | pinch cayenne pepper |
| salt | salt |
| freshly ground white pepper | freshly ground white pepper |
| To garnish: | For garnish: |
| unpeeled shrimps | unshelled shrimps |
| lemon slices | lemon slices |
| 4 parsley sprigs | 4 parsley sprigs |

Setting to use: HIGH

Place the butter in a small bowl. Cook, uncovered, for 2½ minutes or until melted.

Stir the shrimps, cayenne, and salt and pepper to taste into the butter. Pour the mixture into four small ramekin dishes. Refrigerate until the butter has set.

Garnish with unpeeled shrimps, lemon slices and sprigs of parsley.

NOTE: This recipe can also be used for Potted Fish or Potted Meat. For Potted Fish, use 350 g/³⁄₄ lb flaked cooked or canned fish in place of the prawns, and for Potted Meat, use minced cooked meat.

# Beef Olives

| METRIC/IMPERIAL | AMERICAN |
|---|---|
| 175 g/6 oz mushrooms | 1½ cups mushrooms |
| 1 onion, quartered | 1 onion, quartered |
| 1 tablespoon brandy | 1 tablespoon brandy |
| 1 tablespoon orange juice | 1 tablespoon orange juice |
| 2 tablespoons beef stock | 2 tablespoons beef stock |
| grated rind of 1 lemon | grated rind of 1 lemon |
| ½ teaspoon dried rosemary | ½ teaspoon dried rosemary |
| salt | salt |
| freshly ground black pepper | freshly ground black pepper |
| 25 g/1 oz fresh white breadcrumbs | ½ cup soft white bread crumbs |
| 500 g/1 lb topside beef, cut into 4 slices and lightly beaten | 1 lb beef top round, cut into 4 slices and lightly beaten |
| ½ red pepper, cored, seeded and finely chopped | ½ sweet red pepper, cored, seeded and finely chopped |
| 40 g/1½ oz butter | 3 tablespoons butter |
| 1 tablespoon plain flour | 1 tablespoon all-purpose flour |
| 150 ml/¼ pint dry white wine | ²⁄₃ cup dry white wine |

Setting to use: HIGH

Put 50 g/2 oz of the mushrooms, the onion, brandy, orange juice, stock, lemon rind, rosemary, and salt and pepper to taste in a blender or food processor and process until fine.

Work in the breadcrumbs.

Divide the mixture between the beef slices and roll up. Secure each roll with wooden cocktail sticks. Place in a shallow dish and cook, uncovered, for 6 minutes. Turn over after 3 minutes. Set aside, covered.

Slice the remaining mushrooms and place in a large jug with the red pepper. Cover and cook for 4 minutes. Stir in the butter until melted.

Gradually blend in the flour, then add the wine and juices from the beef rolls. Season to taste with salt and pepper. Cook for 3 minutes, stirring every minute.

Arrange the beef rolls on a serving platter and spoon over the sauce.

# Beetroot with Savoury Cream

| METRIC/IMPERIAL | AMERICAN |
|---|---|
| 500 g/1 lb beetroot | 1 lb beets |
| 150 ml/¼ pint chicken stock | ²⁄₃ cup chicken stock |
| 1 large onion, sliced | 1 large onion, sliced |
| 15 g/½ oz butter | 1 tablespoon butter |
| 150 ml/¼ pint double cream | ²⁄₃ cup heavy cream |
| salt | salt |
| freshly ground black pepper | freshly ground black pepper |

Setting to use: HIGH

Place the beetroot (beets) and chicken stock in a shallow container. Cook, covered, for 10 minutes. Rearrange halfway through cooking. Set aside covered.

Place the onion and butter in a medium bowl. Cover and cook for 3½ minutes.

Drain, peel and quarter the beetroot (beets). Mix with the remaining ingredients. Place in a warm serving dish. Cook for 2 minutes or until hot. Do not let the cream boil.

## RAISE YOUR GLASSES

Follow these guidelines for enjoyment of wines and liqueurs.

# Buttered Leeks

| METRIC/IMPERIAL | AMERICAN |
|---|---|
| 3 tablespoons water | 3 tablespoons water |
| pinch of salt | pinch of salt |
| 500 g/1 lb leeks, finely sliced | 1 lb leeks, finely sliced |
| 40 g/1½ oz butter | 3 tablespoons butter |

Setting to use: HIGH

Place the water, salt and leeks in a large bowl. Cook, covered, for 10 minutes. Stir halfway through cooking. Let stand, covered, for 5 minutes.

Drain the leeks and toss in the butter until melted. Arrange in a warm dish. Garnish with the chopped chives if liked.

# Lemon Meringue Pie

| METRIC/IMPERIAL | AMERICAN |
|---|---|
| Pie Case: | Pie Case: |
| 100 g/3 oz butter | ½ cup butter |
| 250 g/8 oz digestive biscuits, crushed | 2 cups crushed graham crackers |

| Filling: | Filling: |
|---|---|
| grated rind and juice of 2 lemons | grated rind and juice of 2 lemons |
| 25 g/1 oz cornflour | ¼ cup cornstarch |
| 175 g/6 oz caster sugar | ¾ cup sugar |
| 2 eggs separated | 2 eggs, separated |

Setting to use: HIGH/Conventional Grill (Broiler)

For the pie case, place the butter in a small jug. Cook, uncovered, for 2 minutes or until melted. Stir in the crushed biscuits (crackers) and press into an 18 cm/7 inch shallow pie pan to cover the bottom and sides evenly.

Add enough water to the lemon juice to make 300 ml/½ pint (1¼ cups). Put a little of this liquid into a large jug, add the cornflour (cornstarch) and stir to make a smooth paste. Stir in the remaining liquid and lemon rind. Cook, uncovered, for 3½ minutes or until the mixture thickens. Stir every minute. Beat in 50 g/2 oz (¼ cup) of the sugar and egg yolks. Pour into the pie case and set aside to cool.

Whisk the egg whites until stiff and fold in the remaining sugar. Pile over the lemon mixture. Cook, uncovered, for 1½ minutes. Brown under a preheated grill (broiler).

Many people feel ignorant about wines and the correct way to serve them. There really are no hard and fast rules, only simple guidelines, which will enable you to avoid any disasters on the drinks front.

Generally there is a great deal of snobbery attached to wines and how to serve them, but you need not get too embroiled in debates. Choose plain glasses for wine – and the thinner the glass the better. The top of the glass should turn in slightly to hold the aroma which is a distinct part of the pleasure of wine drinking. Don't go for metallic goblets, as they invariably taint the wine.

## Get in shape
There are three shapes of glass that will provide a good, working basic set to accommodate all types of wine or fortified wine. The Paris goblet, which comes in three sizes: 70 ml/2½ fl oz suitable for liqueurs; 140 ml/5 fl oz good for sherry and port; 225 ml/8 fl oz ideal for table wine. Next on your list should be a Flute, which is shaped like a long 'vee' and has a shortish stem; this is good for sparkling wines and Champagne – much more suitable than the previously favoured 'sweet-coup' shape as the bubbles cannot get to the surface quickly, so your champers stays sparkling longer. Finally, the traditionally shaped brandy balloon, but don't go for too big a size as these let the aroma escape too quickly and your precious brandy sticks to the vast side – such a waste!

One last tip about the glasses: always rinse them thoroughly in hot water after washing to remove detergent and give a good shine.

# Fruity Combination

## crab bisque

## apricot-stuffed roast chicken
## croquette potatoes
## glazed sprouts

## loganberry cheese mousse

### Serves 4

*A refreshing mixture of flavours that can be served any time of year since frozen alternatives can be used throughout the menu.*

**WINE NOTE** *Verdelho Madeira* makes a sumptuous partner for any seafood soup, while the rich, spicy flavours of *Alsace Gewürztraminer* will match the apricot-stuffed chicken admirably.

**ACTION PLAN**
*On the day before or in the morning:*
1. Make the crab bisque and refrigerate.
2. Prepare the stuffing for the chicken and refrigerate.
3. Make and shape the croquette potatoes.
4. Make the loganberry mousse and refrigerate.

*Later in the day:*
1. Decorate the loganberry mousse.
2. Stuff and truss the chicken.

*Before serving:*
1. Start cooking the chicken 25 minutes before serving the first course.
2. Fry the potato croquettes conventionally and reheat the soup in the microwave while the chicken is in the conventional oven.
3. Cook the sprouts in the microwave while eating the first course.

## Crab Bisque

| METRIC/IMPERIAL | AMERICAN |
|---|---|
| 15 g/¹/₂ oz butter | 1 tablespoon butter |
| 1 small piece fennel, finely chopped | 1 small piece fennel, finely chopped |
| 1 clove garlic, crushed | 1 clove garlic, crushed |
| 1 medium onion, finely chopped | 1 medium onion, finely chopped |
| 50 g/2 oz fresh white breadcrumbs | 1 cup fresh white breadcrumbs |
| 500 g/1 lb crab, meat, half white and half dark meat | 1 lb crab, meat, half white and half dark meat |
| salt | salt |
| freshly ground black pepper | freshly ground black pepper |
| 750 ml/1¹/₄ pint hot fish stock | 3 cups hot fish stock |
| bayleaf | bayleaf |
| 150 ml/¹/₄ pint double cream | ²/₃ cup heavy cream |
| flakes of white crab meat to garnish | flakes of white crab meat for garnish |

Setting to use: HIGH

Place the butter, fennel, garlic and onion in a large bowl. Cook covered for 3 minutes. Stir in the breadcrumbs, crab meat, salt and pepper. Cook, covered, for 4 minutes, stirring halfway through cooking.

Stir in the stock and bayleaf and cook, covered, for a further 8 minutes. Stir halfway through cooking. Remove the bayleaf, pour the soup into a blender or food processor and blend until smooth. Cool slightly.

Stir in the cream, check and adjust the seasoning. If necessary reheat in the microwave for a minute or so but do not boil. Garnish with pieces of white crab meat and serve.

## Apricot-Stuffed Roast Chicken

| METRIC/IMPERIAL | AMERICAN |
|---|---|
| 1 tablespoon chopped parsley | 1 tablespoon chopped parsley |
| 1 medium onion, finely chopped | 1 onion, finely chopped |

| METRIC/IMPERIAL | AMERICAN |
|---|---|
| 1 eating apple, peeled, cored and chopped | 1 dessert apple. peeled. cored and chopped |
| 15 g/½ oz butter | 1 tablespoon butter |
| 25 g/1 oz fresh white breadcrumbs | ½ cup soft white bread crumbs |
| 175 g/6 oz dried apricots, soaked overnight and chopped | 1 cup dried apricots, soaked overnight and chopped |
| salt | salt |
| freshly ground black pepper | freshly ground black pepper |
| 1 × 1.5 kg/3 lb roasting chicken | 1 × 3 lb roasting chicken |
| **To garnish:** | **For garnish:** |
| fresh apricot slices | fresh apricot slices |
| watercress | watercress |

Setting to use: HIGH/Conventional Oven

Place the parsley, onion, apple and butter in a medium bowl. Cook, covered, for 3½ minutes. Stir in the breadcrumbs, apricots, and salt and pepper to taste.

Spoon the stuffing into the chicken cavity, and truss. Place the bird in a roasting bag, secure with a non-metallic tie and prick the bag.

Place the bird breast side down in a shallow dish. Cook the chicken for 12 minutes. Turn over and cook for a further 12 minutes.

Remove the bag and place the chicken in a conventional oven preheated to 190°C/375°F/Gas Mark 5. Cook for 15 to 20 minutes until brown and the juices run clear.

Garnish the chicken with apricot slices and watercress.

# Glazed Sprouts

| METRIC/IMPERIAL | AMERICAN |
|---|---|
| 500 g/1 lb frozen Brussels sprouts | 1 lb frozen Brussels sprouts |
| 3 tablespoons water | 3 tablespoons water |
| 25 g/1 oz butter | 2 tablespoons butter |
| 1 teaspoon caster sugar | 1 teaspoon sugar |
| salt | salt |
| freshly ground black pepper | freshly ground black pepper |

Setting to use: HIGH

Place the Brussels sprouts and water in a medium bowl. Cook, covered, for 12 minutes. Stand, covered, for 2 to 3 minutes.

Place the butter and sugar in a small jug. Cook, uncovered, for ½ minute or until the butter has melted. Stir in the salt and pepper to taste.

Drain the sprouts and toss in the butter mixture. Serve immediately.

# Loganberry Cheese Mousse

| METRIC/IMPERIAL | AMERICAN |
|---|---|
| 125 g/4 oz cream cheese | ¼ lb cream cheese |
| 50 g/2 oz caster sugar | ¼ cup superfine sugar |
| 500 g/1 lb fresh loganberries, puréed | 1 lb fresh loganberries, puréed |
| 2 tablespoons water | 2 tablespoons water |
| 2 tablespoons white wine | 2 tablespoons white wine |
| 3 teaspoons powdered gelatine | 3 teaspoons unflavored gelatin |
| 150 ml/¼ pint double cream whipped | ⅔ cup heavy cream |
| 2 egg whites | 2 egg whites |
| **To decorate:** | **To decorate:** |
| 150 ml/¼ pint double cream, whipped | ⅔ cup heavy cream, whipped |
| few fresh loganberries | few fresh loganberries |
| langues de chat biscuits, to serve | sponge fingers, to serve |

Setting to use: HIGH

Beat together the cheese and sugar, until soft and smooth. Stir in the fruit purée. Set aside.

Place the water and wine in a small jug. Cook, uncovered, for ½ minute or until the liquid is very hot. Sprinkle over the gelatine and stir well until dissolved. Cool slightly, then stir into the cheese mixture. Ensure that it is well incorporated. Set aside.

Whisk the cream until firm but not very stiff, gently fold into the purée. Whisk the egg whites until stiff then gently fold into the mixture.

Pour into a 900 ml/1½ pint (3¾ cup) glass serving dish. Refrigerate until set.

Decorate with the whipped cream and fresh loganberries. Serve with Langues de chat biscuits.

NOTE: Any puréed, canned or frozen fruit can be used in place of the loganberries.

◁ Fruity combination: from top right: crab bisque; glazed sprouts: apricot-stuffed roast chicken; croquette potatoes; left: loganberry cheese mousse

# Best of British

*baked trout*
*green salad*

---

*rare roast beef with*
*gravy*
*potato bake*
*broccoli with cheese sauce*

---

*chocolate mountain*

---

*brandy coffee*

### Serves 4

*A menu to choose when entertaining those guests
who you know are inclined to be conservative
in their tastes.*

**WINE NOTE** Look out for one of the full-bodied whites of the *Franken* region of Germany (in their distinctive flask-shaped bottles) to accompany lemon trout. Red wine from the Rhône valley – like a *Cornas* or *St-Joseph* –would be as richly flavoured as the garlic roast beef.

**ACTION PLAN**

*On the day before or in the morning:*
1. Prepare the chocolate mountain but do not cover with the cream.

*Later in the day:*
1. Clean the trout if necessary, place the lemon slices inside each fish, cover and refrigerate.
2. Prepare the vegetables, the salad ingredients and the salad dressing. Refrigerate. (Cover the potatoes with water to prevent discoloration).
3. Make the cheese sauce for the broccoli, cover and refrigerate.

*Before serving:*
1. Cook the beef in the microwave and leave to stand.
2. Cook the fish in the microwave. Meanwhile prepare the potato bake.
3. Cook the potato bake in the microwave and cook the broccoli on the conventional hob while serving the first course.
4. Make the gravy and reheat the cheese sauce while browning the beef under the grill.
5. Cover the chocolate mountain with whipped cream and decorate with the grated chocolate just before sitting down to the main course.

112

# Baked Trout

| METRIC/IMPERIAL | AMERICAN |
| --- | --- |
| *1 lemon, sliced* | *1 lemon, sliced* |
| *4 sprigs parsley* | *4 sprigs parsley* |
| *4 small trout, cleaned* | *4 small trout, cleaned* |
| *grated rind of 2 lemons* | *grated rind of 2 lemons* |
| *50 g/2 oz butter* | *¹⁄₄ cup butter* |
| **To garnish:** | **For garnish;** |
| *lemon twists* | *lemon twists* |
| *parsley sprigs* | *parsley sprigs* |

Setting to use: HIGH

Place lemon slices and one of the sprigs of parsley inside each trout. Place the fish on a shallow dish, cover and cook for 4 minutes.

Rearrange the trout. Sprinkle the fish with the lemon rind and dot with butter. Cover and cook for a further 5 minutes, basting the fish with the juices halfway through the cooking.

Leave to stand, covered, for 3 minutes then serve, garnished with the lemon twists and parsley.

## Rare Roast Beef

| METRIC IMPERIAL | AMERICAN |
|---|---|
| *1.5 kg/3 lb topside of beef* | *3 lb beef eye rib roast* |
| *vegetable oil* | *vegetable oil* |
| *3 cloves garlic, peeled* | *3 cloves garlic, peeled* |
| *salt* | *salt* |
| *freshly ground black pepper* | *freshly ground black pepper* |
| *watercress sprigs, to garnish* | *watercress sprigs, for garnish* |

Setting to use: HIGH/Conventional Grill

Rub the beef with a little oil, one of the garlic cloves and salt and pepper. Stand the beef on an upturned saucer in a shallow container and cook for 10 minutes.

With a sharp knife, cut the remaining garlic cloves into slivers. Make incisions in the meat and insert the slivers of garlic. Cook for a further 10 minutes.

Remove the meat from the microwave and wrap it tightly in foil. Leave to stand for 20 minutes then brown under a preheated conventional grill. Transfer to a serving dish, garnish with sprigs of watercress and serve.
NOTE: The beef can be cooked in a roasting bag.

△ *The best of British: from right: green salad; baked trout; rare roast beef with gravy; potato bake; broccoli with cheese sauce*

## Thickened Gravy

| METRIC/IMPERIAL | AMERICAN |
|---|---|
| *2 tablespoons cold water* | *2 tablespoons cold water* |
| *2 tablespoons meat sediment from the roasting bag or plate* | *2 tablespoons meat sediment from the roasting bag or plate* |
| *1 tablespoon plain flour* | *1 tablespoon all-purpose flour* |
| *300 ml/½ pint hot beef stock* | *1¼ cups hot beef stock* |
| *a few drops of gravy browning* | *a few drops of gravy coloring* |

Setting to use: HIGH

Place the water in a large jug. Stir in the meat sediment and flour. Add the stock and gravy browning. Cook, uncovered, for about 2 minutes, stirring twice.

NOTE: For a clear gravy, use 2 teaspoons arrowroot, (made into a paste with a little water), in place of the flour and for extra flavour add 1 tablespoon dry sherry.

113

△ The best of British: chocolate mountain

===== **Potato Bake** =====

**METRIC/IMPERIAL**
500 g/1 lb onions, thinly sliced
625 g/1¼ lb potatoes, thinly
  sliced
salt
freshly ground black pepper
2 teaspoons dried mixed
  herbs
scant 75 ml/3 fl oz milk

**AMERICAN**
1 lb onions, thinly sliced
1¼ lb potatoes, thinly sliced
salt
freshly ground black pepper
2 teaspoons dried mixed
  herbs
⅓ cup milk

Setting to use: HIGH

Place the onions in a medium bowl, cover and cook for 5 minutes, stirring halfway through cooking.

Layer the potatoes and onions in a 1.2 1/2 pint (5 cup) casserole dish. Sprinkle each layer with a little salt, pepper and herbs. Finish with a layer of neatly arranged potatoes. Pour in the milk and sprinkle on a little more mixed herbs.

Cover and cook for 9 minutes, turning the dish round halfway through cooking.

===== **Broccoli with Cheese** =====
**Sauce**

**METRIC/IMPERIAL**
3 tablespoons water
salt
500g/1 lb broccoli. stalks
  halved lengthways
1 tablespoon toasted
  almonds. optional

**AMERICAN**
3 tablespoons water
salt
1 lb broccoli, stalks halved
  lengthways
1 tablespoon toasted
  almonds. optional

**Sauce:**
25 g/1 oz butter
25 g/1 oz plain flour
300 ml/½ pint milk
1 teaspoon made mustard
salt
freshly ground black pepper
50 g/2 oz Cheddar cheese,
  grated

**Sauce:**
2 tablespoons butter
¼ cup all-purpose flour
1¼ cups milk
1 teaspoon made mustard
salt
freshly ground black pepper
½ cup grated Cheddar cheese

Setting to use: HIGH

Place the water and salt in a large bowl. Arrange the broccoli in the water with stalks standing upwards. Cover with plastic wrap and cook for 7 minutes. Set aside.

For the sauce, place the butter in a large jug. Cook for 1 minute or until melted.

Blend in the flour, milk, mustard and salt and pepper to taste. Cook for 3 minutes stirring every minute. Stir in the cheese and cook for a further minute.

Drain the broccoli and arrange in a serving dish. Pour the sauce over the broccoli, scatter the toasted almonds over the top and serve.

===== **Chocolate Mountain** =====

**METRIC/IMPERIAL**
125 g/4 oz margarine, softened
125 g/4 oz caster sugar
25 g/1 oz cocoa powder
100 g/3½ oz self raising flour
teaspoon baking powder
2 drops vanilla essence
2 tablespoons milk
2 large eggs, lightly beaten
8 large marshmallows, diced
150 ml/¼ pint warm coffee
3 tablespoons medium sherry
sugar to taste
250 ml/8 fl oz double cream,
  whipped
**To decorate:**
flaked chocolate
2 to 3 sparklers (optional)

**AMERICAN**
½ cup margarine, softened
½ cup sugar
2 tablespoons unsweetened
  cocoa
scant cup self-raising flour
teaspoon baking powder
2 drops vanilla
2 tablespoons milk
2 large eggs, lightly beaten
8 large marshmallows, diced
⅔ cup warm coffee
3 tablespoons medium sherry
sugar to taste
1 cup heavy cream, whipped
**To decorate:**
flaked chocolate
2 to 3 sparklers (optional)

Setting to use: HIGH

Place the margarine, caster sugar, cocoa, flour, baking powder, vanilla, milk and egg into a large bowl. Using an electric mixer, beat together until smooth. Do not overbeat.

Line a 1 l/2 pint (8 cup) heatproof bowl with plastic wrap. Spoon the mixture into the bowl and cover. Place in the microwave on an upturned pie dish and cook for 4½ to 5 minutes or until the base of the pudding is cooked. Set aside, covered for 10 minutes.

Leaving the pudding in the bowl, use a small sharp knife to cut a circle about 10 cm/4 inches in diameter. Scoop out the mixture from the pudding to form a well.

Leave the pudding to cool completely then fill the well with the diced marshmallows. Cut a lid from the pudding mixture and cover the marshmallows. Prick the pudding.

Mix the warm coffee with the sugar and sherry. Pour it over the pudding and refrigerate, uncovered, for about 2 hours. Turn the pudding out onto a serving plate and remove the plastic wrap. Cover with whipped cream and sprinkle with the grated chocolate.

For special occasions, push sparklers into the top of the pudding and set alight just before serving.

# COFFEE & CO

*Coffee is an often-neglected course — make more of it.*

Coffee is the last course of the meal — but this should not deter you from making the effort to complete your guests' gastronomic enjoyment, as it is often the most social part of the meal — there will be more conversation over coffee than at any other point.

Select good quality coffee, use whichever blend you like best, but ring the changes with the presentation and accompaniments to this important course.

## The in tray

Whether you like to linger at the table or retire to more comfortable chairs placing a good looking coffee pot on a tray with some accompanying nibbles will be both pretty and portable.

Cover the tray with an attractive tray cloth — ensure the tray is large enough to accommodate everything you need. The cups can be handed out individually, but the coffee and nibbles could reside on the tray

## Sweet as sugar

One simple idea is to present the coffee with different types of sugar — they could be demerara, brown sugar cubes, rainbow sugar or coffee crystals (all available from delicatessens). Place each type in a small round bowl and serve the three bowls grouped together on a plate.

## Coffee kicks

The wonderful thing about coffee is its versatility. In the summer, instead of serving hot coffee to your guests try iced coffee or caffé granita — for this simply freeze sweetened black coffee in ice trays and when ready to serve, crush, place in tall glasses and top with a liqueur or cream.

Hot coffee can be, and usually is, served with a liqueur. If you are lucky enough to have a good selection then your guests can choose to have their final drinks separately or combined in a liqueur coffee. The combinations are virtually endless — they will stretch as far as your imagination, palate and drinks cabinet will permit.

It is a matter of personal taste if cream is added to the liqueur coffee. The effect of it floating on top is achieved by much practise; but this method should work. Place sugar in the bottom of a heatproof glass, add the liqueur, then the hot coffee, then stir. Pour the cream over the back of a spoon while the coffee is still spinning.

## A sticky end

Many people are bored with the perennial chocolate peppermints. If your guests are healthy types try serving fresh dates. If they are less dedicated serve chocolate covered peanuts or raisins, or sugared almonds. If they are averagely wicked try such goodies as chocolate eggs, turkish delight or chocolate pastilles. Tiny mint imperials will do for the purists who merely wish to refresh their palate.

TECHNICAL • KNOW-HOW

Cooking by microwave energy must be the greatest revolution since man dropped raw food into a fire and found that it was still palatable. This twentieth century method of cooking must naturally raise a few eyebrows and mutterings as it is unique in the world of cuisine. Electro-magnetic energy has been available since time began. Light is the only form which is visible but the energy is also harnessed with electricity to give other uses to man – radar, X-rays, television, radio and of course microwaves.

## How The Microwave Works

To obtain the greatest benefits of cooking by microwave energy it is important to appreciate how the energy works. Traditionally, heat is applied to the outside of food and is cooked by this heat being conducted through the food layers to the centre. Whether grilling [broiling], frying, baking or boiling, the principle remains the same. As this cooking process is carried out, the outer layer of the food being exposed to heat often browns. Cooking by microwaves is very similar, although the energy penetrates rather more than the outside layer of food. However, the method of cooking by conduction still occurs. As a rule, browning of meats and cakes is not usual as there is no heat produced by burners or elements.

The microwave cooker may appear to be a simple box, but it is one of the most highly engineered appliances in the home. Today, these cookers are becoming more sophisticated, with many extra features, but in essence the basic method of producing microwaves is the same.

Behind the controls there are various components which enable the electricity to be used to generate microwave energy. This invisible energy is channelled along a tunnel which opens into the cooking cavity.

The microwaves emerging from the tunnel (or wave-guide) need to be distributed to ensure a good energy pattern. In order to achieve this, a paddle or stirrer, slowly turning, is generally fitted. As it turns, so the microwaves are deflected off the paddle onto the metal cooking cavity surfaces.

Microwaves cannot pass through metal, thus the floor, roof, walls and door of the cooker are all constructed of metal, which in turn contributes to an even energy pattern.

Although microwaves cannot pass through metal they can pass through many other materials as if the materials were invisible. As a result virtually any commonly available culinary material can be used to contain, support or cover food. This includes china, paper, cardboard and plastics. However, there may be exceptions – for example, plastics of the type which cannot withstand the high temperature of the food being cooked.

Finally, microwaves are attracted to moisture and as food itself contains moisture it is the perfect medium for the energy. All food and liquid is made up of moisture or water molecules and the presence of microwave energy excites them to such a degree that they begin to oscillate back and forth at over two thousand million times a second. In doing so they create heat in the food itself and it is this heat which cooks the food. The greatest penetration of the microwaves is 4 to 5 cm/1½ to 2 inches from all directions and decreases with subsequent food layers. Nevertheless, with thicker items of food the cooking continues by conduction.

When the energy is used to cook food the molecules will oscillate, but as soon as the energy is switched off they stop. Simply like switching a light on and off.
Microwave cookers are exceedingly safe to operate.
Microwave energy can only be generated when the door of the cooker is fully closed and the appropriate controls switched on. It cannot be generated if the door is even slightly ajar, added to which all cookers must have at least two safety interlocks.

### CONVECTION/MICROWAVE COOKERS

Some manufacturers now produce microwave cookers which incorporate conventional electric heating elements.

The majority of these models are designed as tabletop appliances. For those who require a small secondary conventional oven in the kitchen as well as a microwave cooker, the benefits of this new technology are twofold, giving the choice of either form of cooking. In addition, many of these cookers can be set automatically to carry out the microwave operation and then complete the cooking by conventional oven cooking. This extends the cooking range of the microwave cooker and introduces the benefit of browning foods such as meat and pastry within the same cooking cavity.

With these new combined microwave cookers, careful thought should be given to the type of container used, once conventional heat is to be applied then the microwave advantage of using any material such as paper, table glass, cardboard and china is lost because the heat could break,

# THE GOLDEN RULES

**There are many tips which can increase the efficiency of your cooker and the results obtained...**

☐ Select the most suitable size and type of container as this will be beneficial to the cooked result.

☐ Unlike conventional cooking, greasing and flouring a cake or pudding container is unnecessary. Also, it results in an unpleasant flour surface on the cooked product.

☐ It is possible to use small pieces of foil to prevent overcooking the thinner areas of food such as meat and poultry. However, do not allow the foil to come into contact with the microwave walls as this can cause arcing (flashes of blue light).

☐ Prick foods with membranes such as egg yolks, tomato skins, apples and potatoes as this will ensure that they will not burst during cooking.

☐ Remember that the more food placed in the microwave, the longer the cooking time.

☐ It is not necessary to use water when steaming in the microwave unless instructions are given to the contrary as it only increases the cooking time and cost of energy.

☐ If thawing poultry or a large piece of meat, ensure that it is fully thawed before cooking.

☐ When cooking vegetables and fruit avoid using too much liquid. Usually 3 tablespoons is sufficient as there is enough water within the food itself to obtain the desired results.

☐ Cover fatty foods like bacon with kitchen paper to absorb the grease and stop the food from spattering or splashing.

☐ Stir liquid foods like soups and stews to ensure speedy and even cooking.

☐ To ensure even cooking arrange foods of equal size in a ring pattern on the cooking dish but foods of uneven shapes should be arranged with the thicker areas towards the outside edge.

crack, scorch or melt the material. Also the appliance will require more cleaning because, with the conventional heat, the food being cooked will spatter and burn.

The latest innovation in microwave cooking is a tabletop convection oven which can be used with the support of the microwave energy. With the simultaneous benefit of hot air and microwave energy, results compare very favourably to foods cooked in a conventional oven, but cooking time is drastically reduced. The simultaneous use of both energies ensures that conventional heat draws off moisture thus browning the food while the microwaves cook moister parts.

General recipes for the dual energy cookers are not readily available as each manufacturer employs a different wattage and design, but the majority do give a recipe book with the appliance which includes many basic recipes that may be adapted by the user.

☐ If cooking food by a variety of power levels, for example, HIGH and then DEFROST (30%), ensure that the food, such as meat and poultry, soups and stews, is brought to the boil and cooked for several minutes on HIGH before reducing the energy.

☐ Follow instructions for standing times after cooking as this will contribute to a better thawed or cooked product.

☐ Clean the cooking cavity thoroughly and frequently. Although it does not get very dirty, it is important to ensure that it is free of bacteria – much like any other kitchen surface.

☐ Do remember the output (wattage) of your cooker and this will help you determine the timing of recipes taken from microwave cookbooks other than the one produced by the manufacturer of your microwave cooker.

☐ Always follow the manufacturer's instructions with respect to use, care and maintenance of the appliance.

There are few limitations to the basic microwave cooker and these can be listed very quickly.

*DO NOT* use the microwave in isolation. Do get the benefit from other kitchen appliances. For example, it is cheaper and quicker to boil 600 ml/1 pint (2½ cups) water in an electric kettle.

*DO NOT* attempt to deep-fat fry in the microwave as it is not possible for the cook to have complete control over the temperature of the fat.

*DO NOT* boil an egg in its shell as pressure will build up within the egg and cause it to explode

*DO NOT* leave an oven thermometer in the cooking cavity unless it is specifically recommended by the microwave manufacturer.

*DO NOT* attempt to bottle [can] fruit or vegetables in the microwave unless instructions are given by the microwave manufacturer.

*DO NOT* tamper with your microwave. If you have problems, call in a fully qualified service technician.

## THE FREEZER AND THE MICROWAVE

When domestic microwave cookers first appeared on the market, one manufacturer advertised his model as 'the unfreezer'. Indeed, for those who have a freezer the microwave cooker gives added dimension to speedy and convenient food preparation. Today many frozen-food companies include instructions for both conventional and microwave thawing and cooking of their products. Nevertheless, it is a myth that all frozen foods can be thawed and heated in minutes. Much will depend upon the type, density and quantity of the food. For example, a bread roll can be thawed in seconds, whereas a piece of meat the same weight takes minutes. In some instances the microwave can be used to speed up thawing but the standing time to complete the operation is quite long. An example of this is frozen éclairs, which are microwaved for 1½ minutes but are not totally thawed until they have stood for 30 minutes.

There are many small foods which can be thawed and reheated within the same operation. This would apply to food such as hamburgers, plated meals and frozen raw fish. It is, therefore, important to understand your particular microwave and wherever possible seek guidance from the manufacturer's instruction book.

### Thawing frozen foods in the microwave

☐ If thawing foods which are very liquid; such as soups and stews, or foods in a sauce, select a container which is just large enough to accommodate the thawed liquid close to the frozen block.

☐ Unless instructions are given to the contrary always cover the food. This is not so necessary with cakes, pastries and bread.

☐ When thawing soups, stews and sauces, break up the partially frozen block with a fork as soon as possible as this speeds up the process.

☐ Always thaw large cuts of meat and birds *completely* before use. To avoid any cooking of the food during thawing it is wiser to start the thawing by microwave but then to let it stand until no ice remains in the food (and all the joints of birds are flexible).

☐ Always ensure that thawed cooked meat and poultry dishes are throughly heated through, they should be heated in the microwave for several minutes before serving.

☐ If thawing foods of which the liquid is simply water, remove any lumps of ice to speed up the thawing process.

☐ Always slightly undercook fish and meat dishes that are to be frozen. This compensates for further cooking that takes place during the heating up time when the food is being thawed and reheated.

### SUITABILITY TEST

It is not always possible to judge if a container material is suitable for use in the microwave but a simple test can be carried out to check its suitability.

Stand a cup of water next to or on the container being tested. Using the maximum setting, microwave for 1½ to 2 minutes. If the container feels cool to the touch it is suitable for cooking operations. If the container feels warm to the touch it should only be used for short heating operations. If it feels hot it is unsuitable for use in the microwave.

Should the container spark during the test this indicates that there is metal within the material. The container should be removed immediately and not used in the microwave.

When testing plastic materials check the container every 15 seconds to ensure that it is not softening.

Almost any container, except metal and some plastics can be used for microwave cooking, but like conventional cooking the best results will be obtained if the right material, shape and size are used. The following information will prove helpful...

ALUMINIUM FOIL: Small quantities of foil can be used but the microwave manufacturer's instructions should always be followed. Foil must never be allowed to touch the walls of the cooking cavity as this can cause arcing i.e. sparking. Use to cover thin areas of food, e.g. the wings of poultry to prevent overcooking, or the corners of sharp-angled containers to prevent dehydration.

BASKETS (straw/wicker): These can be used for short reheating operations, but they may split if left in the microwave for too long. Avoid using baskets that have wire or metal staples to hold them together. Use when reheating bread rolls.

BOIL-IN-BAGS (high density): Suitable for most cooking or reheating operations but always replace the metal ties with an elastic band, plastic tie or piece of string. Use when cooking fresh vegetables and meat, frozen foods in sauce, and blanching vegetables.

BROWNING DISHES (skillets): These dishes are made of a ceramic material with a special base coating of tin oxide. By preheating the dish in a microwave, the bottom gets searing hot. Food placed on the bottom sears and browns so it is especially useful for browning meat and poultry.

CARDBOARD: Cardboard cups, plates and containers can be useful disposable containers. Avoid cardboard containers which are lined with foil, or which have a wax coating as this could melt from the heat of the food.

CHINA: Most china is suitable for use in the microwave providing it does not have metal decorations or metal in the material ingredients. Antique china should not be used as heat from the food could damage it.

COTTON & LINEN: Suitable for short heating operations. Refresh bread by wrapping the loaf in a damp napkin and microwaving for a minute or two. Damp flannels or napkins can be heated in the microwave and presented to your guest, to wipe their hands before an oriental meal.

EARTHENWARE OR POTTERY: These materials are usually porous and can, if used, increase the cooking time or get very hot. Use for pot roasting and casseroles. In some instances glazed chicken pots can be used but follow the manufacturer's instructions.

GLASS (heatproof): Providing the glass is suitable for use in a conventional oven and/or freezer it can generally be used in the microwave.

GLASS (table): Table glass can be used for short heating operations providing the heat of the food will not cause it to crack. Lead crystal or antique glass should not be used.

METAL: As a rule, metal must not be used in the microwave oven unless the manufacturer states otherwise. This applies to metal containers, tags, metal decoration on glass and china and metal which is an integral part of the material. If used, metal may cause damage to the component parts of the cooker, arcing and/or pitting of the cooking cavity walls.

MELAMINE (plastic): This is not usually suitable for use in the microwave as the material absorbs microwave energy and may scorch giving off an unpleasant smell.

MICROWAVE COOKWARE: This is cookware specially designed for microwave use. Usually the cookware is intended to be used both in the microwave and conventional oven (up to 200°C/400°F, Gas Mark 6), some may be disposable. (See below.)

OVENABLE BOARD: Such board is usually coated with a range of polyester and can be used in a microwave cooker and conventional oven (up to 200°C/400°F, Gas Mark 6). It is an ideal replacement for foil containers.

PAPER: Paper cups, plates, towels, serviettes, greaseproof sheets, and parchment can all be used in the microwave, providing the paper does not have a waxed finish. Kitchen paper towel is useful when moisture of food needs to be absorbed to prevent soggyness, or to prevent splashing.

PLASTICS: The best type to use in the microwave are thermoplastics which can withstand very high temperatures 150-200°C/300-400°F. Other types should be used with care for short reheating operations. Plastic storage bags should not be used as the heat of the food will cause them to melt. Most plastic wrap is suitable but some thinner types tend to shrivel very quickly so check the package instructions.

ROASTING BAGS: These bags are perfect for cooking meat, fish or vegetables in the microwave or conventional oven. However, for microwave cooking replace any metal ties and pierce the bag to allow the steam to escape.

THERMOMETER: It is essential to use a thermometer specially designed for use in a microwave.

WOOD: Wooden spoons for stirring, toothpicks for securing meat, long wooden sticks for kebabs can all be used in the microwave for short term operations.

## SIZE AND SHAPE

Round or regular shapes are better than those with acute corners as the food in the corner areas will tend to dry out. Food cooked in oval shapes may also show the same tendencies to dry out at the narrower ends. Some manufacturers suggest these corner areas be masked with small pieces of foil which will reflect the microwaves away.

☐ Large shallow containers are usually a better choice for solid food than tall deep ones as there is a greater surface area giving the food the maximum exposure to the microwave energy.

☐ Liquids and sauces are better heated in a tall narrow container such as a jug, but the capacity should be large enough to allow the liquid to rise in the container without it boiling over.

☐ Frozen food with a sauce should be placed in a container which matches the shape of the frozen food. The container should be small enough to contain the liquid when thawed, it should not spread out in a thin layer.

☐ Preserves such as jams and chutneys should be cooked in a bowl made of a material that can withstand the very high sugar temperatures, and large enough to hold the contents when they boil.

## IMPROVISE

As metal or metal decorated containers cannot be used you may battle to find the right shape container in your cupboard. The following container tips may help you to solve the problem without you having to spend a fortune on a new container...

☐ Non-waxed cardboard boxes of different shapes, lined with plastic wrap can be used for cooking cakes. For example, a shallow oblong box could be divided down the centre and used to make a Battenberg cake.

☐ A straight-sided soufflé dish can be used for making cakes.

☐ Cups or mugs make ideal containers for individual puddings.

☐ Teacups or ramekin dishes can be used for poaching eggs, or making individual custards.

☐ Plastic jelly moulds can be used for making the less usual animal-shaped cakes.

☐ A ring mould can be devised by using a straight-sided soufflé dish with a tumbler inverted in the centre. This is useful for cooking pâtés and cakes.

☐ Inexpensive wine glasses can be lined with plastic wrap and used for madeleines.

☐ Ice cream wafer cones can be filled with cake mixture and supported in a paper cup.

☐ Use paper cake cases; support them by standing them in unwaxed cardboard drinking cups with the base cut off to the correct height to hold them.

## ADAPTING RECIPES FOR MICROWAVE COOKING

Most conventional recipes can be adapted for microwave cooking but it may take several attempts before you achieve success. (This has to be expected since conventional recipes have been developed for cooking by heat whereas microwave recipes are cooked by energy.) However, the following guidelines will prove useful for those people who wish to experiment and convert their favourite conventional recipes.

☐ Where possible look for, and follow, a similar recipe in your microwave cooker's manufacturer's recipe book.

☐ Food cooked in the microwave is likely to take a quarter to a third of the conventional cooking time. However, for small items, the cooking time may be even quicker – four potatoes baked in the microwave cooker will take about 15 minutes and in a conventional oven 1¼ to 1½ hours.

☐ Timing is important. Initially it will be necessary to check the food frequently and err on the side of undercooking – food can always be returned to the microwave cooker for a few extra minutes. Overcooking will result in dehydration and once this stage is reached it will not be possible to recover the texture or flavour.

☐ As liquid does not evaporate at the same rate in a microwave cooker, some soups, casseroles and stews may require less liquid or more thickening agent. Puddings and cakes however have so little moisture within the recipe it may be necessary to add extra liquid.

☐ If the recipe requires more than 600 ml/1 pint (2½ cups) of liquid it is quicker and more economical to use a liquid that has been boiled conventionally rather than to heat it in the microwave cooker.

☐ The full bouquet of spices and herbs will not develop fully due to the speed of cooking most microwave recipes. Therefore a little more flavouring may be required.

☐ Cake or pudding containers should not be greased and floured as this results in an unpleasant flour film on the cooked product. Grease, or grease and sugar containers, or line them with plastic wrap or greaseproof paper.

☐ When cooking an adapted recipe for the first time it is best to stay close to the microwave cooker so that you can check on the cooking progress.

---

### A GUIDE TO COMPARATIVE POWER SETTINGS

Not all manufacturers utilize the same terminology for the variable power settings.
The following guide gives some indication of how the levels compare, but use it for guidance only.
It is advisable to check in your own microwave cooker manufacturer's instruction book.

| 1 | 2 | 3 | 4 | 5 | 6 | 7 |
|---|---|---|---|---|---|---|
| Keep Warm | Simmer | Stew | Defrost | Bake | Roast | High |
| Low | Defrost | Med-Low | Medium | High | Med-High | Full |
| 150 watts | 200 watts | 250 watts | 300 watts | 400 watts | 500 watts | 650/700 watts |
| (25%) | (30%) | (40%) | (50%) | (60%) | (75%) | (100%) |

*Table by courtesy of The Microwave Association*

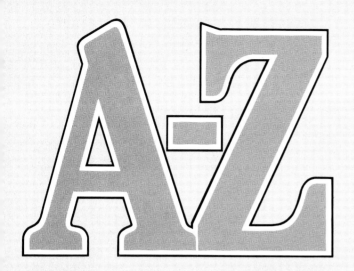

# GUIDE · TO · THAWING AND · COOKING · TIMES

The times given should be used for guidance only. Remember the thawing and cooking times will depend upon the size and thickness of portions, and the age, density and temperature of the food when it goes into the microwave. The information was compiled using a 700 watt microwave, if your cooker has a lower wattage it may be necessary to increase the thawing and cooking times by a minute or two.

You may also need to increase thawing times a little if you use the DEFROST (30%) control rather than the HIGH setting. Remember, it is best to thaw large pieces of dense food on defrost, otherwise you may find that the outside of the food begins to cook before the inside is thawed through.

## APPLES

| To THAW & COOK | |
|---|---|
| Quantity: | 500 g/1 lb |
| Time: | 8 to 10 minutes |
| Setting: | High or Defrost (30%) |
| Additions: | None |
| Container: | Medium bowl, covered or uncovered |

ADVICE: Break up with a fork once or twice during thawing.

| To COOK FRESH | |
|---|---|
| Quantity: | 500 g/1 lb |
| Time: | 5 minutes |
| Setting: | High |
| Additions: | 2 tablespoons water, sugar to taste |
| Container: | Large bowl, covered |

ADVICE: Peel, core and quarter fruit. Stir halfway through cooking.

| To BAKE | |
|---|---|
| Quantity: | 1 medium |
| Time: | 2½ minutes |
| Setting: | High |
| Additions: | None |
| Container: | Shallow dish, uncovered |

ADVICE: Core and make a cut around the middle of the apple. Leave to stand for 1 to 2 minutes before serving.

## APPLE PIE (Frozen)

| To THAW | |
|---|---|
| Quantity: | 1 |
| Time: | 1 minute |
| Setting: | High or Defrost (30%) |
| Additions: | None |
| Container: | Stand on kitchen paper towel on plate |

ADVICE: Remove the foil container before thawing. Stand for 5 to 10 minutes before serving.

## APRICOTS

| To COOK FRESH | |
|---|---|
| Quantity: | 500 g/1 lb |
| Time: | 5 minutes |
| Setting: | High |
| Additions: | 3 tablespoons water, sugar to taste |
| Container: | Medium bowl, covered |

ADVICE: Remove stones [pits] and cut into quarters. Stir halfway through cooking.

## ARTICHOKES, GLOBE

| To COOK FRESH | |
|---|---|
| Quantity: | 4 |
| Time: | 20 minutes |
| Setting: | High |
| Additions: | 300 ml/½ pint [1¼ cups] water, 1 tablespoon lemon juice |
| Container: | Shallow dish, covered |

ADVICE: Trim and wash the artichoke, cut a cross in each stem. Turn over halfway through cooking. Leave to stand for 10 minutes before serving.

## ARTICHOKES, JERUSALEM

| To COOK FRESH | |
|---|---|
| Quantity: | 500 g/1 lb |
| Time: | 9 minutes |
| Setting: | High |
| Additions: | 3 tablespoons water, salt |
| Container: | Medium bowl, covered |

ADVICE: Scrub or thinly peel, then slice the artichokes. Stir halfway through cooking. Leave to stand for 5 minutes before serving.

## ASPARAGUS

| To THAW & COOK | |
|---|---|
| Quantity: | 500 g/1 lb |
| Time: | 8 to 10 minutes |
| Setting: | High or Defrost (30%) |
| Additions: | 5 tablespoons water, salt |
| Container: | Shallow dish, covered |

ADVICE: Arrange with the tips facing the centre. Separate halfway through cooking.

| To COOK FRESH | |
|---|---|
| Quantity: | 500 g/1 lb |
| Time: | 13 minutes |
| Setting: | High |
| Additions: | 3 tablespoons water, salt |
| Container: | Shallow dish, covered |

ADVICE: Remove the woody part of the stems and cut into even-length spears. Arrange with the tips facing the centre. Rearrange halfway through cooking.

## AUBERGINES (EGGPLANT)

To COOK
FRESH
Quantity: 500 g/1 lb
Time: 6 minutes
Setting: High
Additions: 2 tablespoons water, salt
Container: Medium bowl, covered

ADVICE: Trim and dice the aubergine. Sprinkle with salt and leave to stand for 30 minutes, then rinse well and pat dry. Cover and cook, stirring halfway through cooking.

## BACON, Large Cuts

To THAW
Quantity: As required
Time: 9 to 10 minutes per 500 g/1 lb
Setting: High or Defrost (30%)
Additions: None
Container: Stand meat on a trivet in a shallow dish

ADVICE: Turn over once during thawing. Wrap in foil and leave to stand for 15-30 minutes. Smaller cuts will thaw more quickly than larger so check during cooking and stand for only 15 minutes. Meat should be completely thawed before cooking.

To COOK
Quantity: As required
Time: 7½ minutes per 500 g/1 lb
Setting: High
Additions: None
Container: Stand meat on a trivet in a shallow dish

ADVICE: Turn over once during cooking. If practical, place meat in a pricked roasting bag with the metal tag replaced with string. After cooking, remove bag, wrap in foil and leave to stand for 20 minutes.

## BACON RASHERS

To THAW
Quantity: 200 g/7 oz pack – 6 rashers
Time: 1 minute
Setting: High
Additions: None
Container: Plate

ADVICE: Cover with kitchen paper towel. After thawing for 30 seconds, separate rashers [slices] where possible and return to the microwave for a further 30 seconds. After thawing use a pointed knife to separate.

To COOK
Quantity: 200 g/7 oz
Time: 3 to 4 minutes
Setting: High
Additions: None
Container: Bacon rack or plate

ADVICE: Cover the bacon with a piece of kitchen paper towel. The longer the bacon is cooked the crisper it will be. Cook until the desired degree of cooking is achieved.

## BAKED BEANS

To COOK
Quantity: 1 × 220 g/7¾ oz can
Time: 2 minutes
Setting: High
Additions: None
Container: Bowl or plate

ADVICE: Stir halfway through heating.

## BASS

To COOK
FRESH
Quantity: 500 g/1 lb
Time: 5 to 7 minutes
Setting: High
Additions: None
Container: Shallow dish, covered

ADVICE: Clean the fish and cover the head and tail with foil. Cover and cook rearranging halfway through cooking. Stand for 3 minutes.

## BATTENBERG CAKE (Frozen)

To THAW
Quantity: 275 g/9 oz
Time: 30 to 45 seconds
Setting: High
Additions: None
Container: Stand on a piece of kitchen paper towel on a plate

ADVICE: Check after 30 seconds, as the marzipan can oversoften if over-heated. Leave to stand for 15 minutes before serving.

## BEANS, BROAD or LIMA

To COOK
FRESH
Quantity: 500 g/1 lb
Time: 7 minutes or until tender
Setting: High
Additions: 3 tablespoons water
Container: Medium bowl, covered

ADVICE: Stir halfway through cooking.

## BEANS, GREEN

To COOK
FRESH
Quantity: 500 g/1 lb
Time: 14 minutes
Setting: High
Additions: 3 tablespoons water, salt
Container: Medium bowl, covered

ADVICE: Top, tail and slice the beans. Cover and cook, stirring halfway through cooking. Leave to stand for 4 minutes before serving.

To THAW &
COOK
Quantity: 500 g/1 lb
Time: 12 minutes
Setting: High
Additions: 2 tablespoons cold water
Container: Large bowl, covered

ADVICE: Stir halfway through cooking.

## BEAN SPROUTS

To COOK
Quantity: 250 g/8 oz
Time: 4½ minutes
Setting: High
Additions: None
Container: Large bowl, covered

ADVICE: Rinse in water, drain and cook. Stir halfway through cooking; stand for 1 minute. Serve tossed in a little butter or soy sauce.

## BEEF, Large cuts

To THAW    Quantity: As desired
                Time: 9 to 10 minutes per 500 g/1 lb
                Setting: Defrost (30%)
                Additions: None
                Container: Stand meat on a trivet or upturned plate in a shallow dish

ADVICE: Turn over once during thawing. Wrap in foil and leave to stand for 15 to 30 minutes. Smaller cuts will thaw more quickly than larger ones so check during thawing and stand for only 15 minutes. Meat should be completely thawed before cooking.

To COOK    Quantity: As desired
                Time: 5 minutes per 500g/1 lb – rare
                      6 to 7 minutes per 500g/1 lb – medium rare
                      8 to 10 minutes per 500g/1 lb – well done
                Setting: High
                Additions: None
                Container: Stand meat on a trivet or upturned plate in a shallow dish

ADVICE: Place small pieces of foil over thinner areas of meat. If practical, place the meat in a pricked roasting bag replacing the metal tag with string. Turn over halfway through cooking. After microwaving, remove the bag, wrap in foil and leave to stand for 20 to 30 minutes before serving.

## BEEFBURGERS

To THAW &   Quantity: 2
COOK         Time: 3 to 3½ minutes
                Setting: High
                Additions: None
                Container: Plate

ADVICE: Cover with kitchen paper towel to avoid splashing.

To COOK    Quantity: 4 made from 250 g/8 oz meat
FRESH       Time: 5 minutes
                Setting: High
                Additions: None
                Container: Shallow dish, uncovered

ADVICE: Any chopped onion should be sautéed in butter before adding to the raw mince.

## BEEF, Fillet

To THAW    See BEEF, Large cuts

To COOK    Quantity: 500 g/1 lb
                Time: 2 minutes - rare
                      2 to 3 minutes - medium rare
                      3 minutes - well done
                Setting: High
                Additions: None
                Container: Stand meat on a trivet or upturned plate in a shallow dish

ADVICE: Turn halfway through cooking. No standing time required.

## BEEF MINCE

To COOK    See MINCED MEAT

## BEEF STEAK

To THAW    Quantity: 250 g/8 oz
                Time: 4 minutes

Setting: Defrost (30%)
                Additions: None
                Container: Plate, covered

ADVICE: Stand covered for 10 minutes before cooking. If time allows thaw naturally.

To COOK    Quantity: As desired
                Time: 2 minutes per 500 g/1 lb rare
                      2 to 4 minutes per 500 g/1 lb medium rare
                      4 minutes per 500 g/1 lb well done
                Setting: High
                Additions: None
                Container: A browning dish is recommended, if not a plate

ADVICE: If a browning dish is not used, then sear under a pre-heated grill [broiler] or in a frying pan.

## BEETROOT

To COOK    Quantity: 500 g/1 lb
RAW          Time: 10 minutes
                Setting: High
                Additions: 150 ml/¼ pint [⅔ cup] water
                Container: Shallow dish, covered

ADVICE: Select small beetroot. Rearrange halfway through cooking. Leave to stand for 5 minutes before serving.

## BISCUITS (Frozen)

To THAW    Quantity: 6
                Time: 1 minute
                Setting: High
                Additions: None
                Container: Piece of kitchen paper towel

ADVICE: Arrange the biscuits in a circle. Check frequently and remove any which are thawed.

## BLACKBERRIES

To THAW    Quantity: 500 g/1 lb
                Time: 4½ minutes
                Setting: High
                Additions: None
                Container: Large bowl, covered

ADVICE: Stir halfway through cooking.

To THAW &   Quantity: 500 g/1 lb
COOK         Time: 9 minutes
                Setting: High
                Additions: Sugar to taste
                Container: Large bowl, covered

ADVICE: Stir the blackberries and sugar together. Stir halfway through cooking.

To COOK FRESH
Quantity: 500 g/1 lb
Time: 5 minutes
Setting: High
Additions: Sugar to taste
Container: Large bowl, covered

ADVICE: Rinse the blackberries in water. Stir halfway through cooking.

## BLACKCURRANTS

To THAW
Quantity: 500 g/1 lb
Time: 3 minutes
Setting: High
Additions: None
Container: Medium bowl, covered

ADVICE: After thawing, leave to stand for 5 minutes.

To THAW & COOK
Quantity: 500 g/1 lb
Time: 8½ minutes
Setting: High
Additions: 4 tablespoons sugar
Container: Medium bowl, covered

ADVICE: Stir the blackcurrants and sugar together. Stir halfway through cooking.

## BLACK FOREST GATEAU (Frozen)

To THAW
Quantity: 1
Time: 1½ to 2 minutes
Setting: High
Additions: None
Container: Stand on a plate

ADVICE: Remove the board and paper covering before thawing. Check after 1½ minutes to ensure the cake is not overheating. Leave to stand for 15 to 20 minutes before serving.

## BREAD (Frozen)

To THAW
Quantity: 1 large loaf
Time: 2½ minutes
Setting: High
Additions: None
Container: Wrap loaf in a cotton or linen towel, greaseproof paper or kitchen paper towel.

ADVICE: After thawing for 2½ minutes, leave to stand for 5 minutes. If necessary return to the microwave for 2 more minutes.

To THAW
Quantity: 1 slice or 1 bread roll
Time: 1 to 1½ minutes
Setting: High
Additions: None
Container: Place on kitchen paper towel

ADVICE: Remove when warm to the touch. Leave to stand for a minute or two before using.

## BROCCOLI

To THAW & COOK
Quantity: 250 g/8 oz
Time: 12 minutes
Setting: High or Defrost (30%)
Additions: 2 tablespoons water
Container: Shallow dish, covered

ADVICE: Arrange with florets facing centre of dish. Separate halfway through cooking.

To COOK FRESH
Quantity: 500 g/1 lb
Time: 8 minutes
Setting: High
Additions: 3 tablespoons water, salt
Container: Shallow dish, covered

ADVICE: Split the stalks and arrange with the florets facing the centre of the dish. Rearrange halfway through cooking. Leave to stand for 5 minutes before serving.

## BRUSSELS SPROUTS

To THAW & COOK
Quantity: 250 g/8 oz
Time: 9 minutes
Setting: High
Additions: 2 tablespoons water
Container: Large bowl, covered

ADVICE: Stir halfway through cooking.

To COOK FRESH
Quantity: 500 g/1 lb
Time: 10 minutes
Setting: High
Additions: 3 tablespoons water, salt
Container: Medium bowl, covered

ADVICE: Cut a cross in the base of each sprout. Stir halfway through cooking. Leave to stand for 5 minutes before serving.

## BUBBLE AND SQUEAK

To COOK    Conventional cooking recommended

## BUTTER (Frozen)

To THAW
Quantity: 250 g/8 oz
Time: 30 to 45 seconds
Setting: High
Additions: None
Container: Plate

ADVICE: Check often to ensure the butter is not getting too soft. The outside may seem cool but leave to stand for 2 to 3 minutes. If necessary, return to the microwave to repeat the process.

## CABBAGE

To COOK FRESH
Quantity: 350 g/12 oz
Time: 8 minutes
Setting: High
Additions: 3 tablespoons water, salt
Container: Large bowl, covered

ADVICE: Discard the stalk and shred the cabbage. Stir halfway through cooking. Leave to stand for 4 minutes before serving.

## CABBAGE, RED with APPLE (Frozen)

To THAW & COOK
Quantity: 500 g/1 lb
Time: 10 minutes

Setting: High
Additions: None
Container: Medium bowl, covered
ADVICE: Break up the cabbage with a fork after 4 minutes. Stir after 6 and 8 minutes.

## CANNELLONI

To COOK    Quantity: 12 tubes
Time: 9 minutes
Setting: High
Additions: Filling and sufficient sauce to cover, approx 600 ml/1 pint [2½ cups]
Container: Oblong dish, covered
ADVICE: Fill the tubes with the filling and cover with the sauce. Leave to stand for 10 to 15 minutes before serving.

## CARROTS

To THAW &    Quantity: 250 g/8 oz
COOK    Time: 7 minutes
Setting: High
Additions: 4 tablespoons water
Container: Medium bowl, covered
ADVICE: Stir halfway through cooking.

To COOK    Quantity: 500 g/1 lb
FRESH    Time: 8 minutes
Setting: High
Additions: 3 tablespoons water
Container: Bowl, covered
ADVICE: Peel and slice young carrots. Stir halfway through cooking. Leave to stand for 4 minutes before serving. Old carrots are not successful as they toughen on cooking.

## CAULIFLOWER, FLORETS

To THAW &    Quantity: 250 g/8 oz
COOK    Time: 8 minutes
Setting: High
Additions: 4 tablespoons water
Container: Large bowl, covered
ADVICE: Stir halfway through cooking.

To COOK    Quantity: 500 g/1 lb
FRESH    Time: 9 minutes
Setting: High
Additions: 4 tablespoons water, salt
Container: Large bowl, covered
ADVICE: Trim the florets. Add a pinch of salt to the bowl. Stir halfway through cooking. Leave to stand for 5 minutes before serving.

## CAULIFLOWER, WHOLE

To COOK    Quantity: 750 g/1½ lb
FRESH    Time: 10 minutes
Setting: High
Additions: None
Container: Large bowl, covered
ADVICE: Trim and cut a cross in the stalk. Rinse in cold water. Turn halfway through cooking. Leave to stand for 5 minutes before serving.

## CELERY

To COOK    Quantity: 500 g/1 lb
FRESH    Time: 12 minutes
Setting: High
Additions: 3 tablespoons water, salt
Container: Shallow oblong dish, covered
ADVICE: Trim and halve the sticks, Rearrange halfway through cooking. Leave to stand for 5 minutes before serving.

## CHEESECAKE (Frozen)

To THAW    Quantity: 1 × 500 g/1 lb
Time: 1 to 1¼ minutes
Setting: High
Additions: None
Container: Plate
ADVICE: Remove the cheesecake from the foil container before thawing. Check after 1 minute. Leave to stand for 15 to 20 minutes before serving.

## CHERRIES

To THAW    Quantity: 500 g/1 lb
Time: 3 minutes
Setting: High
Additions: None
Container: Medium bowl, covered
ADVICE: Leave to stand for 5 minutes.

To THAW &    Quantity: 500 g/1 lb
COOK    Time: 9 minutes
Setting: High
Additions: Sugar to taste
Container: Medium bowl, covered
ADVICE: Stir the cherries and sugar together. Stir halfway through cooking.

To COOK    Quantity: 750 g/1½ lb
FRESH    Time: 4½ minutes
Setting: High
Additions: 1 tablespoon water
Container: Large bowl, covered
ADVICE: Stir halfway through cooking.

## CHICKEN

To THAW    Quantity: Whole or portions
Time: 7 to 9 minutes per 500 g/1 lb
Setting: High or Defrost (30%)

Additions: None
Container: Shallow dish, bird standing on a plate or trivet, covered with paper kitchen towels
ADVICE: Shield the thin parts of the bird with foil. Remove the giblets as soon as possible. Turn over halfway through thawing. Leave to stand for 10 to 15 minutes before cooking. (Not necessary with portions.) Do not cook until fully thawed.

| To COOK WHOLE BIRD | Quantity: As required<br>Time: 6 to 7 minutes per 500 g/1 lb<br>Setting: High<br>Additions: None<br>Container: Shallow container, bird standing on an upturned plate or trivet. |
|---|---|

ADVICE: Shield the thin parts of the bird with foil. Place in a pricked roasting bag (replacing the metal tag with string). Turn over halfway through cooking. After cooking wrap in foil and leave to stand for 15 to 20 minutes before serving. Brown under a preheated grill [broiler] before serving if desired.

| To COOK (Portions) | Quantity: As required<br>Time: 6 to 7 minutes<br>Setting: High<br>Additions: None<br>Container: Shallow dish, chicken covered with kitchen paper towels |
|---|---|

ADVICE: Cover the thin parts of the portions with foil. Arrange with the thin parts towards the centre. Leave to stand, covered, for approximately 4 minutes before serving. If portions require browning, brown under a preheated grill [broiler] instead of standing.

## CHIPS (Frozen)

| To THAW | Quantity: 500 g/1 lb<br>Time: 3 minutes<br>Setting: High<br>Additions: None<br>Container: Flat plate |
|---|---|

ADVICE: Spread the chips evenly over the plate, leaving a space in the centre. Rearrange halfway through thawing. Cook conventionally. NEVER deep-fat fry in the microwave.

## CHIPS, OVEN

| To THAW & COOK | Quantity: 250 g/8 oz<br>Time: 9½ minutes<br>Setting: High<br>Additions: None<br>Container: Large browning dish, uncovered |
|---|---|

ADVICE: Preheat empty browning dish for 3½ minutes then arrange chips in a single layer. Cook for 6 minutes, turning over halfway through cooking.

## CHOCOLATE

| To MELT | Quantity: 250 g/8 oz<br>Time: 2 to 3 minutes<br>Setting: High<br>Additions: None<br>Container: Bowl |
|---|---|

ADVICE: Break into pieces. Stir once during melting. Check frequently once it starts to melt.

## CHOCOLATE CAKE (Frozen)

| To THAW | See CREAM SPONGE CAKE |
|---|---|
| To COOK | See CHRISTMAS PUDDING |

## CHOCOLATE ECLAIRS (Frozen)

| To THAW | See ECLAIRS |
|---|---|

## CHOPS (Pork, Lamb or Veal)

| To THAW | Quantity: As required<br>Time: 8 to 10 minutes per 500 g/1 lb<br>Setting: High or Defrost (30%)<br>Additions: None<br>Container: Plate or shallow dish, chops covered with kitchen paper towel |
|---|---|

ADVICE: Arrange with thin parts of the chops towards the centre. As chops vary in thickness, check frequently. After cooking wrap in foil and leave to stand for 10 to 15 minutes, or brown under a preheated grill [broiler] instead of standing.

| To COOK FRESH | Quantity: as required<br>Time: 3 to 4 minutes<br>Setting: High<br>Additions: None<br>Container: Shallow dish or plate |
|---|---|

ADVICE: After cooking, leave to stand for 3 to 4 minutes before serving, or brown under a preheated grill [broiler] or in a frying pan instead of standing.

## CHOW CHOW (CHAYOTE)

| To COOK FRESH | Quantity: 500 g/1 lb<br>Time: 5 minutes blanching<br>      6½ minutes cooking<br>Setting: High<br>Additions: Water<br>Container: Large bowl, covered |
|---|---|

ADVICE: Cut into 8 wedges, removing the soft 'stone'. Cover with boiling water and cook or 'blanch' for 5 minutes. Pour off this water then add 3 tablespoons water and return to the microwave to cook for 6½ minutes. Stand covered, for 3 minutes before serving.

## CHRISTMAS PUDDING

| To REHEAT | Quantity: 1 × 1 kg/2 lb<br>Time: 5 minutes then rest 5 minutes, then microwave a further 5 minutes<br>Setting: High<br>Additions: 1-2 tablespoons water<br>Container: China or heatproof glass bowl, covered |
|---|---|

ADVICE: Sprinkle the pudding with water. Due to the high sugar and alcohol content of Christmas pudding, it is wise to keep a close watch on the pudding and remove it as soon as it is the required temperature.

| To COOK | Always use a microwave recipe and follow instructions carefully to ensure the pudding does not overheat or dry out. |
|---|---|

## COD AND WHITE FISH

To THAW & COOK — Quantity: 250 g/8 oz
Time: Fillets – 5 minutes
Steaks – 6 minutes
Setting: High or Defrost (30%)
Additions: None
Container: Shallow dish, covered
ADVICE: Gently separate fillets or pieces halfway through cooking. Butter can be added at this stage for extra flavour.

## COD FILLETS

To COOK FRESH — Quantity: 500 g/1 lb
Time: 4 to 5 minutes
Setting: High
Additions: None
Container: Shallow dish, covered
ADVICE: Fold the fish, or place tail ends under the thicker ends. Rearrange halfway through cooking. Leave to stand for 2 minutes before serving. Break up with a fork once or twice during thawing.

## COD, IN SAUCE (Frozen)

To THAW & COOK — Quantity: For one
Time: 3 minutes
Setting: High
Additions: None
Container: If a pouch, pierce and stand on a plate
ADVICE: After cooking, bag will be hot therefore handle with caution.

## COD STEAKS

To COOK FRESH — Quantity: 500 g/1 lb
Time: 6 minutes
Setting: High
Additions: None
Container: Shallow dish, covered
ADVICE: Arrange the thin ends of the fish steaks towards the centre of the dish. Rearrange halfway through cooking. Leave to stand for 3 minutes before serving.

## CORN (Frozen)

To THAW & COOK — Quantity: 175 g/6 oz
Time: 10 minutes
Setting: High
Additions: 15 g/½ oz [1 tablespoon] butter
Container: Shallow dish or bowl, covered
ADVICE: Break up and stir halfway through cooking.

## CORN-ON-THE-COB

To THAW & COOK — Quantity: 2
Time: 6 to 8 minutes
Setting: High
Additions: None
Container: Wrap individually in greaseproof paper or parchment and stand on a plate
ADVICE: Rearrange during cooking.

To COOK FRESH — Quantity: 4
Time: 12 minutes
Setting: High
Additions: Brush with butter
Container: Wrap individually in greaseproof or parchment paper and stand on a plate
ADVICE: Strip the corn of outer leaves and husks. Rearrange halfway through cooking. Leave to stand for 3 minutes, wrapped, before serving.

## COURGETTES (ZUCCHINI)

To THAW & COOK — Quantity: 500 g/1 lb
Time: 10½ minutes
Setting: High
Additions: 3 tablespoons water, salt
Container: Large bowl, covered
ADVICE: Place the courgettes [zucchini] on top of the salted water. Stir halfway through cooking.

To COOK FRESH — Quantity: 500 g/1 lb
Time: 9 minutes
Setting: High
Additions: 2 tablespoons water, salt
Container: Medium bowl, covered
ADVICE: Trim and slice. Stir the courgettes [zucchini] halfway through cooking. Leave to stand for 5 minutes before serving.

## CRAB, DRESSED (Frozen)

To THAW — Quantity: 1
Time: 1 minute
Setting: High
Additions: None
Container: The plastic container provided, standing on a plate
ADVICE: Remove covering. Do not microwave for longer than necessary or plastic container may distort. Leave to stand for 20 to 25 minutes before serving.

## CRABMEAT (Frozen)

To THAW — Quantity: 400 g/14 oz
Time: 2 minutes
Setting: High
Additions: None
Container: Plate
ADVICE: Turn the meat over halfway through cooking. Break the meat up with a fork then leave to stand for 10 minutes before serving. If in a hurry remove any thawed crab and microwave the remaining frozen pieces.

## CREAM (Frozen)

To THAW — Quantity: 250 g/8 fl oz
Time: 30 to 40 seconds, stand for 10 minutes, then 25 seconds and stand for 30 minutes
Setting: High
Additions: None
Container: Small bowl large enough

ADVICE: Best thawed naturally in case of separation but if short of time follow above instructions. Break cream up with a fork after the first 40 second's thawing. Stir and mash before final standing period.

## CREAM SLICES (Frozen)

To THAW — Quantity: 2 individual slices
Time: 15 to 30 seconds
Setting: High
Additions: None
Container: Stand on a piece of kitchen paper towel on a plate

ADVICE: Check after 15 seconds as the icing may get overheated. Leave to stand for 30 to 45 minutes before serving. If desired, return to the microwave after 20 minutes' standing time.

## CREAM SPONGE CAKE (Frozen)

To THAW — Quantity: 1
Time: 1 minute
Setting: High
Additions: None
Container: Plate

ADVICE: Check after 30 seconds. Leave to stand for 10 to 15 minutes before serving.

## DOUGHNUTS, RING (Frozen)

To THAW — Quantity: 1
Time: 45 seconds to 1 minute
Setting: High
Additions: None
Container: Plate with doughnut standing on kitchen paper towel

ADVICE: Check the doughnut frequently. Leave to stand for 2 to 3 minutes before serving.

## DOUGHNUTS, CREAM (Frozen)

To THAW — Quantity: 4
Time: 15 to 30 seconds
Setting: High
Additions: None

ADVICE: Arrange the doughnuts so that they face the centre of the plate. Check after 15 seconds to ensure the cream is not melting. Leave to stand for 5 to 10 minutes before serving.

## DOUGHNUTS, JAM (Frozen)

To THAW — Quantity: 1
Time: 10 seconds
Setting: High
Additions: None
Container: Plate, with doughnut standing on kitchen paper towel

ADVICE: The jam inside the doughnut gets very hot so beware when eating.

## DRIED FRUIT

To RECONSTITUTE — Quantity: 250 g/8 oz
Time: 6 minutes
Setting: High
Additions: 600 ml/1 pint [2½ cups] water
Container: Bowl, covered

ADVICE: Pour the water over the fruit and microwave. Leave to stand for 30 minutes, then drain and use as required.

## DUCK

To THAW — Quantity: Whole or portions
Time: 7 to 9 minutes per 500 g/1 lb
Setting: High
Additions: None
Container: Shallow dish, bird standing on a trivet, covered with kitchen paper towel

ADVICE: Shield the thin parts with foil. Remove the giblets as soon as possible. Turn over halfway through thawing. Leave to stand for 10 to 15 minutes before cooking. (This is not necessary with portions.) Ensure the duck is thawed thoroughly before cooking.

To COOK (Whole bird) — Quantity: 1 × 2.5 kg/5 lb
Time: 40 minutes
Setting: High
Additions: None
Container: Shallow container, bird standing on an upturned plate or trivet

ADVICE: Shield the thin parts with foil. If practicable, place the duck in a pricked oven bag (replacing the metal tag with string). Start cooking, breast side down. Pour off the juices and turn over halfway through cooking. After cooking, remove the bag, wrap in foil and leave to stand for 10 minutes. If desired, brown under a pre-heated grill [broiler] before serving.

## ECLAIRS (Frozen)

To THAW — Quantity: 4
Time: 45 seconds to 1 minute
Setting: Defrost (30%)
Additions: None
Container: Stand on a piece of kitchen paper towel on a plate

ADVICE: Check before 30 seconds to ensure the chocolate does not melt. Leave to stand for 20 minutes before serving.

## EDDOES

To COOK FRESH — Quantity: 500 g/1 lb
Time: 9 minutes
Setting: High
Additions: 3 tablespoons water
Container: Medium bowl, covered

ADVICE: Peel and dice. Stir halfway through cooking. Stand covered for 3 minutes before draining. Toss in butter, mash or serve plain.

## EGGPLANT

To COOK    See AUBERGINES

## EGGS

To POACH   Quantity: 2 × size 2 (large) eggs
           Time: 1 minute
           Setting: High
           Additions: 4 fl oz/125 ml (½ cup) water,
           2 tablespoons vinegar
           Container: 2 ramekin dishes
ADVICE: Divide the water and vinegar between the dishes, cook uncovered until boiling then break an egg in to each dish, prick the yolk and cook. Leave to stand for 1 minute before draining. Never attempt to boil eggs in their shells, and always prick an egg yolk with a toothpick before cooking.

## ENDIVE (CHICORY)

To COOK    Quantity: 350 g/12 oz
FRESH      Time: 5 minutes
           Setting: High
           Additions: None
           Container: Large bowl, covered
ADVICE: Trim and separate the endive. Rinse in cold water with 1 tablespoon lemon juice. Stir and check frequently through cooking. Leave to stand for 3 minutes before serving.

## FAGGOTS IN SAUCE

To THAW &  Quantity: 6 × 500 g/1 lb
COOK       Time: 9 minutes
           Setting: High
           Container: Casserole, covered
ADVICE: Remove from the foil container. Halfway through heating break up the mixture and arrange the faggots around the outer edge of the casserole.

## FENNEL

To COOK    Quantity: 500 g/1 lb
FRESH      Time: 8 minutes
           Setting: High
           Additions: 4 tablespoons water, salt
           Container: Medium bowl, covered
ADVICE: Trim and slice. Stir the fennel halfway through cooking. Leave to stand for 4 minutes before serving.

## FISH

To COOK    See COD

## FISH CAKES (Frozen)

To THAW &  Quantity: 4
COOK       Time: 3½ to 4 minutes
           Setting: High
           Additions: None
           Container: Plate
ADVICE: Turn over halfway through cooking and rearrange if necessary.

## FISH FINGERS (Frozen)

To THAW &  See FISH CAKES
COOK

## FRUIT SALAD (Frozen)

To THAW    Quantity: 400 g/14 oz
           Time: 3 minutes
           Setting: High
           Additions: None
           Container: Medium bowl, covered
ADVICE: Stir and separate the fruit after 1½ minutes. Leave to stand for 5 minutes before serving.

## GAMMON STEAKS

To THAW    Quantity: 250 g/8 oz
           Time: 4 minutes
           Setting: High
           Additions: None
           Container: Shallow dish or plate, meat covered
           by kitchen paper towel
ADVICE: Rearrange halfway through thawing.

To COOK    Quantity: 250 g/8 oz
           Time: 3 to 4 minutes
           Setting: High
           Additions: None
           Container: Shallow dish or plate, meat covered
           by kitchen paper towel
ADVICE: Use of a browning dish may be preferred to obtain searing. For thick steaks the time may need to be increased.

## GOOSE

To THAW    Quantity: As required
           Time: 7 to 8 minutes per 500 g/1 lb
           Setting: High or Defrost (30%)
           Additions: None
           Container: Shallow container, bird standing on
           an upturned plate or trivet.
ADVICE: Shield the thin parts with foil and cover bird with kitchen paper towel. Remove the giblets as soon as possible. Turn over three times during thawing. If a large bird, immerse in cold water for 30 minutes after thawing. Remove, drain and dry. Cook only when completely thawed.

To COOK    Quantity: As required
           Time: 6 to 7 minutes per 500 g/1 lb
           Setting: High
           Additions: None

Container: Shallow container, bird standing on a trivet or upturned plate

ADVICE: Shield the thin parts of the bird with foil. If practical, place the goose in a pricked roasting bag (replacing the metal tag with string). Start cooking breast side down. Pour off the juices and turn over halfway through cooking. After cooking, remove the bag, wrap in foil and leave to stand for 15 minutes before serving. If desired, brown under a preheated grill [broiler] before serving.

## GOOSEBERRIES

To COOK FRESH
Quantity: 500 g/1 lb
Time: 6 minutes
Setting: High
Additions: 4 tablespoons water, sugar to taste
Container: Large bowl, covered

ADVICE: Top and tail the gooseberries. Stir halfway through cooking.

## HADDOCK, SMOKED

To THAW & COOK
Quantity: 250 g/8 oz
Time: Fillets: 5½ minutes
Smoked: 5½ minutes
Steaks: 6 minutes
Setting: High or Defrost (30%)
Additions: Butter
Container: Shallow dish, covered

ADVICE: Halfway through cooking, gently separate fillets or pieces. Butter can be added at this stage for extra flavour.

## HADDOCK FILLETS

To COOK FRESH
Quantity: 500 g/1 lb
Time: 4 to 5 minutes
Setting: High or Defrost (30%)
Additions: None
Container: Shallow dish, covered

ADVICE: Fold or place the tail ends under the thicker ends. Rearrange the fish halfway through. Leave to stand for 2 minutes before serving.

## HERRINGS

To THAW & COOK
Quantity: 2
Time: 6 minutes
Setting: High
Additions: None
Container: Shallow dish, covered

ADVICE: Leave to stand for 2 to 3 minutes before serving.

To COOK FRESH
Quantity: 4 gutted herrings
Time: 5 minutes
Setting: High
Additions: None
Container: Shallow dish, covered

ADVICE: Stand covered for 3 minutes before serving.

## JELLY

To DISSOLVE
Quantity: 1 packet
Time: 2 to 3 minutes
Setting: High
Additions: 150 ml/¼ pint water
Container: Bowl or jug

ADVICE: Once melted, add sufficient cold or hot water to make up to 600 ml/1 pint [2½ cups].

## KIDNEY

To THAW
See LIVER

To COOK
Quantity: 500 g/1 lb
Time: 5 to 6 minutes
Setting: High
Additions: None
Container: Shallow dish, covered

ADVICE: Remove the membrane, halve and core before cooking. Stir halfway through cooking.

## KIPPERS

To COOK FRESH
Quantity: 1
Time: 2 to 3 minutes
Setting: High
Additions: Butter
Container: Shallow dish, covered

ADVICE: Rearrange halfway through cooking. Leave to stand for 1 minute before serving.

## KOHL RABI

To COOK FRESH
Quantity: 500 g/1 lb
Time: 9 minutes
Setting: High
Additions: 3 tablespoons water
Container: Medium bowl, covered

ADVICE: Peel and dice. Stir halfway through cooking. Leave to stand covered for 3 minutes then drain. Toss in butter and serve the Kohl rabi immediately.

## LAMB, BREAST

To COOK
Quantity: 500 g/1 lb boned, rolled and stuffed roast
Time: 12 minutes
Setting: High
Additions: None
Container: Stand the meat on a trivet or upturned plate in a shallow dish.

ADVICE: If practical, place the meat in a pricked roasting bag (replacing the metal tag with string).
Turn the lamb halfway through the cooking time, then wrap in foil and leave to stand for 25 to 30 minutes before serving and carving.

## LAMB, CHOPS

To COOK    See CHOPS

## LAMB, CROWN

To COOK    Quantity: As required
Time: 5 minutes per 500 g/1 lb
Setting: High
Additions: None
Container: Stand the meat on a trivet or upturned plate in a shallow dish

ADVICE: Turn halfway through cooking, then wrap in foil and leave to stand for 10 minutes before serving.

## LAMB, Large Cuts

To THAW    Quantity: As required
Time: 9 to 10 minutes per 500 g/1 lb
Setting: High or Defrost (30%)
Additions: None
Container: Stand meat on a trivet or upturned dish in a shallow dish

ADVICE: Turn over once during thawing. After thawing, wrap in foil and leave to stand for 15 to 20 minutes. Smaller cuts will thaw more quickly than larger, so check during thawing and leave to stand for only 15 minutes. Meat should be completely thawed before cooking.

To COOK    Quantity: As required
Time: Leg on the bone: 7 minutes per 500 g/ 1 lb – medium
8 to 9 minutes per 500 g/1 lb – well done
Leg, boned: 7 minutes per 500 g/ 1 lb – medium
9 minutes per 500 g/1 lb – well done
Loin: 10 minutes per 500 g/1 lb
Setting: High
Additions: None
Container: Shallow dish, meat on trivet or upturned dish covered with greaseproof paper or parchment

ADVICE: If practical, place the meat in a pricked roasting bag (replacing the metal tag with string). Cover the thin parts of the meat with foil. Turn over once during cooking. After cooking, remove from the bag, wrap in foil and leave to stand for 25 to 30 minutes. For loin, leave to stand for 5 to 10 minutes. If more browning is required, brown under a preheated grill [broiler] after standing.

## LASAGNE (Frozen)

To THAW &    Quantity: 1 × 400g/14 oz
COOK    Time: 5 minutes, leave to stand 5 minutes and return for 5 minutes
Setting: High
Additions: None
Container: Shallow dish, covered

ADVICE: Remove from foil container and transfer to a flameproof dish close in size to the original foil container. If desired, brown under a grill [broiler].

## LASAGNE, Sheets

To COOK    Quantity: 175 g/6 oz
Time: 9 minutes
Setting: High
Additions: 1.7 l/3 pints [4 pints] water, 1 tablespoon oil and 1 teaspoon salt
Container: Long oblong dish, covered

ADVICE: Ensure that the pasta is covered throughout the cooking. Leave to stand for 8 minutes before using.

## LEEKS

To COOK    Quantity: 500 g/1 lb
FRESH    Time: 10 minutes
Setting: High
Additions: 3 tablespoons water, salt
Container: Large bowl, covered

ADVICE: Trim and slice. Stir halfway through cooking. Leave to stand for 5 minutes before serving.

## LETTUCE

To COOK    Quantity: 750 g/1½ lb
Time: 7 minutes
Setting: High
Additions: 150 ml/¼ pint [⅔ cup] water and 25 g/ 1 oz butter
Container: Large bowl, covered

ADVICE: Trim and cut the lettuce into 4. Stir halfway through cooking.

## LIVER

To THAW    Quantity: 250 g/8 oz
Time: 2 to 2½ minutes
Setting: High
Additions: None
Container: Dish, covered

ADVICE: Separate the pieces after 2 or 3 minutes. Leave to stand for 5 to 8 minutes.

To COOK    Quantity: As required
Time: 5 to 6 minutes
Setting: High
Additions: None
Container: Dish, covered

ADVICE: Rearrange halfway through cooking.

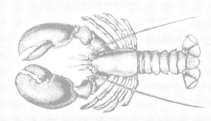

## LOBSTER (Fresh)

To COOK    Conventional cooking recommended

## LOBSTER (Frozen)

To COOK    Quantity: 1 × 400g/14oz
& SERVE    Time: 1 minute, stand for 5, 1 minute, stand for 5,
COLD    1 minute, stand for 5, turn over, 1 minute, stand for 30 minutes
Setting: High

Additions: None
Container: Plate
ADVICE: Rinse with cold water before cooking.

## MACARONI

To COOK    See PASTA

## MACKEREL (Fillets)

To THAW &    Quantity: 2
HEAT    Time: 3¼ minutes
    Setting: High
    Additions: None
    Container: Plate, covered
ADVICE: If necessary, rearrange halfway through cooking.

To COOK    Quantity: 2
    Time: 1¼ minutes
    Setting: High
    Additions: None
    Container: Plate, covered
ADVICE: Stand uncovered, 5 to 10 minutes before serving.

To COOK    Quantity: 500 g/1 lb
(Whole)    Time: 5 minutes
    Setting: High
    Additions: None
    Container: Shallow dish, covered
ADVICE: Clean the fish. Rearrange the fish halfway through cooking. Leave to stand for 3 minutes before serving.

## MANGE-TOUTS (SNOW PEAS)

To THAW &    Quantity: 250 g/8 oz
COOK    Time: 9 minutes
    Setting: High
    Additions: 3 tablespoons water, salt
    Container: Large bowl, covered
ADVICE: Stir halfway through cooking.

To COOK    Quantity: 500 g/1 lb
FRESH    Time: 8 minutes
    Setting: High
    Additions: 3 tablespoons water, salt
    Container: Large bowl, covered
ADVICE: Top and tail the mange-touts. Stir halfway through the cooking. Leave to stand for 5 minutes before serving.

## MARROW

To COOK    Quantity: 750 g/1½ lb
FRESH    Time: 14 minutes
    Setting: High
    Additions: None
    Container: Shallow dish, covered
ADVICE: Halve the marrow lengthways and remove the seeds. Rearrange halfway through cooking. Leave to stand for 4 minutes before serving.

## MEATBALLS (Frozen)

To THAW &    Quantity: 500 g/1 lb
COOK    Time: 6 minutes
    Setting: High
    Additions: None
    Container: Large plate
ADVICE: Rearrange if necessary after 3 and 5 minutes.

## MEAT, Canned

To HEAT    Quantity: 500 g/1 lb
    Time: 5 minutes
    Setting: High
    Additions: None
    Container: Medium bowl, covered
ADVICE: Stir halfway through cooking.

## MINCED MEAT (Beef, Lamb, Pork)

To THAW    Quantity: 500 g/1 lb
    Time: 2 minutes, stand for 5 minutes, return for 1 to 2 minutes
    Setting: High
    Additions: None
    Container: Bowl, covered
ADVICE: Break up the meat with a fork and stir as often as possible as this will speed up the operation.

To COOK    Quantity: 500 g/1 lb
    Time: 5 minutes
    Setting: High
    Additions: 4 tablespoons water
    Container: Bowl, covered
ADVICE: Stir once or twice during cooking.

## MUSHROOMS

To COOK    Quantity: 250 g/8 oz
FRESH    Time: 5 minutes
    Setting: High
    Additions: 2 tablespoons
    Container: Medium bowl, covered
ADVICE: Wipe the mushrooms and leave them whole.

## MUTTON, Boneless diced

To THAW    Quantity: 500 g/1 lb
    Time: 4 minutes
    Setting: High
    Container: Medium bowl, covered
ADVICE: Stir halfway through thawing. Stand for 5 minutes before using.

# OKRA

To COOK FRESH
Quantity: 500 g/1 lb
Time: 9 minutes
Setting: High
Additions: 3 tablespoons
Container: Large bowl, covered

ADVICE: Wash and trim, sprinkle with salt and stand for 30 minutes. Rinse and dry before cooking. Stir halfway through cooking and stand, covered, for 3 minutes before serving.

# ONIONS

To THAW
Quantity: 500 g/1 lb
Time: 5 to 6 minutes
Setting: High
Additions: None
Container: Medium bowl, covered

ADVICE: Stir halfway through thawing.

To COOK FRESH
Quantity: 500 g/1 lb
Time: 8 minutes
Setting: High
Additions: None
Container: Medium bowl, covered

ADVICE: Peel and slice the onions. Stir halfway through cooking.

# OYSTERS

To COOK RAW
Quantity: 6
Time: 3 minutes
Setting: High
Additions: 150 ml/¼ pint [⅔ cup] boiling water
Container: Shallow dish, covered

ADVICE: Stand covered for 2 minutes before serving.

# PARSNIPS

To COOK FRESH
Quantity: 750 g/1½ lb
Time: 8 minutes
Setting: High
Additions: 3 tablespoons water, salt
Container: Large bowl, covered

ADVICE: Trim and cut the parsnips into quarters, Stir halfway through cooking. Leave to stand for 5 minutes before serving.

# PASTA (Macaroni, Noodles, Tagliatelle)

To COOK DRIED
Quantity: 250 g/8 oz
Time: 8 minutes
Setting: High
Additions: 1.7 l/3 pints [4 pints] water, 1 tablespoon oil and 1 teaspoon salt
Container: Very large bowl, covered

ADVICE: Ensure that the pasta stays covered with water throughout cooking. Leave to stand for 8 minutes before using.

# PASTRY (Frozen)

To THAW
Quantity: 250 g/8 oz
Time: 30 seconds
Setting: High or Defrost (30%)
Additions: None
Container: Stand on a plate

ADVICE: Check frequently. Ensure that the fat in the pastry does not start to melt. Leave to stand for 4 to 5 minutes before using.

# PASTRY FLAN CASES

To COOK
Quantity: 1 × 18 cm/7 inch
Time: 3 to 4 minutes
Setting: High
Additions: None
Container: China or ovenproof glass flan dish

ADVICE: Prick the pastry well and check frequently after the first 2½ minutes.

# PEACHES

To COOK FRESH
Quantity: 500 g/1 lb
Time: 5 minutes
Setting: High
Additions: 3 tablespoons water, sugar to taste
Container: Medium bowl, covered

ADVICE: Stone [pit] the fruit and cut into quarters. Stir halfway through cooking.

# PEARS

To COOK FRESH
Quantity: 4 medium
Time: 5 minutes
Setting: High
Additions: 3 tablespoons water, sugar to taste
Container: Shallow dish, covered

ADVICE: Peel, core and halve the pears. Rearrange halfway through cooking.

# PEAS

To THAW & COOK
Quantity: 250 g/8 oz
Time: 7 minutes
Setting: High
Additions: 3 tablespoons water
Container: Bowl, covered

ADVICE: Stir halfway through cooking.

To COOK FRESH
Quantity: 500 g/1 lb
Time: 12 minutes
Setting: High
Additions: 3 tablespoons water, pinch of sugar
Container: Large bowl, covered

ADVICE: Pod the peas. Stir halfway through cooking.

# PEPPERS

To THAW
Quantity: 250 g/8 oz
Time: 3½ minutes
Setting: High or Defrost (30%)
Additions: None
Container: Medium bowl, covered

ADVICE: Stir halfway through cooking.

## PLAICE, FILLETS (Frozen)

To THAW & COOK — Quantity: 250 g/8 oz
Time: 5 minutes
Setting: Full
Container: Shallow container, covered

ADVICE: Gently separate the fillets halfway through cooking. Butter can be added at this stage for extra flavour.

## PLAICE FILLETS

To COOK FRESH — Quantity: 500 g/1 lb
Time: 4 minutes
Setting: Full
Container: Shallow dish, covered

ADVICE: Arrange the fish with tails under thicker parts. Rearrange fish halfway through cooking. Leave to stand for 2 minutes before serving.

## PLUMS

To COOK FRESH — Quantity: 500 g/1 lb
Time: 5 minutes
Setting: High
Additions: 3 tablespoons water, sugar to taste
Container: Large bowl, covered

ADVICE: Remove the stones from the plums. Stir halfway through cooking.

## PORK, BONELESS DICED

To THAW — Quantity: 500 g/1 lb
Time: 4 minutes
Setting: High
Additions: None
Container: Medium bowl, covered

ADVICE: Stir halfway through thawing. Leave to stand for 5 minutes.

## PORK, Large Cuts

To THAW — Quantity: As required
Time: 9 to 10 minutes per 500 g/1 lb
Setting: High or Defrost (30%)
Additions: None
Container: Stand meat on a trivet or upturned plate in a shallow dish

ADVICE: Turn over once during the thawing operation. After thawing wrap in foil and leave to stand for 15 to 30 minutes. Smaller cuts will thaw more quickly than large ones so check during thawing and leave to stand for 15 minutes. Meat should be completely thawed before cooking.

To COOK — Quantity: As required
Time: 10 minutes per 500 g/1 lb
Loin: 10 to 13 minutes per 500 g/1 lb
Setting: High
Additions: None
Container: Stand on a trivet or upturned plate in a shallow dish.

ADVICE: Wrap thin parts with foil. If practical place the meat in a pricked roasting bag (replacing the metal tag with string). Drain off juices and turn over halfway through cooking. After cooking, remove the bag, wrap in foil and leave to stand 25 to 30 minutes. If crispy crackling is desired, the skin can be removed and crisped in a browning dish or under a preheated grill [broiler].

## PORK CHOPS

To COOK — See CHOPS

## PORK FILLET (TENDERLOIN)

To THAW — See PORK

To COOK — Quantity: 500 g/1 lb
Time: 8 minutes
Setting: High
Additions: None
Container: Shallow dish

ADVICE: Rearrange halfway through cooking. Cover and leave to stand for 5 minutes before serving.

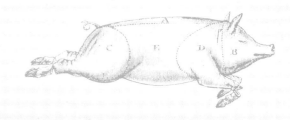

## PORK PIES (Frozen)

To THAW — Quantity: 2 individual
Time: 1½ minutes
Setting: High
Additions: None
Container: Pies standing on kitchen paper towel on a plate

ADVICE: Avoid overheating as the aspic jelly will melt. Useful in an emergency but not recommended for everyday practice. Leave to stand for 10 to 15 minutes before serving.

## PORK SPARERIBS

To COOK — Quantity: 750 g/1½ lb
Time: 18 minutes
Setting: High
Additions: None
Container: Large bowl, covered

ADVICE: Rearrange halfway through cooking. Stand for 5 minutes before serving.

## PORRIDGE

To COOK — Quantity: 125 g/4 oz [1 cup]
Time: 5 minutes
Setting: High
Additions: 600 ml/1 pint [2½ cups] water, ¼ teaspoon salt, 1½ to 2 tablespoons sugar
Container: Bowl, covered

ADVICE: Stir once or twice during cooking.

## POTATOES

To BAKE — Quantity: 4 × 275 g/10 oz
Time: 15 minutes
Setting: High
Additions: None
Container: Shallow dish

ADVICE: Scrub and prick the potatoes. Turn over halfway through cooking. Leave to stand for 5 minutes, wrapped tightly in foil, before serving.

To BOIL    Quantity: 500 g/1 lb
           Time: 8 minutes
           Setting: High
           Additions: 3 tablespoons water, salt
           Container: Large bowl, covered

ADVICE: Peel and cut the potatoes into equal size pieces. Stir halfway through cooking. Leave to stand for 5 minutes before serving.

## PRAWNS

To THAW    See SHRIMPS and PRAWNS

## RABBIT (Frozen)

To THAW    Quantity: 1 kg/2 lb in portions
           Time: 9 minutes
           Setting: High
           Additions: None
           Container: Large bowl, covered

ADVICE: Rearrange the rabbit pieces halfway through thawing. Leave to stand for 10 minutes before using.

## RASPBERRIES

To COOK    Quantity: 500 g/1 lb
FRESH      Time: 5 minutes
           Setting: High
           Additions: Sugar to taste
           Container: Large bowl, covered

ADVICE: Rinse the raspberries in water. Add sugar and stir halfway through cooking.

## RHUBARB

To THAW &  Quantity: 500 g/1 lb
COOK       Time: 12 minutes
           Setting: High
           Additions: 3 tablespoons sugar
           Container: Large bowl, covered

ADVICE: Stir once or twice during cooking.

To COOK    Quantity: 500 g/1 lb
FRESH      Time: 8 minutes
           Setting: High
           Additions: 3 tablespoons water, sugar to taste
           Container: Large bowl, covered

ADVICE: Trim and cut the rhubarb into pieces. Stir halfway through cooking.

## RICE

To COOK    Quantity: 250 g/8 oz
           Time: 13 minutes
           Setting: High
           Additions: 900 ml/1½ pints [3½ cups] water
           Container: Large bowl, covered

ADVICE: Stand covered for 10 minutes after cooking. Brown or untreated rice will take about twice as long to cook.

## RUM BABA (Frozen)

To THAW    Quantity: 2 individual
           Time: 30 seconds
           Setting: High
           Additions: None
           Container: Pláte

ADVICE: Check after 20 seconds to ensure the rum babas are not thawing too quickly. Leave to stand for 15 minutes before serving.

## RUTABAGA

To COOK    See SWEDE

## SALMON, SMOKED (Frozen)

To THAW    Quantity: 200 g/7 oz
           Time: 30 seconds
           Setting: High
           Additions: None
           Container: Plate

ADVICE: Turn over after 15 seconds. After cooking, gently separate the salmon from the plastic wrap and spread out the salmon over the plate. Leave to stand for 25 to 30 minutes.

## SALMON, STEAKS

To COOK    Quantity: 500 g/1 lb
FRESH      Time: 4 to 5 minutes
           Setting: High
           Additions: None
           Container: Shallow dish, covered

ADVICE: Arrange the fish with the thin ends towards the centre of the dish. Rearrange halfway through cooking. Leave to stand for 3 minutes before serving.

## SALMON TROUT

| To COOK FRESH | Quantity: 4 gutted fish |
| --- | --- |
| | Time: 7 minutes |
| | Setting: High |
| | Additions: None |
| | Container: Shallow dish, covered |

ADVICE: Rearrange fish halfway through cooking.

## SAUSAGES (Frozen)

| To THAW | Quantity: 250 g/8 oz |
| --- | --- |
| | Time: 2½ minutes |
| | Setting: High |
| | Additions: None |
| | Container: Plate |

ADVICE: Cover sausages with kitchen paper towels. Separate sausages after 1½ minutes. Remove any sausages once thawed. Stand for 3 to 4 minutes before cooking. Cook conventionally. Never fry in the microwave.

## SCALLOP

| To COOK | Quantity: 4 sliced scallops |
| --- | --- |
| | Time: 2 to 3 minutes |
| | Setting: High |
| | Additions: None |
| | Container: Shallow dish, covered |

ADVICE: Stir halfway through cooking and leave to stand for 1 minute before serving.

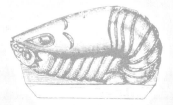

## SCAMPI (Breaded)

| To THAW & COOK | Quantity: 250 g/8 oz |
| --- | --- |
| | Time: 4 minutes |
| | Setting: High |
| | Additions: None |
| | Container: Plate |

ADVICE: Spread the scampi around the plate. This method is only suitable if an uncrisp exterior is acceptable. If not, cook by the conventional method.

## SHRIMPS AND PRAWNS (Frozen)

| To THAW | Quantity: 500 g/1 lb |
| --- | --- |
| | Time: Loose 7 to 8 minutes |
| | Block 14 minutes |
| | Setting: High |
| | Additions: None |
| | Container: Shallow dish |

ADVICE: Stir or break up the block halfway through thawing. Leave to stand for 10 mintues. Drain before use.

| To COOK RAW | Conventional cooking recommended. |
| --- | --- |

## SNAILS, IN SAUCE (Frozen)

| To THAW & COOK | Quantity: 12 |
| --- | --- |
| | Time: 1 minute, stand for 1 minute, return for 1½ to 2 minutes |
| | Setting: High |
| | Additions: None |
| | Container: Non-metallic escargot dish or a plate |

ADVICE: Remove from the foil and place on the special dish or in a circle on the plate. Check and turn plate around once during second cooking time.

## SOLE

| To THAW & COOK | Quantity: 250 g/8 oz |
| --- | --- |
| | Time: Fillets: 5 minutes |
| | Setting: High |
| | Container: Shallow dish, covered |

ADVICE: Halfway through cooking gently separate the fillets. Butter can be added at this stage for extra flavour.

## SOLE

| To COOK FRESH | Quantity: 500 g/1 lb |
| --- | --- |
| | Time: 4 minutes |
| | Setting: High |
| | Container: Shallow dish, covered |

ADVICE: Rearrange halfway through cooking and leave to stand for 2 minutes before serving.

## SNOW PEAS

| To COOK | See MANGE-TOUTS |
| --- | --- |

## SPAGHETTI

| To COOK DRIED | Quantity: 250 g/8 oz |
| --- | --- |
| | Time: Cook uncovered 1 minute, then return for 9 minutes |
| | Setting: High |
| | Additions: 1.7 l/3 pints [4 pints] water, 1 teaspoon salt, 1 tablespoon oil |
| | Container: Very large bowl, covered |

ADVICE: Cook for 1 minute, then push the remaining spaghetti under the water. Cook for a further 9 minutes, ensuring the spaghetti is covered with water throughout cooking. Leave to stand for 10 minutes before serving.

## SPINACH

| To THAW & COOK | Quantity: 250 g/8 oz |
| --- | --- |
| | Time: 8 minutes |
| | Setting: High |
| | Additions: None |
| | Container: Medium bowl, covered |

ADVICE: Stir to break up several times during thawing.

| To COOK FRESH | Quantity: 500 g/1 lb |
| --- | --- |
| | Time: 12 minutes |
| | Setting: High |
| | Additions: None |
| | Container: Very large bowl, covered |

ADVICE: Wash but don't dry the spinach. Stir halfway through cooking.

## SPONGE CAKE

To COOK          These are best cooked conventionally unless you follow a microwave recipe and appropriate instructions.

## SPONGE PUDDING (Frozen)

To THAW          Quantity: 1 × 350 g/12 oz
                 Time: 1 minute
                 Setting: High
                 Additions: None
                 Container: Invert onto a plate
ADVICE: Remove the foil container. Leave the greaseproof covering in position. Peel off after thawing. Leave to stand for 10 minutes.

To THAW &        Quantity: 1 × 350 g/12 oz
COOK             Time: 3½ minutes
                 Setting: High
                 Additions: None
                 Container: Invert onto a plate
ADVICE: Remove the foil container. Leave the greaseproof covering in position. Peel off after 1 minute. Serve immediately.

## STEAK AND KIDNEY (Frozen)

To THAW          Quantity: 500 g/1 lb
                 Time: 4½ minutes
                 Setting: High
                 Additions: None
                 Container: Large bowl, covered
ADVICE: Stir halfway through thawing. Leave to stand for 5 minutes before using. Serve immediately.

## STEAK & KIDNEY PUDDINGS (Frozen)

To THAW &        Quantity: 2 individual
COOK             Time: 5½ minutes
                 Setting: High
                 Additions: 2 teaspoons water
                 Container: 2 large cups or mugs or 2 small bowls
ADVICE: Remove the foil cases. Stand each pudding on a large piece of plastic wrap. Drop the puddings into the containers. Sprinkle the water over the top of each pudding. Cover with plastic wrap. After 2 minutes, pierce the lid of each pudding.

## STRAWBERRIES (Frozen)

To THAW          Quantity: 500 g/1 lb
                 Time: 2½ minutes
                 Setting: High
                 Additions: None
                 Container: Medium bowl
ADVICE: Gently rearrange after 1 and 2 minutes. Leave to stand for 5 to 10 minutes before using.

## SWEDE [RUTABAGA]

To COOK          Quantity: 500 g/1 lb
FRESH            Time: 9 minutes
                 Setting: High
                 Additions: 3 tablespoons water, salt
                 Container: Large bowl, covered
ADVICE: Peel and dice the swede. Stir halfway through cooking. Leave to stand for 5 minutes before serving.

## SWEETBREADS

To COOK          Quantity: 1 kg/2 lb
                 Time: 8 minutes
                 Setting: High
                 Additions: 1.2 l/2 pints [5 cups]
                 Container: Large bowl, uncovered
ADVICE: Soak in lukewarm water with a dash of vinegar added for 2 hours before cooking. Change water halfway through soaking. Trim off fat and skin before cooking. Once cooked, plunge into cold water and stand for 10 minutes. Reheat or fry conventionally.

## SWEET POTATOES

To COOK          Quantity: 500 g/1 lb
                 Time: 9 minutes
                 Setting: High
                 Additions: 3 tablespoons water
                 Container: Medium bowl, covered
ADVICE: Peel and dice the potatoes. Stand for 3 minutes.

## TAGLIATELLE

To COOK          See PASTA

## TINDOORI

To COOK          Quantity: 250 g/8 oz
                 Time: 6 minutes
                 Setting: Maximum
                 Additions: 3 tablespoons water
                 Container: Medium bowl, covered
ADVICE: Rinse and slice tindoori. Stand covered for 3 minutes after cooking then drain before serving as an accompaniment to curry.

## TURBOT

To COOK          See FISH, WHITE

## TOMATOES

To COOK          Quantity: 500 g/1 lb
FRESH            Time: 5½ minutes
                 Setting: High

Additions: None
Container: Medium bowl, covered
ADVICE: Slice the tomatoes and stir halfway through cooking.

# TROUT

| To THAW & COOK | Quantity: 2 |
| | Time: 8 minutes |
| | Setting: High |
| | Additions: 25 g/1 oz [2 tablespoons] butter |
| | Container: Large or oval plate, covered |

ADVICE: Turn over after 3 minutes. Smear with the butter and continue cooking. Leave to stand for 3 minutes before serving.

| To COOK FRESH | Quantity: 500 g/1 lb |
| | Time: 2½ minutes |
| | Setting: High |
| | Additions: None |
| | Container: Shallow dish, covered |

ADVICE: Clean the fish and cover the head and tail with foil. Leave to stand for 3 minutes before serving.

# TURKEY

| To THAW | Quantity: As required |
| | Time: 7 to 8 minutes per 500 g/1 lb |
| | Setting: High or Defrost (30%) |
| | Additions: None |
| | Container: A trivet or upturned plate standing in a shallow dish |

ADVICE: Shield the thin parts with foil. Cover with kitchen paper towel. Remove the giblets as soon as possible. Turn over three times during thawing. If a large bird, immerse in cold water for 30 minutes after thawing operation. Remove, drain and dry. Cook only when it has completely thawed and no ice is present.

| To COOK | Quantity: As required |
| | Time: Under 4 kg/8 lb: 8 mins per 500 g/1 lb; |
| | 4 to 5 kg/8 to 10 lb: 7½ mins per 500 g/1 lb; |
| | 5 to 7 kg/10 to 12 lb: 7 mins per 500 g/1 lb; |
| | 7 to 10 kg/12 to 20 lb: 6½ to 7 mins per 500 g/1 lb |
| | Setting: High |
| | Additions: None |
| | Container: Shallow dish, bird on a trivet or upturned plate |

ADVICE: Cover the thin parts with foil. If practical place in a pricked roasting bag. Start cooking breast side down. Pour off juices and turn over halfway through cooking. After cooking, remove bag and wrap in foil; stand for 30 minutes before serving.

# TURNIP

| To COOK FRESH | Quantity: 500 g/1 lb |
| | Time: 10 minutes |
| | Setting: High |
| | Additions: 3 tablespoons water, salt |
| | Container: Large bowl, covered |

ADVICE: Peel and dice the turnip. Stir halfway through cooking. Leave to stand for 5 minutes before serving.

# VEAL

| To COOK | See CHOPS and BEEF |

# VEGETABLES, CANNED

| To HEAT | Quantity: 350 g/12 oz |
| | Time: 3 to 4 minutes |
| | Setting: High |
| | Additions: None |
| | Container: Medium bowl, covered |

ADVICE: Stir halfway through cooking.

# WHITEBAIT

| To COOK | Best cooked conventionally. |

# ZUCCHINI

| To COOK | See COURGETTES |

## ── ACKNOWLEDGMENTS ──

Photography by Martin Brigdale
Food for Photography prepared by Jacki Baxter and Maureen Pogson
Photographic styling by Sue Leighton.

Table Dressing Features written by Joan McLeod
Photographed by Nick Carman
Photographic styling by Shân Lang
Photograph top right p. 88, by Laurie Evans

The Publishers would like to thank the following companies
for the loan of accessories for photography:
Philips Appliances; Lakeland Plastics; David Mellor and Harrods

The line drawings used in the A-Z Guide were taken from
Food and Drink: A Pictorial Archive from
Nineteenth Century Sources published by Dover Publications, Inc.
180 Vanick Street, New York, NY. 10014, USA

The author would like to thank Editor Helen Martin,
Art Editor Carole Thomas and Assistant Editor Debbie Lines
for their invaluable help on this book.